Praise for *THE LAST OF THE PRESIDENT'S MEN*

"An intimate but disturbing portrayal of Nixon in the Oval Office."

—David Hoffman, *The Washington Post*

"Brisk, provocative . . . Woodward's engrossing volume gives us an Alexander Butterfield of enormous complexity."

—Stephen L. Carter, *BloombergView*

"A head-shaker . . . a great read."

—John W. Dean, former White House counsel to President Nixon, *Verdict*

"A short and riveting look into the files and memory of Alexander Butterfield. . . . Here Butterfield gives Woodward access to files and photos even the seasoned journalist had never seen before. . . . Nixon's vulgarities and general ugliness of manner somehow shocked this usually unshockable reader."

—Sara Nelson, *Amazon Best Book of October 2015*

"Full of new insights for the public and scholars. . . . [A] largely overlooked window into the Nixon personality . . . a service to history."

—Tim Naftali, former director of the Nixon Presidential Library

"A cringe-worthy portrayal of the 37th president. . . . Woodward puts the petty Nixon on vivid display."

—Evan Thomas, *The Washington Post*

"Woodward returns to the scandal to profile Alexander Butterfield, the Richard Nixon aide who revealed the existence of the Oval Office tapes and effectively toppled the presidency. . . . [the book is] pure Woodward: a visual, dialogue-heavy, blow-by-blow account of Butterfield's tenure. . . . a close-up view of the Oval Office in its darkest hour."

—*Kirkus Reviews*

## Praise for *PLAN OF ATTACK*

"A remarkable book. . . . The American people seldom have been given this clear a window on their government's most sensitive deliberations."

—Tim Rutten, *Los Angeles Times*

"Instantly essential. . . . By far the most intimate glimpse we have been granted of the Bush White House, and the administration's defining moment."

—Michiko Kakutani, *The New York Times*

## Praise for *STATE OF DENIAL*

"Woodward's trilogy on the Bush administration at war is essential, and compelling, reading."

—*Foreign Affairs*

"Serious, densely, even exhaustively reported, and a real contribution to history in that it gives history what it most requires, first-person testimony. . . . This is a primer on how the executive branch of the United States works, or rather doesn't work, in the early years of the 21st century."

—Peggy Noonan, *The Wall Street Journal*

"The most revealing in-the-room glimpse of the Bush administration that we have so far."

—Walter Shapiro, Salon.com

## Praise for *THE WAR WITHIN*

"This is the stuff of history . . . wonderfully illuminating, and cumulatively these books may be the best record we will ever get of the events they cover. . . . They stand as the fullest story yet of the Bush presidency and of the war that is likely to be its most important legacy."

—Jill Abramson, *The New York Times Book Review*

"The *In Cold Blood* of national security journalism."

—Robert Dreyfuss, *The Nation*

"Bob Woodward is the latest to remind us that it is presidents, not their understudies, who shape the destiny of nations."

—Fouad Ajami, *The Wall Street Journal*

## Praise for *OBAMA'S WARS*

"*Obama's Wars* plows relentlessly forward like a shark."

—Michiko Kakutani, *The New York Times*

"A saga of tragedy: about the snares and illusions of war in Afghanistan, the corruption of war generally, and the jangle of motives—the convergence and clash of bureaucratic interest, personal ambition, and earnest strategic analysis."

—Fred Kaplan, Slate.com

"Compelling and immensely readable. . . . The best account we have of an extraordinarily important decision by a wartime president."

— *Gen. David Barno (U.S. Army, ret.), Foreign Policy*

## Praise for *THE PRICE OF POLITICS*

"A remarkable achievement. . . . Woodward, being Woodward, digs deeper and draws more out of the protagonists than anyone else has."

—Jeff Shesol, *The Washington Post*

"Required reading."

—*Politico*

ALSO BY BOB WOODWARD

The Price of Politics

Obama's Wars

The War Within: A Secret White House History, 2006–2008

State of Denial

The Secret Man
(with a Reporter's Assessment by Carl Bernstein)

Plan of Attack

Bush at War

Maestro: Greenspan's Fed and the American Boom

Shadow: Five Presidents and the Legacy of Watergate

The Choice

The Agenda: Inside the Clinton White House

The Commanders

Veil: The Secret Wars of the CIA, 1981–1987

Wired: The Short Life and Fast Times of John Belushi

The Brethren
(with Scott Armstrong)

The Final Days
(with Carl Bernstein)

All the President's Men
(with Carl Bernstein)

# BOB
# WOODWARD

# THE LAST

## OF THE

# PRESIDENT'S

# MEN

SIMON & SCHUSTER PAPERBACKS

NEW YORK · LONDON · TORONTO · SYDNEY · NEW DELHI

*In memory of Ben Bradlee*

 Simon & Schuster Paperbacks
An Imprint of Simon & Schuster, Inc.
1230 Avenue of the Americas
New York, NY 10020

First Simon & Schuster paperback edition October 2016

SIMON & SCHUSTER PAPERBACKS and colophon are registered
trademarks of Simon & Schuster, Inc.

For information about special discounts for bulk purchases,
please contact Simon & Schuster Special Sales at 1-866-506-1949
or business@simonandschuster.com.

The Simon & Schuster Speakers Bureau can bring authors to your
live event. For more information or to book an event contact the
Simon & Schuster Speakers Bureau at 1-866-248-3049 or visit our
website at www.simonspeakers.com.

Interior design by Joy O'Meara

Manufactured in the United States of America

10  9  8  7  6  5  4  3  2  1

Library of Congress Control Number 2015947987

ISBN 978-1-5011-1644-5
ISBN 978-1-5011-1645-2 (pbk)
ISBN 978-1-5011-1646-9 (ebook)

# AUTHOR'S PERSONAL NOTE

Evelyn M. Duffy has assisted me on three previous books, one on President George W. Bush, and two on President Obama. This is the fourth in the last eight years. She dove into this book on President Nixon with determination and ingenuity. The one characteristic, above all others, you want in an assistant is a capacity for hard work. It is a central feature of her character.

She is relentless, focused and driven by a natural curiosity and deep sense of fairness. She reads, absorbs, comprehends and interprets rapidly. A simple question will yield a one-to-five-page memo.

Evelyn transcribed my first long interview with Alexander Butterfield and immediately alerted me to the possibility and importance of getting the story and documents from the last of Nixon's men. She was intimately involved in planning our approach. She made two solo trips to La Jolla and spent days interviewing Butterfield and reviewing files and documents.

We discussed the importance of getting a fourth wind on this project. She supplied that fourth wind. I can pay her no greater compliment. Even after we had emptied Butterfield's memory and records and sifted through the boxes, she saw the necessity to go back again—to review, check and dig deeper.

She helped me with some initial drafts of sections, and edited *every-*

*thing* many, many times. She spent days at the Nixon Library in California searching for a few specific needles in one of the largest archival haystacks in America. This became not just a project but a passion. Her stamina to address the unanswered questions is unmatched. I enjoyed watching her relish the inner workings of this strange White House, the twists and turns of the Nixon inner sanctum.

When we started together in 2007, she would carefully make discreet suggestions. Now she says we have to do certain things and challenges me, directly but in her friendly, genuine way. I immediately—or later—realize she is right. And she understands the lessons of Nixon, his presidency and Butterfield, who became our witness—hers as much as mine.

# PROLOGUE

Near the end of July 2014 I flew to California to meet with Alexander P. Butterfield, the former aide to President Richard Nixon who disclosed the secret White House taping system 41 years earlier.

The tapes provided the proof of Nixon's direct role in the cover-up of Watergate, other crimes and government abuses. Without that evidence, Nixon certainly would have been able to stay in office.

"There's more to the story of Nixon," Butterfield told me.

He picked me up at the airport in his Cadillac and we drove to his condominium two blocks from the Pacific Ocean in La Jolla. For 20 years before joining the Nixon White House staff, he had been one of the Air Force's most accomplished pilots. He drove confidently and fast.

At age 88, Butterfield, 6-foot-2 with salt white hair, walked with a slight stoop. But he was energetic and vital. He chatted comfortably, and he was dressed neatly in freshly pressed slacks and shirt.

He pulled into his space beneath his building and put a key in the elevator, which slowly took us to his second-floor penthouse. We got off the elevator and entered his bachelor residence of five large rooms.

I quickly scanned the open-plan living area with its modern furnishings and a dark, heavy-wood circular table used as much for work as dining.

What really snapped me to attention were 20 boxes and piles of documents and files he had agreed to bring out of storage for my assistant, Evelyn Duffy, and me to read and copy. Here, after all these decades, was a vast new archive, unknown until now.

One of Butterfield's jobs in the Nixon White House had been to prevent departing staffers from leaving with official documents. But when he left in 1973, he carted off literally thousands of documents from the White House. Many are originals. Though Butterfield is normally very neat and organized—even fastidious—the arrival of new boxes and files from storage had created an unusual disorder.

I immediately began dipping into the boxes and opening files. They contained everything from routine chronologies to bizarre memos outlining Nixon's orders. Included were some previously undisclosed Top Secret exchanges with Henry Kissinger, Nixon's national security adviser, and a few highly classified bulletins of the CIA.

Some were neatly organized, including copies on onionskin paper of all memos Butterfield wrote. These were in a monthly file about two inches thick for each of the 50 months he was in the White House— a virtual diary. Other files were scattered about the five rooms, cluttering his bedroom, office and study. Closets contained more boxes, books, folders and dossiers—some from the White House and others from his time in the Air Force. One tall stack of boxes was housed in an unused shower stall.

The boxes also contained parts of an unpublished memoir he had written in the 1990s. Butterfield gave me a copy of the chapter drafts that he still retained, and he has given me permission to quote from them.

In all, over 11 months in 2014 and 2015, I interviewed him for more than 40 hours on digital audio recordings or digital video.

His documents, the interviews and his memoir chapter drafts provide a remarkable stream of anecdotes, recollections and new episodes not found in the public record or histories. The result is a deeper, more disturbing and baffling portrait of Nixon. Though Butterfield has given occasional interviews and speeches over the decades, his personal odyssey, precisely how and why he decided to disclose the existence of the taping system, is largely untold. In some respects he has been waiting in plain sight to share the intimate details of his experience in the Nixon White House.

I did not realize this until July 18, 2011, when he visited a house my wife and I have on the South River near Annapolis, Maryland. We spent the day together with the tape recorder going. In 2014 he agreed to let me tell his story in full and gave me access to his voluminous records in La Jolla.

Butterfield has had prostate cancer for years. Despite this and other minor health problems, I found his memory to be superb. He is an excellent witness. During the course of our interviews he would quote Nixon, participants or himself verbatim about an important incident. Then months later we would review the incident and he would give the same account, often recalling the same quotations.

He is not seeking employment. He neither asked for nor has he received money from me or my publisher.

He is a proud man but over the course of the interviews he made what lawyers call "admissions against interest." He recalled with unusual candor incidents that he knows are embarrassing and do not reflect well on him.

Seen up close through Butterfield's eyes and documents, Nixon is both smaller and larger.

The focus of this book is on these two men—Nixon and Butterfield. Three months after leaving the White House, Butterfield disclosed Nixon's secret taping system to the Senate Watergate Committee.

The hundreds of hours of the secret recordings made public in a piecemeal fashion over four decades have come to define Nixon and his five and a half years in the White House.

As a deputy assistant to the president, Butterfield occupied the office next to Nixon's Oval Office for three of his four years in the White House. He became a witness to, and extension of, Nixon's strategies, likes, dislikes and whims. When Nixon was in Washington, Butterfield was the first to see him in the morning and the last to see him at night. He was one of only a very few who knew about the secret taping system.

In his memoir, *RN*, Nixon said he was "shocked" that Butterfield betrayed the secret. "I had believed that the existence of the White House taping system would never be revealed," Nixon wrote.

The secret taping system was not put in place until February 1971. There are no tapes of the first two years of the Nixon presidency. By virtue of his proximity to the center of the Nixon universe and his extraordinary memory, Butterfield himself essentially became that tape recorder.

After Nixon resigned in August 1974 he spent much of the remaining 20 years of his life conducting a war on history, trying to diminish his role in Watergate and other crimes, while attempting to elevate his foreign policy and other accomplishments.

But nearly each year since 1974 new tapes and documents have been released showing the depth of his criminality and abuse of power.

Yet history is never complete, never fully told or settled. I thought the story of Nixon was over for me in 2005 when former FBI associate director Mark Felt publicly revealed that he was the secret source known as Deep Throat. He was among the key sources that Carl Bernstein and I used in reporting the Watergate story for *The Washington Post*.

Alex Butterfield was not a typical presidential aide. Most aides get their jobs as rewards for longtime service to the successful candidate. Butterfield came in as an outsider, spent four years in the Nixon White House as a key insider, and then left as an outsider, files in tow.

So the story, like most of history, does not end.

# 1

Colonel Butterfield was in a foul mood. The 42-year-old Air Force officer was on the path to four stars, and maybe the top uniformed job in the Air Force. "I was an ambitious son of a bitch," he said later, "and I'd been lucky. I had a very good record. I was in this thing to go all the way . . . to be the chief of staff."

He was, however, stuck in Australia as the senior U.S. military officer and representative of CINCPAC, the Commander in Chief Pacific—a reward for years in Vietnam and in the Office of the Secretary of Defense as liaison to the Lyndon Johnson White House. He had been promised he would only be in Australia for two years, but now they, the mysterious they, wanted to extend him another two years.

He saw it as a career disaster, keeping him out of the action, the "smoke" as he called it—the center of things. The "smoke" was Washington or Vietnam, where he had flown 98 combat reconnaissance missions.

On this particular day, November 20, 1968, he was in Port Moresby, New Guinea, the giant island in the Pacific, just north of Australia, traveling with the U.S. ambassador to Australia.

Butterfield picked up a copy of the *Tok-Tok*, the local newspaper. Here would be some intel on what was going on in the smoke. He took the paper back to his motel room and settled in with a sandwich. The main story was Richard Nixon, who had just won election as president 15 days earlier. Butterfield had voted for him.

He stopped cold. Nixon's top aide was identified as H.R. "Bob" Haldeman. Was it possible? Haldeman was an old college acquaintance. It was astonishing that Haldeman was running the transition team preparing to take over the White House and the U.S. government.

Butterfield and Haldeman had known each other as students at the University of California at Los Angeles (UCLA) in the mid-1940s. Their girlfriends, whom they each later married, were Kappa Kappa Gamma sorority sisters and close friends. The couples had doubledated. Haldeman was quiet, a somewhat colorless man, austere, not very political. He often came across as a bit of an asshole who was brusque with his girlfriend, Jo. Butterfield had lost touch with Haldeman but Jo and Butterfield's wife, Charlotte, exchanged Christmas cards and snapshots of their children.

It wasn't much to hang on to. But a fighter pilot knew about coincidence and chance, the quick maneuver in the air. It was the difference between ace or dead.

Haldeman! He tried to recall everything about him. How much could you learn from a double date and hanging around Fraternity Row? They had been in different fraternities. Haldeman was a Beta, which was considered the best. Old Harry Robbins, H.R. "Bob." Butterfield needed an exit strategy and now he thought, "Here's my out." It was worth a try.

Butterfield had almost perfect Efficiency Reports, the formal evaluations that drive promotions. He had served as aide to two generals. With a gentle, relaxed charm he knew how to please the boss without fawning. He had earned early promotions, and his personnel file was stuffed with letters of commendation from top civilians at the Pentagon and from Vice President Hubert Humphrey. He looked the part of the classic Air Force officer. "He was drop-dead handsome," said Charlotte in 2014, nearly 30 years after their divorce.

"If you're going to get promoted to general officer," Butterfield told me later, "you've got to be where the smoke is . . . in a really important, highly visible job in either Washington, D.C., or back in Vietnam.

And command of a tactical fighter wing in Vietnam is what I wanted in the worst way.

"I was desperate to get back to Vietnam. If I have to be delayed [in Australia] for another two years, I'm dead in the water. I'm frantic, I'm actually frantic. I hate to admit that." The urgency, he said, was simply because no one knew how long the war would last, and he did not want to miss out.

Butterfield awoke the next morning to heavy rain in New Guinea, and lay in bed thinking. If only he could talk with Haldeman, an unhurried session to tout his record: Defense Secretary Robert McNamara had employed him as a contact point in the White House. He had prepared McNamara's regular military reports to the cabinet and accompanied him whenever he visited the White House. He knew a lot about power levers in Washington. He wanted to tell his UCLA pal about how crucial it was for him to be in an important, high-visibility assignment when he would became eligible for promotion to brigadier general, the one-star generalship, and the road to the smoke.

Would Haldeman understand? Could he possibly pull some strings? There were lots of strings to be pulled, especially from the vantage of the White House.

The weather stayed bad. Good. He wanted time. He grabbed the shuttle bus to the tiny airport terminal. Scanning the day-old paper from Sydney, he saw nothing about Nixon or his transition. Damn it! He thumbed through the other newspapers and several magazines. Nothing. At the counter, he sipped orange juice and coffee. The rain continued. Butterfield's mind was churning hard. He bought an inexpensive bag of cookies and returned to the motel and hung the pidgin sign on the door: NO WAKIM MANISLIP (Do Not Disturb). Shedding his damp clothes, he put on a robe and sat to write. "Dear Bob . . ."

At first Butterfield wanted to describe his plight and see if Haldeman would intervene and assist with a new Air Force assignment. He wanted to get back to Vietnam with a wing command, a large unit of 75 or more planes. That seemed incredibly audacious. But Butterfield's strong suit was personality. At UCLA he had been named the Most Collegiate Looking Male, and in high school the Most Popular. He had been class president twice in two different high schools, and student body president at the end of his junior year. He had earned letters and gold awards in football, basketball and track. Soon the letter to Haldeman was a direct appeal for a face-to-face meeting at the Pierre Hotel in New York, where the president-elect had set up his transition shop. Just 20 to 30 minutes. That was a bold request but Butterfield was a solid and respectable voice from the past.

He was running out of motel stationery, down to the last sheet. Going over to the bed, he lay down. What did he really want? Was it just an assist with a new assignment? Or was it more?

Butterfield imagined himself in an office talking to Haldeman. Would Bob still have that businesslike aura? The cold efficiency had doubtless appealed to Nixon. Butterfield knew the type from the Air Force. If he could get an audience, he would be able to establish a rapport. That was what he did, that was one of his talents. He knew that it was also dicey. If he went outside the chain of command to Haldeman, it could be seen as an impropriety. So he had to ask himself, What is my true objective? Why is it suddenly so important to put myself in front of Haldeman and try to impress him?

But in one of those rationalizations common to all and for which Butterfield forgave himself, he decided he could offer his professional services for a post on Nixon's National Security Council staff. That would position him to return to Vietnam. That could be easy, he figured. He had to present himself as a clear-eyed colonel of excellent character and deportment. He was a graduate of the National War College, had a master's degree in foreign affairs, had lived in six foreign countries. He pretty well knew the world and the issues. Not a bad package, he concluded. He was also combat ready and trained in every facet of tactical aviation—air-to-air, air-to-ground, air defense and reconnaissance. He was one of the few Air Force colonels with that range of experience. For two years, he also had been a member of the Air Force Skyblazers, America's only formation aerobatic team in Europe.

Out of motel stationery, he went to the front desk and got more. Soon back in Australia, he revised his letter, making it into a biographical résumé, and sent it off. Later he tried to call Haldeman in New York. No luck.

Finally, Butterfield reached Larry Higby, Haldeman's executive assistant, on the phone. Higby was Mr. Step-and-Fetch-It. (Later in the Nixon White House the staff assistants were called "Higbys." Even Higby eventually had a Higby who was known as "Higby's Higby.")

"Colonel Butterfield, this is Larry Higby. Bob is busy now. Can I be helpful? Bob knows you're calling and he told me you two knew each other at UCLA."

Butterfield explained that he was coming to Washington on business. Of course the only business was to see Haldeman but he didn't say that. He said he wanted no more than 30 minutes on an important personal matter. He knew he wasn't fooling Higby, who replied they should talk the next day, and that he would probably have more to go on.

In Australia Butterfield was his own boss in charge of his schedule so he arranged to take leave and set up his travel. Within days he was in a room at the Washington Statler Hilton watching Nixon on television announce his cabinet.

Butterfield would later write in his memoir draft, "I took note of the Cabinet selectees' names and as I did so a strange feeling came over me. It was one I've never forgotten—a good feeling, one of confidence, a premonition of sorts that I was closing in on my destiny, that I would definitely be a part of this upcoming Administration."

The next morning, in freshly pressed uniform, Butterfield took a cab across the Potomac River to the Pentagon, which was familiar territory. He had worked there in several assignments. During the morning he tracked down colleagues who pulled the strings on the many military programs in Australia.

At noon he walked to the vast Pentagon Concourse, a mini-mall of retail stores, found a pay phone and called Higby.

"Mr. Higby is not available. Would you care to leave a message?"

Goddamnit! Butterfield muttered. He stared at the coin box of the pay phone, his long legs extended out of the booth. Now he was in the delicate minuet of making sure Haldeman knew he was available but not appearing overanxious. He calculated that if he called back in 30 minutes, and then again and again, his call slips could pile up and he would look like a pest. Not persistent, but annoying. Difficult and un-welcome. He decided to play a version of Hard to Get. He would wait until mid-afternoon to call again.

He went into D.C. and lunched alone at Duke Zeibert's, then one of the most famous and busiest restaurants with the power set. He could think of many restaurants to have a belt—the Jockey Club, Rive Gauche, or Sans Souci. He'd dined and drunk in all of them. No city brought back more stirring memories because over the years he had been in and out of Washington, especially as the senior aide to General Rosy O'Donnell, who had been commander-in-chief of the Pacific Air Forces in the early 1960s.

At 3 p.m. he picked up the phone.

Bob will be able to see you tomorrow afternoon here in New York, Higby said. They agreed on 2 p.m.

The next day, Butterfield flew to New York City and checked his bags at the Plaza Hotel. As soon as the meeting with Haldeman was over, he was heading back to Australia. He then went down to the Oys-ter Bar for a light lunch and a little meditation—a comforting stream of hope punctuated with flashes of deep worry. He needed to present himself as a competent potential addition to Nixon's team. There was much to think about. What exactly was the course he wanted to take? And was he going about it in the right way? How many acquaintances from decades back did Haldeman have knocking on his door? There was a bit of effrontery in it, but Haldeman also might find it comfort-ing. The top aide to the president might be suspicious of new friends.

Butterfield stopped at the men's room to gargle and brush his teeth, a ritual he practiced before important meetings. Soon he was out the door with briefcase in hand. It was cold but sunny, just right for the walk of several blocks to the Pierre, which had an elegance of its own. He visited the men's room again to comb his hair. Whenever he went hatless, even in the slightest breeze, his wispy hair would go standing up on end. He was conscious of not wanting to look unkempt or goofy as though he had just stuck a finger in an electrical socket.

"I'm walking in for the final exam," he recalled.

At the front desk, he asked for the main floor of the Nixon Transition Office and headed for the elevators.

Suddenly there was a commotion behind him, men moving fast. As he turned, he saw this wave sweeping in from the chilly air outside. He knew at once it was Secret Service moving with that special urgency and self-importance. "There's this rush of humanity," Butterfield recalled. "It looked like 40 or 50 people. Some of them had cameras. So this was the press. And lo and behold, Richard Nixon. I'd never laid eyes on Richard Nixon, but he comes rushing in. I'd thought at the time he looked a little more handsome than I thought he was, and a bit taller."

Nixon smiled and nodded to the hotel staff and bystanders and did not turn Butterfield's way. In 30 seconds Nixon and his Secret Service agents, and perhaps a handler or two, had crowded into an elevator and were gone.

Butterfield marveled at the way the old Haldeman connection was going, the timing, the prospect . . . the sense of destiny. In the back of his mind was the question: how far to push this? Well, he was pushing it to the limit, and the main event was to come. Maybe his hope was excessive, and he would get a polite brush-off, "Good to see you, Alex, and may the rest of your life turn out well."

# 2

"This meeting meant a lot," Butterfield recalled. "I am a full colonel, and I don't want to leave the military. The whole point is to stay in the military." He was not going to tell Haldeman his ultimate objective. "It was a surreptitious plan of mine. And some people would say it's not cricket. If I just could get with the Nixon team, I thought in a year or a year and a half at the most, I could get out of there and probably get a good assignment back in Vietnam. But of course I couldn't tell Haldeman that what I so desperately sought was only temporary."

After announcing himself to the receptionist, Butterfield took a chair and watched the outer office. Lots of hurried movement but these were happy people. Their candidate, and Butterfield's, had won. Their devotion was paying off for them. They were going to Washington, headfirst into the smoke.

A young man came tearing around the corner. He was grinning. Had to be Higby. They shook hands. Butterfield thought immediately and irreverently of Tweety Bird, the cartoon character, a baby chick popping his head through an eggshell. He looked 17. Thin, slight, blond with blue eyes—barely edging to manhood.

Sir, Higby said, please follow me.

"What a jolt it was to hear from you," said Haldeman, standing and coming forward to shake hands in a warm greeting.

He had not changed. The 1946 crew cut was intact, a trademark of sorts. He was a two-decade-older version of his earlier self.

"What brought you back to the United States? Or maybe I should ask what you're doing in Australia in the first place. Here . . . sit down."

They updated each other on wives and kids. Butterfield outlined his Australia problem.

Nearly everyone signing up or designated for the White House staff was an out-of-towner, Haldeman said. He joked that Nixon, the former congressman, senator and vice president, was the only one who had been to Washington before. They needed people with "Washington experience" like Butterfield.

Army Colonel Alexander Haig, promoted to colonel only 18 months earlier, had returned from Vietnam and was slated to be the military assistant to Dr. Henry Kissinger, the newly announced Nixon national security adviser.

Butterfield knew Haig well from the Pentagon. They had both served in Secretary of Defense McNamara's office.

Air Force Colonel Don Hughes, another old Butterfield friend, was designated Nixon's senior military aide, Haldeman explained. Hughes had been a military aide to Vice President Nixon.

The Nixon world was moving fast, and Butterfield could feel it slipping away. Well, he proposed, perhaps there would be an open slot on the National Security Council staff?

No, Haldeman said, They planned for only one military officer on the Kissinger staff, and if they made an exception, Butterfield would have to take a job normally filled by a more junior officer. Haldeman assumed that would be worse for his career than being stuck in Australia another year or two.

Butterfield agreed. He wanted no part of an assignment he would be overqualified for, even if it were in the White House. He had obviously arrived a few weeks late to compete with Haig, who was known as an ambitious, driven, wily opportunist.

As the talk was winding down, Butterfield stood and thanked Haldeman for slipping him into his schedule. He tried to feel good about it. He had taken maximum action, hatched a plan, flown to the United

States and done as much as he could within the bounds of propriety—
whatever that might be. So he would return to Australia, where he had
a fine though exquisitely smokeless assignment.

He thought he read an expression of sincere regret on Haldeman's
face.

As they walked out, Haldeman asked, Why does it have to be a
military job? Maybe there were other possibilities, maybe they should
consider another job in the White House?

"Well, yes," Butterfield replied, "maybe we should. I'll think about
that, Bob, and let you know right away. Meanwhile, the best of luck."
He added one of his signature lines. "I mean it."

Back at the Plaza he tamped down his natural instinct to stop at the
Palm Court to have a cold martini. It was a long trek home and he did
not arrive in Canberra until December 16.

Days later he wrote Haldeman a long thank-you letter and said that
if it would help Haldeman build his team he would consider a civilian
position and leave the military. Butterfield later told me: "It seemed
that Haldeman really liked being with me. You really could pull this
off. You are going to need some luck." At the same time, he added that
he was surprised he had so readily offered to cast aside a 20-year ster-
ling Air Force career. But he found there was an excitement in the air
in both Washington and New York.

Weeks passed. On Sunday morning, January 12—eight days before
the Nixon inauguration—Butterfield's phone rang.

"I've been giving a lot of thought to our talk," Haldeman said, "and
wondering where you might fit into all of this. I didn't tell you exactly
what I'll be doing in the White House, and there's still a lot I don't
know but he—the president, Mr. Nixon—has said that I'll be working
directly with him. I'll be ensuring that he gets everything he needs,
that there's proper follow-up to the tasks assigned the staff."

"I know," Butterfield replied. "Like an executive officer," the number two in an organization, the person who gets the operations off the
ground and follows up.

"Well," Haldeman continued, "I'd thought all along that I wouldn't
need a deputy, that I could handle everything I had to do alone." But

General Andrew Goodpaster, the former adviser to President Dwight Eisenhower, who was familiar with the way the White House worked, had a strong view.

"I'm sitting here beside General Andy Goodpaster now and he has convinced me that I should have a deputy. I had never thought of that." Haldeman said he did not necessarily want one but Goodpaster, about to become Supreme Allied Commander, Europe, had persuaded him.

"That seems to be a perfect job for you," Haldeman announced. "How would you like to be part of this and come in as my deputy? I'm really going to be the president's alter ego, and I want you to be mine."

He then put it another way. "You will be to me what I am to the president."

Butterfield was dumbfounded. This was the job offer of a lifetime. He thought, "If I'm going to go as a civilian, I've hit a home run."

"Now, I realize you'll want to think about this and talk to Charlotte, but we've decided here that we want the whole team on board the day after the inaugural. We don't want people drifting into Washington for the next six months."

"Jesus, Bob!" Butterfield almost shouted. "You've really knocked me for a loop." He wanted to find words to express gratitude rather than surprise. "I do have things to think about. I'm not even sure how to get out of the Air Force. You know . . . how to retire. But whatever happens, I want to thank you for the confidence. I'm tremendously flattered and honored to be considered." The wrong words, he later realized. He was not being considered. It was a flat-out job offer to be at the center.

"Just let me know as soon as you can, Alex. And incidentally, you don't have to leave the Air Force. Of course, that's all up to you." They had power, he reminded Butterfield. "Keep in mind also that we can help you right here. Just call me." He gave several phone numbers. "General Goodpaster is our conduit with the Defense Department, and if you need anything done, *anything*, we can do it immediately from here."

Butterfield did not miss the *"anything."* He promised an answer by Tuesday. "Is that okay?"

"Tuesday is fine," Haldeman said. "And Alex . . . I'd encourage you to think carefully about this. It's an opportunity you don't want to miss."

Butterfield loved the prospect. He had not accepted on the spot because he thought it might be improper, perhaps even unlawful for a military officer on active duty to accept a nonmilitary assignment in the White House.

Charlotte, his wife (they had met when he was in the fifth grade), didn't like the idea. "He was a golden boy in the Air Force," she said in a 2014 interview. "He was always promoted ahead of everybody else. And I loved my life. He was such a star. And at the time, everyone knew he was going to be on the next generals list. I liked that."

She could see he was determined to accept and she did not expect him to forgo the opportunity because of her reluctance. "I would not have expected him to change his mind," she said. "It was just my opinion."

Butterfield called his main mentor, now retired Air Force General Rosy O'Donnell.

"When the president of the United States calls, Alex, you don't have much choice," O'Donnell said. Other close friends also said he had to take it.

On Tuesday morning, he called Haldeman and accepted.

Haldeman sounded genuinely pleased. "Do you have a place to stay?"

Butterfield did not ask about title or salary. He, however, decided it was best to resign from the Air Force to avoid any appearance of a conflict or impropriety.

"I'll be an assistant to the president, one of five or six with that title," Haldeman volunteered, "and you'll be deputy assistant to the president."

On January 17, Butterfield flew to the United States and was immediately invited to a black-tie dinner party given by General Earle Wheeler, the chairman of the Joint Chiefs of Staff, the highest-ranking military position in the United States armed forces. "The Honorable Alexander Butterfield" was seated ahead of all the ambassadors as if he were more senior to four-star officers. And he was given a general officer's quarters at Bolling Air Force Base outside Washington.

The next day, Butterfield met Rosy O'Donnell at Rive Gauche, a top Georgetown restaurant. Over a pair of vodka Gibsons, O'Donnell poked him gently on the shoulder. "You know, your highness," he remarked, "you never did tell me how you came by this presidential appointment?"

"Well," Butterfield said, modifying an old vaudeville line, "I was in Moresby, and it was raining like a son of a bitch and . . ."

O'Donnell began to laugh. It was infectious. Soon they were giggling like boys and ordering another round of Gibsons.

It had been a race to get to Washington for the inaugural on January 20, and Butterfield watched snatches of it on television.

The next morning, wearing civilian clothes, he arrived at the White House for the first official day of the Nixon administration. At 8 a.m. Haldeman took the seat at the head of the table in what then was called the Fish Room, now known as the Roosevelt Room, in the West Wing right across from the Oval Office. Some 30 top White House staff crowded into the room, including Henry Kissinger. For Butterfield it was a room full of strangers. They had all, or nearly all, worked on the campaign or had deep associations with Nixon.

Haldeman was stern, all business, very much the man in charge. This is the new man Alex Butterfield, he announced. He is my deputy. He and I will be working together closely, he said.

Damn nice of him, thought Butterfield. It gave him immediate standing.

Keep in mind, Haldeman said, we're here for *eight* years.

What? Looks of mild bafflement appeared on a number of faces. Haldeman explained that though Mr. Nixon had been elected to a four-year term, in this day and age it was virtually impossible to push through Congress any kind of meaningful legislative program and do all the other things—foreign and domestic policy—in four years. So it's eight years for us—1969 through January 1977. Develop that mind-set, Haldeman said. Though he was clearly the top staff person in the new administration, he was adamant that he not be called chief of staff, he said.

Eight years was a bold declaration, boiling with self-confidence. It was a nice, unexpected touch. Butterfield thought it insightful, if they could deliver. Eight years could give them enough time for an era, a Nixon era. He figured Haldeman was acting as a good football coach getting his team mentally prepared: we are here to win our games, not to lose.

We want to start thinking of ourselves as invisible, Haldeman said. Mr. Nixon is the star on the team, the only star. We're here to serve and support. No grandstanding by the staff.

This was all said in utter seriousness, no levity.

Finally, this is important, Haldeman directed, no one of the staff other than communications director Herb Klein, an old Nixon friend from California, and Ron Ziegler, the new press secretary, was to have any contact with a member of the press. "We're going to be the silent staff." Exceptions would have to be approved in advance by him. He would have to be convinced such contact would benefit the president. If not, he would not approve the contact. In case there was any ambiguity, the rule—Butterfield thought it was an edict—goes into effect today, Haldeman said. The atmosphere was clear. White House aide Egil "Bud" Krogh would later call it "a mood of manic resolve."

Be in the East Room of the White House at 12:45 p.m. for a 1 p.m. ceremony in which each of you will take an oath of office, Haldeman said. Go to your assigned office and draw up a list of any repairs, furniture or supplies you might need.

Eight years, invisibility, strict orders not to talk to the press, to-do lists apparently down to how many paper clips they might need? Did Haldeman think of everything? Butterfield wondered. It was as if Nixon, and his presidency, was being wrapped in an impenetrable cocoon.

# *3*

---

Butterfield was assigned a cozy, low-ceilinged office in the West Wing basement, across from the one-chair barbershop and next door to the photo studio.

He strolled down the hall to the Situation Room and found Colonel Al Haig, the new military assistant to Kissinger. The two laughed about all the times they had been in the West Wing during the Johnson years. That was their secret, they joked, and agreed that it was better not to advertise or even let it be known they had served in a Democratic administration.

At 1 p.m., Butterfield was standing with Haldeman and other White House staffers in the East Room. He had not seen Nixon since mid-December in the lobby of the Pierre Hotel.

"Ladies and gentleman," a voice boomed, "the president of the United States and the chief justice of the United States."

Soon the president was directly in front of Butterfield—four feet away on a slightly raised platform. The expression on Nixon's face signaled apprehension. He had a way of smiling with his mouth but not his eyes, Butterfield noticed. He knew how expressive the eyes could be. A genuine smile tended to move to the eyes. But Nixon's eyes looked hollow. How strange, Butterfield thought. Nixon had been high visibility for decades, had spoken to countless people in every imaginable setting. Why couldn't he be at ease surrounded by his own people and in what was now his own house? Maybe he was just not feeling well.

Nixon spoke for five minutes. He made several awkward jokes telling the wives that the men on his staff would be working nights. "If they are away after midnight," he added, "don't blame me, blame them."

"I'm right there by the platform," Butterfield remembered. "I'm the first guy. And Nixon's standing there. And I see he's looking at me funny, like he doesn't want to stare at me, but he has never seen me before." Butterfield laughed, recalling the moment. "I couldn't say, 'Hey, don't you remember me in the Pierre lobby!' And I wondered if I'm the guy making him uncomfortable."

After the ceremony, Haldeman invited Butterfield to his office, which adjoined the Oval Office on the west side. It was large with windows and a fireplace. He wanted to talk about an important topic: paper flow. How paper would move to and from Nixon, how to manage and control it, somehow get their arms around the vast amount of business in the largest of enterprises: the American presidency, and the procedures for making decisions large and small.

I want you to work right here in my office for most of each day, Haldeman said, so you can see how both Nixon and I think, our style, our every mode of operating. "I want you to take notes like I do when you're in with the president. You know, to use the same format." Format was important. "Even to act and react as I would."

"I couldn't believe he was saying that," Butterfield recalled. He asked, Why?

"Because it will be easier on the president." Presidential ease was critical. "He's a funny guy. It's hard for him to deal with people he doesn't know well."

"I wanted to say, 'Now you're telling me,' " Butterfield recalled. "I'm just in from Australia." He thought he might have asked: How about people he has not even met?

"The chemistry has to be there," Haldeman went on. "So, until he gets used to your company, to your presence, to the extent that you can be a carbon copy of me, or a near carbon copy, you will put the president increasingly at ease. It isn't going to happen overnight. I know that; but I'll tutor you. Every time I come out of the Oval Office, I'll review with you what went on, how I responded, and how I plan to follow up on items that require staff action."

"That scared me to death," Butterfield said later. Haldeman had intimated on the phone that Nixon was a bit odd and Butterfield had read that in news reports. But this was extraordinary. Was it really necessary? He knew about the importance and subtlety of personal chemistry. But this exercise, apparently designed to create a staff clone, sounded not only weird but ridiculous.

"So," Haldeman told him, "I'm going to have to work you in rather slowly. If you don't do things exactly as I do, it could upset him."

It wasn't over. "When I go in there, I always sit to the left of the president. We always use yellow pads around here. He uses yellow pads. Don't use a white pad."

Unbelievable, thought Butterfield. He didn't want to hear any more. "It was a strange world I was entering. I wondered if it was as strange as it sounded. I thought, Do I have to get a crew cut too? What have I got myself into? I'm wondering if I can really be a carbon copy of Haldeman." He thought of asking, " 'Do you want me to leave now, Bob? Do you want me to pack my bag and leave?' It was hard to respond. I just had to nod. I couldn't get up and walk out, although I thought about it.

"I can hardly believe this little briefing I'm getting here. It's incredible to me. Where else could this be happening? I can't imagine."

The Air Force could be buttoned down, but this was another dimension entirely.

Shortly after 5 p.m., Haldeman was called into the Oval Office. Butterfield assumed he would be out in a short time to give him his first coaching session in "How to Be a Carbon Copy." At 6:30 Ken Cole, the designated staff secretary who would handle presidential paperwork, came in. He outlined how they would be working together on administrative matters.

Bob is in with the president, Butterfield said, and I'm waiting for him to come out.

"Oh, I don't think so," Cole said. "Bob is across the street with the president. They're taking a sort of tour of the Executive Office Building"—the main staff building next to the West Wing end of the White House.

After 7:30 Haldeman returned to his office, where Butterfield had waited two and one half hours.

Haldeman apologized.

"I didn't mind," Butterfield said. He had met Ken Cole and they had discussed paper flow. "I liked him a lot."

Haldeman apologized a second time for not alerting Butterfield that he and the president had gone on a tour. He had thought of leaving the president for a moment to go back to his office and explain. But, he said, if he had done that he was afraid he might somehow unnerve Nixon—"You know, make him uncomfortable knowing you were in here."

No, Butterfield didn't know. And he didn't understand. Not just his presence but the knowledge that he was in Haldeman's office would somehow stoke the president's worry? This made Butterfield think that the discomfort was about him. Yet he felt it was best to get back to a discussion of paper flow, note taking and carbon-copying Haldeman.

Haldeman was not going to let it go. "He knows we've brought you in as my deputy. In fact, he saw you this afternoon at the swearing-in."

That was not surprising to Butterfield, who had been four feet away from the president for the ceremony.

"He asked if you were the one standing next to me by the podium. So I can tell, he's just a little edgy."

Edgy? Why? How was that possible?

"He knows of the plan—in fact, he's approved the plan—to bring you into the Oval Office operation, but he's apprehensive about our getting started."

Apprehensive? The man has just taken over the leadership of the free world, and he is apprehensive about meeting a midlevel functionary? What was going on?

"That's why I want to wait for just the right time to take you in and introduce you."

"Bob, please," Butterfield lied. "That's fine. I understand perfectly." He did not understand at all.

Haldeman continued to express concern about the coming introduction. Butterfield could remember Haldeman's words 42 years later: "He's such a funny guy," Haldeman said. "I've got to play his moods. And if it happens to be the wrong time, you're dead in the water before you get started.

"I've brought you all the way in here. I have told him about you, but you know, I don't even know if he was paying attention."

Butterfield did not know whether to shriek, cry or walk out. What a thing to say—"I don't even know if he was paying attention"—even if it was true. What an utter put-down, cold, cruel and demeaning.

Given the circumstances, Butterfield smiled and assured Haldeman he would follow his lead. "What do you think it'll take, Bob, a couple of days?"

"Oh, yeah, about that. We'll do it this week for sure—probably late in the day as he's leaving the office. He'll be more relaxed then."

Was this happening? Was it believable? How could the president of the United States need to be relaxed to meet him?


During these early days, Nixon held a private dinner for the Apollo 8 astronauts, the second human spaceflight mission and the first to fly around the moon. Frank Borman, the commander of Apollo 8, was a friend of Butterfield's, an Air Force colonel of the same vintage. The two went for a drink at the Hilton.

"God, Alex, you've got a great job," Borman said, indicating that this was going to be a wonderful presidency. "I mean, working for the president. You're really lucky. You're an integral part of this man's team, the inner sanctum."

"Jesus, Frank, you already know the president better than I do," Butterfield replied. "Believe it or not, I've never even met the man. The truth is I'm supposed to stay out of sight for fear that I'll upset him if he sees me. My orders are to hide out in Haldeman's office."

Butterfield later congratulated Haldeman for shunning the title chief of staff. Haldeman also had been an Eagle Scout, and the Scouts liked a clear hierarchy. And he'd spent all those years at J. Walter Thompson advertising agency, where there was also a defined pecking order. Butterfield liked organizational charts. In the military they always had one on the wall. "Why don't you call yourself executive assistant? That makes your position clear to everyone."

"We don't want to make anything clear," Haldeman replied.

Later the business magazines *Forbes* and *BusinessWeek* inquired about White House organizational arrangements and titles. Haldeman told Butterfield not to answer. "Let them keep fucking guessing," he said.

## 4

———————

Five days into the administration, Saturday, January 25, Haldeman was sitting in his office with Butterfield, going through a manila folder filled with memos that Nixon had dictated to Rose Mary Woods, his personal secretary for 18 years.

One memo began: "To: Mrs. Nixon . . . From: The President."

"Imagine yourself writing this to Charlotte," Haldeman said smiling. He read on. One subject was Nixon's bedside table: "RN needs a table that is larger, something that will allow *him* to get *his* knees under it." Nixon kept referring to himself in the third person and with initials. Butterfield had trouble believing what he was seeing as he read on. "RN . . . RN . . . RN." It was as if Nixon were discussing another person.

"I had never seen anything like it," Butterfield recalled. "I could hardly believe it. In the real world it's a funny memo." He was more fascinated than amused. What was this marriage? And who was Nixon?

In those first days he got to know many of the senior and more junior people working in the West Wing. They seemed friendly, welcoming and savvy. They showed reverence toward Nixon, a devotion and almost worshipfulness when he would pass through. Mention of him was "THE PRESIDENT." Butterfield had seen some of this in the Johnson White House but the intensity was new.

On January 31, Haldeman returned to the touchy subject of the president's marriage. "It was never easy," he explained to Butterfield, "never harmonious." Dick and Pat often saw things differently, and neither gave in easily to the wishes, or demands, of the other. Nixon wanted to eliminate the friction, Haldeman said.

"He went through a long explanation of how he wants us to work with her staff," Butterfield recalled, "and it boils down to our carefully reviewing everything they recommend—all the social function scenarios." Chiefly about receptions, dinners and parties.

"When we can, we'll return the scenarios 'approved as submitted,' " Haldeman said. "But when we can't, when we feel that changes must be made, we'll make those changes and they'll have to accept them without protest."

It hardly sounded like a plan to avoid friction. "Isn't that really a matter for the president to take up with the first lady?" Butterfield asked.

Haldeman chuckled. It was uncharacteristic of him. "You don't understand, Alex," he said. "The president doesn't discuss these kinds of things with Pat. We do.

"And that brings up another subject," he continued. He personally had served as the intermediary between the Nixons over the years. "She hates me," Haldeman said. He usually reflected the president's view and was a pretty straight transmission belt for Nixon's likes and dislikes. The relationship with Pat never took. "I failed." Eventually during one of the campaigns, she refused to see him or talk to him on the phone.

"Finally," Haldeman said, "we made Dwight Chapin the intermediary." Chapin, 28, was currently the appointments secretary. He was also the ultimate choirboy. "Dwight, as you may have noticed already, has the world's nicest manner. He is polite and considerate, and both the president and I thought he'd work out fine."

Chapin lasted a couple of months. "But as soon as Pat felt that he had no personal interest in her view, that he was only seeing her to convey Dick's view—you know, the president's view—she shut him out too. To this day, she doesn't really trust me because she's convinced I will always represent the president's position—she's right, actually."

No surprise, Butterfield thought. Of course she would realize the obvious that anyone in the employ of Nixon would be the advocate for his views.

Butterfield, however, did not see what was coming next.

"I think you could handle Pat perfectly," Haldeman said. "You're a lot older than Dwight. That'll help a lot. And because you're new on the staff, she won't see you as she sees Dwight and me as longtime associates of the president."

Oh, no, Butterfield thought, as the new man he would have to be more inflexible, reflect the president's views unflinchingly to the first lady.

And then there is the Rose Mary Woods problem, Haldeman explained. Rose had been with Nixon since 1951.

"She's almost like an aunt to the girls," he said, referring to the Nixon daughters, Tricia and Julie. "But the fact is that she's outlived much of her usefulness. She's not sophisticated in the least and hasn't grown much. The president likes her but he wants to keep her at a distance. If he doesn't, she'll be in his office every five minutes with some unimportant, irrelevant matter. So I've got to work that out." He said the president was very aware of the Rose problem, and had told him, "I don't want her coming in here every five minutes. She's a pain in the ass."

Butterfield wondered if he was also going to get the Rose account. But the news was almost worse.

"Incidentally," Haldeman added, "you may want to be on the alert. She's already resentful of you. She doesn't like to see new people getting close to her man."

The Nixon inner circle sounded like both snake pit and kindergarten. "I'd say she's a bit premature in her resentment," Butterfield said.

"No," Haldeman said. "As I say, Alex, I don't want to wait any longer." He would take Butterfield to meet the president, he promised, today or tomorrow. "There's too much to be done that depends on your working as closely with the president as I am."

Haldeman added that Butterfield had to understand, "The president only works through me." And the goal was to substitute Butterfield as the alternative Haldeman.

But in the meantime, here was the plan. "If the president comes in, you just walk out." On occasion the president would come into Haldeman's office. If he did, let him only see your back, Haldeman instructed. "It'll spook him if he sees you."

Butterfield recalled, "I'm hiding behind columns, or I'm ready to, you know? I'm sleuthing around the West Wing so I won't spook the president when he sees this different face. It was an uncomfortable period."

Haldeman had one more piece of business. The president was interested in preserving as much detail as possible of his Oval Office history. So the president wanted to start having someone senior on the staff sit in on every meeting and take notes of the highlights. "Not only the substantive things," he explained, "but the mood of the meeting, as well. The president described them as sort of 'anecdotal reports.' And that is something I want you to get launched." Butterfield would be one of the handful of people to sit in once Nixon got to know him. Kissinger, John Ehrlichman, the White House counsel and a longtime aide, and Haldeman himself would do these memos.

It was an agonizing two weeks for Butterfield as he stayed out of sight.

On February 18, Haldeman came racing in to find Butterfield.

"Goddamnit," Haldeman said, "just what I did not want to happen. Jo called and I've got to get out to California." Jo, his wife, had not yet come to Washington and there were papers Haldeman had to sign about the sale of their house in California. It had been almost a month, and Butterfield still had not yet met Nixon. "I've got to take you in to meet him. You have to fill in for me when I'm gone," Haldeman said. He would be away about four days.

Butterfield recalled, "It was terrible. He grabbed me and said, 'I've got a staff car waiting to take me out to Dulles. I'm going back to Los Angeles. This is just what I didn't want to happen. I've got to take you in now to meet the president. Talk about not the right time.' So we run down the hall . . . Haldeman's almost frantic. We burst into the Oval Office breathless and unannounced. Of course, he could do that. I remember the president's face. We startled him. What the hell was going on? It's Haldeman and he's got that mysterious man with him. Still at a trot we move toward the middle of the Oval Office. And the president can see two guys running in and stop in the middle. So he gets up and comes around from his desk."

"Mr. President," Haldeman said. "This is Alex Butterfield. He's the one I've been telling you about. He's coming in as my deputy. He was in the Air Force." He explained that he had no choice but to go to California about the sale of his house.

"I'll be gone three, four days. And Alex will be sitting in my office and I just wanted you to meet him. Alex will be at my desk tomorrow, and he'll be running the Oval Office operation for the next four days."

"It's an honor to meet you, Mr. President," Butterfield said, extending his hand, "and to be here too. I'm really grateful for the appointment. It's a great honor for me to be a member of your team."

It was a good firm handshake. "There are only three of us there," Butterfield recalled, "so it's time for the third guy to speak."

"Ah, uh, hmm, ah, ahh," the president mumbled, clearing his throat and gesturing toward Haldeman. "Urm, urm." His right hand went up to his mouth, covering it briefly. He seemed about to speak, glanced at Butterfield and motioned to Haldeman. But still there were no words. Nixon began to make little circles with his hand as if to recall something to mind. "Urm, urm," he said.

Butterfield looked pleadingly at Haldeman.

Nixon again uttered some low-pitched guttural sounds that were not words. Suddenly he began to move one foot back and forth, almost pawing the carpet.

It was torture. Butterfield was considering a prayer asking for divine intervention, someone to help the president, anything.

Haldeman suddenly shifted his position.

Good idea, Butterfield thought, shifting his own body. But he felt strangely uncoordinated. In the silence he found himself also pawing the carpet with one foot like Nixon. He could not think of a time in his life when he had felt more uncomfortable.

The president seemed as if he were trying mightily to say something. He was perspiring, and no words came out, only a kind of growl. It was nothing intelligible. Someone had to end this suffering, Butterfield thought, and he started to speak. He wanted to say something about getting back to work. But at the same instant Haldeman broke in, firmly and abruptly extinguishing Butterfield's words.

Butterfield did not register what Haldeman said, but the tension seemed relieved.

Haldeman and Butterfield glided toward the door as if they had just adjourned a normal meeting.

Butterfield felt as if he were a zombie.

"Well, thanks, Mr. President," Haldeman said, almost chirping his words out. "Alex will be at my desk in the morning. I'll be working Alex into some of your meetings starting first thing next week."

"Fine, fine," the president responded. "Oh, say, Bob, I've got this goddamned reception over in the East Room. You know, the diplomatic thing. Are you coming over?"

"No, sir. I hadn't planned on it. Do you want me there?"

"Oh, no," the president said. "I'll call you later."

Haldeman grabbed Butterfield by the shoulder and they rushed out of the Oval Office.

"God damn, God damn!" Haldeman said all the way as they ran.

Back in Haldeman's office briefly, Butterfield fell into a chair.

What did I do wrong? he asked.

Nothing, Haldeman insisted. It had been his fault for not finding a more leisurely moment in the president's schedule. "Tomorrow would have been a lot better. He's got a pretty light day. Or Sunday, after the worship service. But you see now, don't you, why I was so insistent that the timing be right?"

"Yeah," Butterfield replied, "I sure do."

"I should have been more patient," Haldeman said. "But I need you in there more than ever now."

Haldeman departed at once. Butterfield was left to worry alone. Not a word! Whatever the reason, it was a total disaster, an experience he would never have thought possible. Three minutes he would never, ever forget. He felt lost. Was he dead in the water, as Haldeman had earlier suggested? Talk about invisible. Talk about not paying attention. Did the president even know he existed? That he had been in the Oval Office pawing the carpet mildly traumatized? Was it because of him? There was no way not to take this personally.

"I can't tell you how bad it was," Butterfield recalled. "And I thought, whoa, where the hell am I? You know? Disneyland? I just didn't understand what the next couple of days were going to hold for me."

# 5

---

Butterfield was in Haldeman's office right next to Nixon's the next day. He wavered between still feeling traumatized and isolated by his wordless and devastating Oval Office encounter the day before and the odd sensation of being right there next to the most powerful man in the world.

How could Nixon avoid speaking with him now? But Nixon went through a busy schedule and did not call or buzz once. It was a long, unnerving day. It seemed that the president was doing everything to avoid him. Normally by evening, Haldeman would have been with the president four or five times. Butterfield was anxious to go back in there, and concluded that the absence of a summons had to be purposeful. "He's trying to run the Oval Office by himself without my help," he concluded.

At 6:30 p.m. the president summoned his personal physician, Air Force Colonel Walter Tkach. Butterfield now worried that Nixon could make a clandestine exit, slip out of the Oval Office through the glass-paneled door leading to the Rose Garden, and be over in the residence before Butterfield noticed. He vowed that he could not let that happen.

So at 7 p.m. sharp, after the president had been with Dr. Tkach for half an hour, Butterfield walked into the Oval Office.

"Excuse me, Mr. President," he said, "but I didn't want you to get away without signing the day's accumulation of bills. Some of these things have to get out tonight."

Nixon glanced at Butterfield, and without a word, looked back at Tkach and resumed their conversation.

Again! thought Butterfield. Again! He walked over to Nixon's desk and placed the open folder of legislation and correspondence that needed his signature near his left elbow. As Haldeman had instructed in clone school, he held the first bill in front of Nixon at an angle convenient for signing. "There aren't really too many of these tonight," he explained, "about a dozen." He expected Nixon to respond, acknowledge the necessity of the often twice-daily ritual of signing.

Instead there was an awkward moment: pure quiet.

Tkach then asked a question, and Nixon answered him as he signed the bills. He put the cap back on his pen and resumed his conversation with Tkach as if they were alone in the room.

Butterfield felt flushed, but he gathered his documents and walked toward the door.

See you later, Alex, said Tkach, perhaps sensing the embarrassment.

"Okay, Walter, see you tomorrow," Butterfield said and exited.

There was no ambiguity. The president had not only been cold, distant and dismissive. He had been rude. Driving home, he could think of nothing else. As he lay in bed, he could not shake it. Not a word. Goddamnit! he thought. Who did he think he was? For a moment, however, he managed a smile. He, of course, knew the answer. After all, Nixon was president of the United States. But that should not provide him with immunity from the niceties of human interaction. When all was said and done, he did not have to be rude and uncivil. Butterfield wondered if he should go to Haldeman when he returned and volunteer to leave. How was this ever going to work out?

Butterfield later described his thoughts to me. "I wondered, is he really rude, or is he just terribly shy? I was really upset. Here I was, and I had given up the whole Air Force deal, my career. Now I've been lured into this thing. Obviously, I was starting to blame it on other people." He laughed. "It was all my decision. I knew that. But it looked like I am toast."

•    •    •

The next morning, February 19, Bryce Harlow, the head of White House liaison with Congress, came to see Butterfield. Harlow was considered a master of congressional relations with a soft-spoken but persistent style. He had held the same congressional liaison job for President Eisenhower, and was widely considered the wise man for congressional and public relations. At 53 he was a World War II veteran and a contemporary of Nixon's.

Butterfield knew enough to listen to Harlow.

Let's make sure the president is brought up to date on a brewing issue in the Virgin Islands legislature, Harlow said. The legislature for the U.S. territory was agitating for Nixon to fill a vacancy in the governorship, arguing that they could not proceed with their budget without a new governor. Lots of the congressional leaders coming in for an 8:30 a.m. meeting with the president were aware of the issue and it might come up.

He was plainly warning Butterfield: Don't let the president be embarrassed.

At 8:10 a.m. Butterfield hurriedly put together a memo on the issue of the Virgin Islands legislature and governorship. He called Harlow and suggested he brief the president so Nixon would not be blindsided.

Harlow called back to say that he had been in with the president but had not had a chance to raise the Virgin Islands problem. Secretary of Defense Melvin Laird was currently in the Oval Office with the president. It would be "prudent," he said, to brief the president. "Prudent" from Harlow meant, Do what I suggest.

Butterfield said he had written a memo on the Virgin Islands legislature and would hand it to the president as soon as Laird left the Oval Office. He knew that Harlow was eager to get to the Cabinet Room to mingle with the congressional leaders—his constituency as head of White House liaison with the Hill.

Butterfield phoned Rose Woods, whose office was strategically placed on the other side of the Oval Office. Her office had direct access to the Cabinet Room. Call me please, he asked, as soon as Laird has left and the president is alone.

The minutes ticked by. No call from Rose.

At 8:27 a.m., three minutes before the leadership meeting was scheduled to begin, Butterfield decided to act. Haldeman would not let this slip. "Feeling duty-bound" as he would later write in his unpublished memoir, his job was to make sure that Nixon was not embarrassed or "caught short." He opened the door directly into the Oval Office, the memo in hand, and walked in. He was just in time. The president and Laird were out of their chairs and heading for the leadership meeting.

"Mr. President," Butterfield said. "It'll only take a minute, but you should read this one-page memo before you go into the leadership meeting." He extended the memo toward Nixon. Something was not right. "Or I can brief you orally," he added lamely.

Nixon was visibly annoyed. The expression on his face was chilling.

Butterfield momentarily felt almost defiant. He didn't give a damn. This was his job. He was representative of the system Haldeman and he were putting in place—looking out for, protecting the president. The president and his new aide stood there for a fraction of a second almost facing off.

"What the hell is it about?" Nixon snapped. "What do you want?"

Butterfield wanted to say, "I'm doing my job." But he realized he was about to step in it. Oh, how insignificant his answer was going to seem. Here was the commander-in-chief meeting with his secretary of defense in the middle of a war, perhaps the most controversial in U.S. history. How could he couch it succinctly to make it sound worthy of stopping the commander-in-chief almost literally in his tracks?

"It's about the Virgin Islands legislature," Butterfield said, "and—"

"The Virgin Islands legislature?" the president shouted. "Jesus Christ! I don't give a good goddamn about the Virgin Islands legislature!" He turned to Laird. "Mel, do you give a damn about the Virgin Islands legislature?" essentially asking if Laird were an idiot like this other guy, Butterfield.

"No, sir, I don't give a damn about the Virgin Islands legislature," Laird dutifully replied. He was obviously enjoying this little bit of Oval Office theater. There was the president chewing out one of his under-

lings, demonstrating command and common sense, which the under-
ling clearly had not.

The president shook his head.

An artful combination of disgust and disbelief, Butterfield could
see. The perfect put-down.

Without another word, Nixon turned back toward the far door and
with Laird close on his heels, walked out.

Butterfield recalled, "I got these two rude sons of bitches. The thing
is about to come apart for me." His first impulse was to tear up the
memo and erase it and the encounter from his mind. Instead, restraint
was the order of the day. He placed the memo on the president's desk
and returned to Haldeman's office.

"I knew I was going to quit," Butterfield later told me after reviewing his notes, memos and book draft. "I was going to quit this job. No
one had ever talked to me that way. In all my years in the military, no
one had ever talked like that.

"Oh, I can't tell you how close I came to walking out. I was mad.
God, I thought that was rude. Rude!

"Haldeman brought me in there, he's away and I'm flunking the
course my first time out of the box. I wanted to say, 'Fuck you,' I mean,
I did want to say that."

He did nothing of the kind. Throughout the balance of that day,
the president did not buzz for him. That would have been unheard of
if Haldeman were there. And Butterfield found no reason to call or go
see the president.

That night Butterfield had dinner in the White House staff mess
and went home late. Brooding, he played back the scene. No, he had
never in his adult life been spoken to or treated with so little respect.
He was in shambles and bewildered. "My mind was made up," he
wrote in his book draft. "I'd tell Haldeman—if the president hadn't
done so already—that I was not the man for the job. Until then, I'd
swallow my pride and perform as well as I knew how." He had been an
aide to two top-level Air Force officers and the secretary of defense. It
was endless work but not difficult. Judgment was the key ingredient,
and he had been tested many times. "I was not a boob."

# 6

---

The next morning, February 20, Butterfield wrote in his book draft: "On the way to the White House Thursday morning I promised myself I'd give no hint to anyone of my anger and disgust. I'd take on a cheery demeanor, smile a lot and hope the day went quickly. It would be my last in an environment I'd suddenly come to loathe.

"I don't like the environment. I don't like anything about him, I have to admit that. And I'm upset as hell."

At 7 a.m., he went into the Oval Office for a routine check to make sure everything was in order before the president arrived, almost religiously, between 7:50 a.m. and 8:10 a.m. A roaring fire was going in both the president's fireplace and Haldeman's. Freshly cut flowers from the White House nursery were in place. He went to the president's outbox. Only Haldeman and he were allowed to remove materials. He noticed that the memo he had written on the Virgin Islands legislature the day before was there. In the memo Butterfield had explained that he did not want the president to be caught short on the issue and suggested it be handed off to the secretary of the interior, who oversaw the U.S. territories.

He glanced at the bottom of the memo where he had listed three options for the president:

Agree _____

Disagree _____

Comments _____

Nixon had initialed his RN in the Agree line.

What a pleasant surprise! Butterfield thought. He expected the president would ignore the memo or return it with no decision. He read the simple "RN" as an apology of sorts. His spirits began to rise. He did some follow-up paperwork so the president could make an appointment for the Virgin Islands governorship. Some documents came back with approving presidential check marks in the upper-right-hand corner—Nixon's way of agreeing. At minimum it was an accommodation.

How a check mark could lift the spirits!

Later in the day in Haldeman's office the buzzer went off. Could this really be? Surely not. The buzzer sounded again.

Butterfield grabbed a pen, the yellow pad and walked into the Oval Office.

"Good morning, Mr. President."

"Yes, well," the president began, "I thought you might have some things to be signed. I don't think we got to that yesterday."

"Yes, sir. I've got a number of things. Let me get the folder." He scurried back to Haldeman's office, struck that the president had observed that there had been no signings the evening before. Butterfield believed they had been playing a little game, aware of the mood swings of the other. Now it was time to kiss and make up. He was glad. He did not want to fail. Perhaps he was over-interpreting, making too much of the president's neglect. Within a minute he was back in the Oval Office.

"Alex," Nixon said. His name sounded weird coming from this weird man. "Maury Stans is coming in, as you know," the president said. Stans, the commerce secretary and chief Nixon fundraiser, wanted to parade his key deputies and assistants through the Oval Office to meet the president. "He's due any minute. You stick around when he comes in because we want to get rid of him quickly. I want it to look like we're working on something—you know, the schedule or some damn thing." Nixon kept signing, bing, bing, bing, paying little attention to each paper. "If we don't do that, they'll never get out of here. It's just supposed to be a handshake but Maury will want to tell me everyone's life history."

Tell Chapin, the appointments secretary, to tip off Stans that the president is having an especially busy day, Nixon ordered.

"Hello, Maury," Nixon said when Stans stepped through the door. "Glad you could drop by. Ah, Alex and I were just going over some scheduling problems, and . . . ah . . . oh, you know Alex, don't you?"

Stans had brought about ten of his top people.

"This is quite a gang you've got here, Maury. Who's minding the store?"

Everyone laughed.

"You stay right here," the president said to Butterfield, signaling the importance of their business, as he extended his hand to Maury's gang.

Butterfield was amused. "The president was an actor," he wrote in his account of the Stans meeting. "I stepped back several paces to be out of the way and stood there, pen in one hand, pad in the other . . . arms folded across my chest. To have heard the president, and seen him, one would have thought I'd been his closest aide for 20 years. I knew he'd fooled Maury's staff, if not Maury himself, and I wondered what the reaction would be if I blurted out the fact that the president had spoken his first words to me only the day before . . . and it was in a fit of exasperation."

The president dispensed cuff links to all the gang, complimented Maury on the "fine team," but said he hoped it would be the last time all of them were out of the building.

Oops, thought Butterfield, a modified rerun of the earlier joke. He took it as his cue to move back to Nixon's desk, where he looked at Stans and waved his pad in a suggested farewell gesture that it was time to depart. The gang filed out.

"You know," Nixon said to Butterfield, "anytime you can get rid of a dozen people in as many minutes, you've had a successful meeting. We ought to remember that. We should make it a rule."

Next, Housing Secretary George Romney was bringing a few of his team. "We've got to time it to handshakes only. And God knows that's not going to be easy with Romney."

Back at Haldeman's desk, Butterfield ordered coffee from the White House mess but was thinking champagne would have been more appropriate. It was the first time Nixon had called him Alex, and the president had made him an accomplice in the effort to expedite the routine and ceremonial. He felt relief. He had been admitted of sorts, perhaps only provisionally, to the Club, a rite of passage. It had been an emotionally exhausting month. He went downstairs to the men's room, washing his hands and face. He felt the muscles in his body relax, probably for the first time in weeks. Nixon had him tied in knots. What a strange bird, he thought, shy and introverted but tough and strong-willed, and in the company of intimates profane. Almost allergic to new people. Jesus H. Christ, Butterfield thought. He had never dreamed, never thought it possible that a politician could be so stressed and tongue-tied. Worse was the realization that he knew he had been the cause in part. Who wouldn't have lost a lot of enthusiasm? At least he had been spoken to now. But the dressing-down—the ranting—in front of Laird still was inexcusable.

Butterfield wrote in the draft of his book: "I had never, in 21 years in the Air Force, been witness to such behavior. He was an ignorant boor, a bumpkin, as far as I was concerned and I readied myself to jump ship."

Ah, but that was then. This morning, he had seen in Nixon what he read as nothing less than the signs of regret. Their indirectness, he believed, suggested their sincerity.

With Haldeman back from California, Butterfield turned to the endless paper flow and orders from Nixon. He sent out these orders in memos to others in the president's name, signed, "Alexander P. Butterfield, Deputy Assistant to the President." On February 22, 1969, his memo to Attorney General John Mitchell and the postmaster general said the president wanted two reports "on your joint effort to stop the mailing of obscene materials to juveniles." Another just to the postmaster general said "The President has directed that the religious inscription—'In the beginning God . . .'—be restored to the Apollo 8 stamp."

With Butterfield and Haldeman's wives still in Australia and Los Angeles respectively, the two men had dinner in the White House mess several times a week, often with Kissinger, a real bachelor. Butterfield liked Kissinger though the national security adviser tended at times to take himself too seriously. But most of the time he sounded good, crafting and talking in elegant paragraphs. He also had a razor-sharp wit, evident as he conducted informal, dinner seminars on foreign policy.

Butterfield also got to know Daniel Patrick Moynihan, the Democrat and Harvard professor on leave to be Nixon's top urban affairs adviser. In the first months, Butterfield found that a calm typically descended over the White House about seven in the evening. Some of his most enjoyable moments later in the day were spent in Moynihan's cozy office, only 40 feet from his own, having a stiff drink.

Moynihan frequently would go swimming and then, with uncombed wet hair and red-stocking feet, pad by Butterfield's office looking for his drinking buddy. "Hi, Alex, ready!"

Once at Haldeman's 7:45 a.m. senior staff meeting, Moynihan grew so frustrated at the wandering discussion that he raised his clenched fist, brought it down hard on the table, and shouted, "Fuck!" There was immediate silence. Butterfield watched everyone turn to Rose Woods, the only woman at the meeting, in horror and embarrassment.

Haldeman began to trust Butterfield more, and the president soon assigned Butterfield the responsibility of working out a strategy and game plan to win congressional approval for the modified Anti-Ballistic Missile (ABM) system. It was the president's major initiative that first summer, and soon Butterfield was churning out memos and directives to cabinet members and key Republicans in Congress. It was an unusual delegation of responsibility to the new man.

•     •     •

On March 18, 1969, Rose Woods and several longtime Nixon staffers arranged a 45th birthday celebration for Paul Keyes, a comedy writer and Nixon friend who had helped on the 1968 campaign. Keyes had been a writer and producer of the television comedy variety show *Laugh-In*. He had arranged for Nixon to appear on the show and deliver the line that was the trademark of the show, "Sock It To Me." Nixon's appearance drew lots of attention, seemed to humanize him, and a number of political commentators later said it got him elected.

Keyes had met Nixon in the 1960s when he was a producer for *The Jack Paar Tonight Show*. His version of his encounter with Nixon before the show went like this: "Hi, Mr. Vice President. I'm Paul Keyes. I just talked to Jack, and he said he won't raise the matter of the fucking fags in the State Department if you won't." Keyes then perfectly mimicked Nixon's distress: "What?! What?! What is that?!"

A bond of sorts had formed after that, and Keyes was frequently on the Nixon payroll as a joke writer. This week he was in Washington helping the White House speechwriters.

Near the end of the day, Butterfield was in the Oval Office when Haldeman mentioned that the small celebration for Keyes's birthday was being held later in the Fish Room. Haldeman knew of Nixon's fondness for Keyes, who had very conservative politics.

Mr. President, Haldeman said, why don't you step across the hall and say hello and happy birthday to Paul?

The president seemed to give it some thought but remained noncommittal, so Haldeman dropped it. The president decided these matters and it was fruitless to press.

Later in the day Haldeman suggested to Butterfield, "Come on. Let's go over and see how the party is going." He first propped open his office door and did the same to the rear door to the Fish Room, which was directly opposite his own. That way he could make a rare appearance at a White House social event and also hear if the president buzzed. The two open doors suggested, and symbolized, the short leash.

Butterfield noticed some nice decorations in the Fish Room. It was festive. A bar cart had been wheeled up from the staff mess, and a

Navy steward was bartending. Several trays of hors d'oeuvres rested on a table to one side. Butterfield was introduced to Keyes and chatted with Rose Woods, Pat Buchanan, a key Nixon speechwriter and strategist, and several others before retreating with his drink to the back of the room with Haldeman.

"Ladies and gentlemen, the president," shouted an aide as Nixon followed him. Nixon walked in and stopped. A hush fell over the room and continued unnaturally.

# 7

---

"Gee, Mr. President," Keyes said, breaking the silence, "you must be losing your touch. They all applauded when I came in."

A good line for TV was followed by a second silence. Tick, tick, tick.

"Shit," Haldeman muttered under his breath. Butterfield wondered why someone like Rose or Haldeman or Buchanan, no shrinking staffer, didn't try to rescue the moment—or the president—with something such as applause or a boo for Keyes. Why not offer him a glass of wine or explain that Paul had been there all week? But the silence continued. No one chanced breaking it, even Keyes, who was about five feet from Nixon. There was not even a handshake.

The president was perspiring, Butterfield noticed. Now there was a persistent stillness. Butterfield nervously cleared his throat. The noise sounded like a cannon shot.

Nixon stepped back slowly and pointed at Keyes, who was wearing a solid green blazer. "Ah, ah, ah . . . uh," he muttered.

Then Nixon pointed down at the carpet, a worn, faded maroon. He spoke in a deep but barely audible voice. "Green coat . . . red rug . . . Christmas colors." He then wheeled around and strode out of the room to the Oval Office.

That was it. Butterfield would remember those six words verbatim 45 years later—"Green coat . . . red rug . . . Christmas colors."

The buzzer in Haldeman's office sounded almost immediately. Three long blasts. It was as if Nixon was sending his anger, distress or embarrassment—who could know which—in some primitive Morse code. The furious summons seemed louder and more intense than normal.

"Oh, boy," Haldeman exclaimed. He heaved a sigh of resignation and headed out. "Don't leave, Alex. I'll talk to you when I come out."

A pall had fallen. Rose and Keyes seemed especially stricken. It was impossible for any of them to feign indifference or overlook such an excruciating display. Butterfield did not know the words to describe it. Could the minutes be likened to a self-immolation? Sometimes you saw things you wish you had not seen.

Butterfield ordered another drink, chugged it down, and went back to Haldeman's office to wait. In the first months, he was finding some things to admire in Nixon—the work ethic, snatches of empathy, the determined, focused effort so evident in nearly everything he did. The humanity barely emerged, and Nixon was quickly becoming the oddest man he'd ever known.

He had noticed how rapidly and easily Nixon's moods rubbed off on, even infected, Haldeman, who did not lighten up. Butterfield thought a more relaxed approach might serve the president.

When Haldeman came back through the Oval Office door he wore his businesslike expression. He was still giving Butterfield lessons in how to deal with Nixon.

Butterfield thought of a film and the song "Six Lessons from Madame La Zonga." The first lines seemed to apply: "Have you ever been embarrassed?"

Haldeman sat down glumly. Do you know what the president said?

"He had to be upset with himself," Butterfield replied. "He was exactly as he was the day you introduced me . . . except for that painful reference to 'Christmas colors.' Was there some significance to that?"

"No, no," Haldeman said. "He just got tied up when he walked in and everyone stopped talking. It's probably my fault for not preparing a briefing paper. If he's given some information—just a line or two, a couple of talking points—he's fine."

Talking points for a small, private birthday party?

"But," Haldeman continued, "he didn't mention anything about himself. Do you know what he raised hell about?"

"No."

"He didn't like the liquor cart there in the Fish Room. He told me he doesn't want to see cocktails served anywhere in the West Wing except in the staff mess."

"And that was it?"

"Yep," Haldeman replied. "That was it."


The president had scheduled his sixth press conference on June 19, and it would be live on national television. He had cleared his calendar and holed up to pore over his briefing books. He did not like to conduct a practice run with staff peppering him with possible questions, as many presidents do.

In preparing the briefing books, Butterfield had asked the speechwriters to divide the questions into the "clean," the basically straightforward inquiries, and the "dirty," the hostile questions that were antagonistic or included possible traps.

Nixon's seclusion gave Butterfield some free time to return home to pick up something he needed. As he was coming back down MacArthur Boulevard, his beeper went off. He was among a handful of aides assigned one. Normally the beep meant Higby was relaying some instruction from Haldeman.

Butterfield spotted a service station ahead on the left and pulled over. He jogged across the street. The only public phone was on the wall in the service station garage. The shop was filled with all kinds of loud noises, including someone banging on a tire with a rubber hammer. The background noise would not be a problem, Butterfield figured, because he would be able to find out what Higby wanted, so he dialed the White House switchboard.

"Oh, yes, Mr. Butterfield. One moment . . . the president's calling."

Damnit. Butterfield took out his pen but he had nothing to write on. He had to prepare for the encounter, and later half joked, "If I'd had my stuff with me, I'd have gargled and brushed my teeth."

Almost instantly the distinctive low muffled voice filled his ear.

"Siff funafunwas pss't negro souse ponopotion." Click!

"WHAT . . . SIR?" But the president was gone, apparently back to the briefing books. It was so fast with no hello, no good-bye. Butterfield stepped outside, leaned against a tree, shut his eyes and played back the muttered sounds as best he could conjure them. He was frantic. And in the hyper-charged world and spooky drama of the White House, part of him felt his life was at stake. One of the words—the only halfway clear one—was "negro," Butterfield was pretty sure. "Ponopotion"? What the hell was that? "Ponopotion, Ponopotion," he played it over again and again in his own mind, slowing it up, "Pon–o–po–tion," speeding it up, "ponpotion" to dig out the meaning. "Negro" for sure and then this new concoction—"PONOPOTION." He felt he was growing brain dead. What was "pss't? It wasn't a word, it was just a sound.

The Haldeman rule was to serve the president—answer his needs, his questions. Cushion his way. If it meant reading between the lines, deciphering his handwriting, or untangling the grunts and half words, then do it. Haldeman and Butterfield were the pipeline from Nixon's mind, and words, to the executive functions of the presidency. Competence meant getting it right, not asking the president to repeat himself. That would have been the easy way, but it was just not done. Butterfield was astonished that this man, so forceful and usually articulate, even eloquent, could mash his words so often. It was as if he were locked in his own deeply personal world, thinking, planning and churning. The staff were the relay stations, and they better get with this strange program.

Butterfield went back to the garage and called his secretary. "Please call the Library of Congress or Bob Brown's office, or both—yes, call them both—and find out what percent of the U.S. population is Negro." Bob Brown was a black special assistant who handled community relations.

It was a guess.

Yes, "ponopotion" was likely "population" and "pss't" or whatever it was could be "percent." All perhaps.

Back at the White House, Butterfield was met by his secretary. "Bob Brown says that Negroes comprise 11 percent of the U.S. population."

In his office, Butterfield retreated to his memory bank, closing his eyes, and actually holding his head in his hands. Maybe he could squeeze Nixon's words out of his brain. He wanted to calm himself, return to that moment in the garage. But pure retrieval was now impossible because his guess got in the way. Logically it seemed it was the kind of thing the president might want to know.

Butterfield took a sheet of White House stationery and wrote: "There are 22,354,000 U.S. blacks in America, which is 11.1% of our 200 million (plus) population. (This comes from three reliable sources.)"

He added the second point for clarity. A one-number answer might seem barren. He took the note over to the residence, where the president was holed up and had it sent up.

He reported to Haldeman what had happened. That evening the two sat in Haldeman's office and watched the press conference on TV.

At one point, Nixon referred to "the 11 million law-abiding Negro citizens in this country."

Oh Jesus, the "11" was the percentage. Butterfield felt sick. By supplying the extra information, he had made the gaffe possible—prime time to the world—that the black population was suddenly half of what it really was.

"Don't worry about it," Haldeman said. "You really didn't do anything wrong. The president made the error and we can have Ziegler straighten it out."

Butterfield, relieved that Haldeman was in a forgiving mood, said he would get a note to Ziegler right away.

"Mistakes like that are nothing new," Haldeman added, "especially when statistics are involved. Besides most people won't have a clue." But then he insisted that Butterfield see both Ziegler and Herb Klein personally to get it corrected. "Don't depend on a note."

Butterfield went to see Ziegler. When he returned to Haldeman's office Kissinger was there, complaining with much emotion that the president had gone too far promising troop withdrawals from Vietnam.

Later that night Butterfield bumped into Bob Brown.

"Hey, Alex. Does the president know something I don't know?" Brown said with a smile. "Man, we lost *half* the brothers!"

Nixon, Butterfield later recalled, "blew it because I gave him too much information. All my life I was told, 'Don't give them too much information, just give what they ask.' "

For Butterfield it was an important study in the consequences of the president's words. What had meaning? What could he change with words? His Vietnam policy, of course. And what could he not change? The population statistics, of course. But the press and the world were focused on Vietnam. What were Nixon—and Kissinger—up to? Where were they going? And with what consequences? Were the strategy and the bombing working?

*8*

There is only the thinnest of membranes separating the unnoticed, largely silent crime, and the one that explodes in the media defining the event if not an era.

Butterfield watched the president in November 1969 as he erupted over a series of press reports by journalist Seymour M. Hersh on the massacre of hundreds of Vietnamese civilians by American soldiers on a search and destroy mission. The attack was led by Army Lieutenant William L. Calley in a village that would become infamous as the scene of the best-documented Vietnam War crime—My Lai.

Anything of concern to Nixon automatically became important to Butterfield. Because Nixon was so fired up about My Lai and Hersh's intense focus and the drumbeat of his reports, Butterfield gathered in his archive numerous documents about the case.

Nixon had learned about My Lai, though apparently not its full dimensions, two months before Hersh's first story. Secretary of Defense Laird had laid it out to Nixon in a confidential two-page memo: "Subject: The My Lai Atrocity.

"The known facts leave no doubt about the necessity of prosecution. . . . Publicity attendant upon such a trial could prove acutely embarrassing to the United States. It might well affect the Paris peace talks and those nations opposed to our involvement in

Vietnam will certainly capitalize upon the situation. Domestically, it will provide grist for the mills of antiwar activists."

A confidential accompanying statement of facts stated that the investigation was triggered by Ronald L. Ridenhour, a former soldier, who wrote a letter to the secretary of defense on March 29, 1969, alleging the American military had committed atrocities against Vietnamese civilians. After a three-month Pentagon investigation, some of the details were reported in the Daily Report to the President on August 5, 1969. It was determined that on March 16, 1968, a large number of Vietnamese were killed, including "women and children." It added, "The villagers were all unarmed and were offering no resistance."

If publicized, this was a clear political threat to Nixon's strategy of Vietnamization. The design was to turn the war over to the South Vietnamese while withdrawing most of the U.S. troops. Nixon said his goal was Peace with Honor. Both the Peace and Honor were threatened by the My Lai revelation. The massacre would stiffen the enemy's spine and justify its resistance. The mass slaughter of Vietnamese civilians, women and children, demolished any notion of honor.

Haig, Kissinger's deputy, sent internal Army and Pentagon memos labeled *SENSITIVE* to Butterfield. They consisted mainly of lists of names of 36 witnesses to the massacre. Hersh, then a freelance reporter, had crisscrossed the country to track down some of the witnesses.

His first article had run November 13, 1969, under the headline "Lieutenant Accused of Murdering 109 Civilians" in various newspapers. The story a week later was filled with first-person witnesses willing to be named, recounting what they had seen. Sergeant Michael Bernhardt was quoted telling Hersh, "The whole thing was so deliberate. It was point-blank murder and I was standing there watching it. . . . One, they were setting fire to the hootches and huts and waiting for people to come out and then shooting them. Two: They were going into the hootches and shooting them up. Three: They were gathering people in groups and shooting them. As I walked in, you could see piles of people all through the village. . . . It's my belief that the company was conditioned to do this."

Another witness, Michael Terry, said, "They had them in a group standing over a ditch—just like a Nazi-type thing. . . . We just treated them like animals."

In his November 25 story, Hersh had the most potent witness, someone who had not only seen the massacre but participated in it. Hersh had located Paul Meadlo, 22, at his mother's home in the farm community of West Terre Haute, Indiana. The on-the-record self-incrimination by Meadlo was horrifying.

"So we stood about 10 or 15 feet away from them, then he [Calley] started shooting them. Then he told me to start shooting them. . . . I started shooting them. I used more than a whole clip—actually I used four or five clips." Hersh noted that there are 17 M-16 shells in a clip, and Meadlo estimated they killed 15 Vietnamese civilians in that one shooting spree. In all he said that he thought 370 had been massacred.

The killings, Meadlo said, "did take a load off my conscience for the buddies we'd lost. It was just revenge, that's all it was."

Though he said he believed he was acting on orders, Meadlo said he had haunting memories. "They didn't put up a fight or anything. The women huddled against their children and took it. They brought their kids real close to their stomachs and hugged them, and put their bodies over them trying to save them. It didn't do much good."

Meadlo's mother told Hersh, "I sent them a good boy and they made him a murderer."

*Time* and *Newsweek* ran cover stories on the massacre. Then television entered the fray. Meadlo appeared on a new CBS television show called *60 Minutes*, interviewed by Mike Wallace.

"Do you ever dream about this?" Wallace asked.

"I still dream about it," Meadlo answered. "I see the women and children in my sleep. Some nights I can't even sleep. I just lay there thinking about it."

Many who didn't believe Hersh changed their minds overnight. Stephen Ambrose, a leading military historian, said, "My Lai and the way it was presented on television just shook me to my roots. My Lai was the single most shocking thing to come out of the Vietnam War for me."

The White House had known for some time that former soldier Ronald Lee Ridenhour had first blown the whistle on the massacre. He had sent a three-page letter to not just the secretary of defense and the Army, but to two dozen others, including some U.S. senators.

Butterfield flew to Florida with Nixon on November 27 for Thanksgiving. How to counter the My Lai incident was very much on Nixon's mind. Across three pages of notes on a yellow legal pad, Butterfield recorded the president's action plan, a classic Nixon attack. The president's comments were so potentially explosive that Butterfield immediately classified his notes Top Secret.

"Check out the Claremont man," since Ridenhour had gone to Claremont Men's College.

"Check all talkers," Nixon said, referring to all those speaking out publicly. "The Army photographer—Cleveland P/D man sold material to Life and to C P/D," references to the *Cleveland Plain Dealer*. "How much?"

Nixon continued, "They're vulnerable on two counts: A, photographer's mother and dad are Cleveland peaceniks; B, Meadlo too smooth for a farmer."

Butterfield noted that the president thought the Pentagon was "too scared to investigate adequately.

"Another vulnerable spot — $ passed
                   — Claremont fellow Jewish
                   — (lib Jew)

"We need some ammo in the hands of some Senators. . . . We need a big senator—a gut fighter—a stand up senator."

Perhaps envisioning a replay of his own crusade on the House Un-American Activities Committee, the president proposed "some congressman who could dig into this one on a personal basis. We can feed info to them."

"Get backgrounds of all involved—all must be exposed—" and he repeated "Meadlo too smooth." John Ehrlichman, the White House counsel, could get an investigation going.

"Extent to which it happened greatly exaggerated.

"Let's check this Mike Wallace (60 Minutes) too. He's far left.

"Discredit witnesses, discredit Time and Life for using this. Get right-wingers with us."


Butterfield was in the president's cabin on Air Force One returning from Florida on November 30 when Nixon again raised My Lai. Nixon voiced sympathy for the young lieutenant who had been on patrol in the village. Nixon was "a Calley advocate," according to Butterfield.

"I think this fellow Calley," Nixon told Butterfield, "he's probably a good soldier. I think we're rushing into this thing. He may be getting a bum rap." Nixon said that this "Goddamn what's-his-name" Ridenhour had squealed to Seymour Hersh. "We ought to get someone on that guy. What is that guy? Learn more about him." John Ehrlichman, the White House counsel, had a network of investigators, Nixon added.

"Now when we get back, you check in with John. John's got people that can get on this guy's tail," the president said. "Tell Ehrlichman, I want the guy tailed. I want to know everything about him, tail him, put a tail on him."

Butterfield passed the orders to Ehrlichman.

"Okay, I'll take care of it," Ehrlichman said, and the White House gumshoe apparatus went to work. In a *SECRET* memo to the president dated December 17, Butterfield reported that Ridenhour "was discreetly interviewed by a confidential investigator posing as a news reporter."

Jack Caulfield, a former New York City police detective who did investigative chores for Ehrlichman, was on the case.

One purpose was to establish the relationship between Ridenhour and Hersh, "the apparent driving force behind the non-government release of alleged massacre information."

Butterfield's report noted that Hersh was a former press secretary to Eugene McCarthy, the antiwar senator, and that Hersh had "received a $1,000 grant to pursue development of the My Lai story. The grant came from the Edgar B. Stern Family Fund which is clearly left-wing and anti-Administration."

Ridenhour had felt that during his interview Hersh had implied he was a "government official," according to the *SECRET* memo, and he was unhappy with Hersh for manipulating the story and making it appear that Ridenhour had conducted extensive interviews with My Lai participants and witnesses. Ridenhour said of Hersh, "He's a no-good son of a bitch," according to the memo.

Future action, Butterfield said in the memo, should include "Putting a good lawyer in touch with Ridenhour, with instructions to make the most of Ridenhour's 'bitter feeling' toward Hersh." In addition, he said they should look more into "the activities of Hersh and the Edgar B. Stern Family Fund."

The White House investigating led nowhere. Hersh won a Pulitzer Prize. Calley was eventually convicted of premeditated murder and given a life sentence. Nixon ordered Calley removed from the stockade and confined to his quarters, where he served only three years.

And My Lai did as much as anything to turn war-weary Americans against Vietnam.

Butterfield thought Nixon had responded defensively to what was clearly an atrocity. In his memoir Nixon wrote, "Calley's crime was inexcusable," but the critics "were not really as interested in the moral questions raised by the Calley case as they were interested in using it to make political attacks against the Vietnam war."

He said that "maintaining public support for the armed services and for the war had to be given primary consideration." It was why he ordered Calley to be released from the stockade and confined to his quarters on his base.

"The whole tragic episode was used by the media and the antiwar forces to chip away at our efforts to build public support for our Vietnam objectives and policies," Nixon concluded.

In Vietnam today there is a My Lai Museum. Hersh visited it in early 2015 for *The New Yorker* and noted the names and ages of the victims listed on a marble plaque. The count of the dead is no longer in dispute: a total of 504 people from 247 families; 24 families lost everyone—three generations, no survivors. Included in the 504 were 60 elderly men, and 282 women (17 of whom were pregnant). A total of 173 children were killed; 53 were infants.

# 9

On Christmas Eve 1969, the president toured the ground floor of the Executive Office Building adjacent to the White House. According to his daily log, he walked around for 18 minutes to wish employees a Merry Christmas. But later that evening, according to Butterfield, the president stopped into several of the offices of the White House support staff, the General Service employees or civil servants. He found something very disturbing. A number of offices prominently displayed pictures of the late president John F. Kennedy.

I want all those pictures down today, Nixon ordered Butterfield. "Down from the walls and off the desks. Jesus Christ! If we've got this kind of *infestation* imagine what [Secretary of State] Bill Rogers has at the State Department."

Since his days as a congressman pursuing Communist and State Department official Alger Hiss, Nixon believed the department was full of liberal, left-leaning bureaucrats.

In one office, Nixon told Butterfield, he had found not just one but *two* pictures of President Kennedy. He wanted this cleaned up immediately. If necessary, to ensure across-the-board loyalty from support staff, he directed they must assign one of their own people, a political appointee, to every support office. Or, he told Butterfield, they should just get rid of the whole support staff.

"Abolish all offices and start over from scratch," he said. He wanted what he called a proper "picture policy" but he didn't want it blamed on him. Coming on the heels of his walk-through, he said, a sweeping order to take down all JFK pictures might be taken as "Presidentially directed." Butterfield was to move discreetly, take the initiative on his own, give the president cover.

Allegiance should be to the sitting president, Nixon said, and forget past presidents or their favorite president.

Butterfield thought this was unreasonable but orders were orders and this one was clear. It was just another day at the office.

A week later, while the president spent New Year's Day in San Clemente at the Western White House, Butterfield made his own inspection. Over the next two weeks they discovered that of the 35 offices, six had photographs of one or more former presidents. All of these also displayed Nixon pictures, as did 21 of the other offices. In eight offices he found no pictures of any president.

Butterfield spoke with Bill Hopkins, the senior civil servant and chief clerk of the White House who oversaw the support staff of some 400.

What a surprise, Butterfield told him, to discover that civilian government employees would display pictures of a past president in federal offices. Taking down the pictures of the former presidents, Butterfield argued, would only be a gesture of common courtesy to a current president and underscore their "pledged loyalty" to him.

Hopkins seemed to understand but he insisted none of his people were disloyal.

Make a detailed check of possible infractions, Butterfield said. He did not tell him the president was ordering this.

Haldeman weighed in with a January 14, 1970, memo to Butterfield: "The president would like you to check to find out who the woman is in the EOB who has the two Kennedy pictures. What's her background . . . is she new, old, someone we can trust, etc. Please get a report back to me on this quickly." Haldeman added a handwritten note: "This has now delayed nearly a month—and he asks about it once a week—at least. H"

The office with the two Kennedy pictures, Butterfield discovered, was occupied by Edna Rosenberg, who had served nearly 41 years on the White House staff—longer than anyone else. Butterfield checked her personnel file and found her described as a "completely loyal American whose character, reputation, and associations are above reproach" by the House Committee on Un-American Activities (Nixon's old committee as a congressman), the Civil Service Commission's Bureau of Personnel Investigation, the State Department and its Passport Office, the CIA, the Secret Service and the FBI.

Leaving nothing unchecked, Butterfield discovered that Rosenberg had remained single and lived with her sister in Silver Spring, Maryland.

Since a new official Nixon photo had just been printed, Butterfield instructed Bill Hopkins to see that everyone received one and in the process of hanging it on the wall made sure all others were taken down "in accordance with normal policy."

By January 14 all 35 offices displayed only Nixon's photograph.

Nixon wanted a progress report. This was followed by a note to Butterfield from Haldeman expressing more impatience. So on January 16, Butterfield outlined all that he had done in a two-page memo to the president entitled "Sanitization of the EOB." The photographic legacy of JFK had been expunged.

As Butterfield also noted in his memo, the second half of the project was under way. That was, he wrote, "to ensure across-the-board loyalty of all White House Support Staff personnel even if we find it necessary to [as the president had directed] 'abolish current office arrangements and start over from scratch.' " It would take him two to three days to screen all the personnel records, he said, but later he found that no purge would be necessary.

As he recalled, Butterfield said, "JFK represented the group that Nixon had a thing about, the privileged class. Nixon called them 'those sons of bitches who had everything given to them.' That was almost visceral with him. And Kennedy was the poster boy for that group.

"I felt that this resentment that we're talking about for those that had it given to them, not only was it very intense, but was always with him. In other words, he didn't just think about it now and then and erupt. It was always there. And the resentment, instead of dissipating with time, it seemed to intensify.

"You would think over time he would mellow. But not Richard Nixon."


"What the hell is the president of Harvard doing on the White House grounds?" Nixon asked Butterfield one day in the spring of 1972 buzzing for him. Butterfield could tell Nixon was really steamed. This called for immediate action.

"Rex," Butterfield said from the phone in the Oval Office to chief usher Rex Scouten, "is Derek Bok, the president of Harvard, on the White House grounds?"

"Yes he is," Scouten answered. "Right now he's with the first lady and about 80 others." Pat Nixon was honorary chairwoman of the Committee for the Preservation of the White House, which sets policy relating to the museum functions of the executive mansion.

Butterfield felt relieved, repeating what Scouten had said, figuring that would solve the problem.

"I don't give a damn," Nixon said, adding, "He's on our Enemies List." As if to say, have you forgotten? "What the hell do we have these lists for?"

Butterfield knew of such an Enemies List with dozens of names, but also of an Opponents List and a Freeze List. He was unsure which took precedence.

"Why do we have these lists if we don't pay any attention to them?" Nixon was furious, as if some electric charge had gone off in him. "I don't ever want that son of a bitch back here on the White House grounds." He put it on Butterfield. "I want you to make damn sure he doesn't show up here again. And you get those Enemies Lists, make sure everybody knows who's on them." Update them. "Redo them, make sure they're correct and we adhere to them."

"Yes, sir."

Butterfield recalled, "I knew he meant business. Derek Bok represented to Nixon the whole, not just Ivy League, but the whole North-eastern part of the United States. If you were from there, went to an Ivy League school, you had it given to you. You were a privileged son of a bitch.

"And as he got older, instead of mellowing, the neuroses intensified and he lumped them all together."


One day Butterfield walked into the Oval Office to retrieve something from the president's desk. Haldeman, staff assistant Steve Bull and he were the only ones who could go in unannounced. Nixon didn't seem to mind. The days of hiding behind columns and slinking around were long gone. Butterfield was a full member of the inner circle.

Nixon and Don Kendall, the CEO of PepsiCo, and a big supporter and campaign contributor, were sitting by the fireplace. Kendall was there to talk about the Soviet Union, where PepsiCo had substantial operations. He wanted to give his advice about how to handle the So-viets. Nixon knew how he wanted to deal with them and had made it clear from comments Butterfield had heard that Kendall's advice would be meaningless. "I don't need this son of a bitch to tell me about the Soviet Union or how to deal with them," he had said. So it was one of Nixon's stroking sessions, intended to make someone feel important and useful to the president, particularly for reelection fund-raising.

As Butterfield fiddled with papers on the desk, he later told me, he would long remember what Nixon was saying, and it wasn't about the Soviet Union. This was before the tapes were installed. The president was talking about New York City, where he had gone to practice law after he had lost the California governor's race in 1962.

"I'd been in Congress and in the Senate and vice president for eight goddamn years," Nixon said, "during which time Ike was in and out of the hospital." This was when he had filled in for Ike at National Secu-rity Council and cabinet meetings, he noted.

"I moved the family to New York City," when he had joined the law firm of Mudge Rose. "Do you think one of those goddamn fat-cat New

York bastards ever invited me to one of his country clubs or his private town club or any of that? *Not one goddamn time!*"

Butterfield reflected, "Nixon was known, I think, by a lot of people as being a bit odd. But that was it. Kind of an odd duck, but in a nice way, often. But I saw a guy there who, with the resentments and the depth of those resentments, and the hatreds. There was a lot of hatred. And I think he had to be an unhappy man, basically an unhappy man. That's why he liked being alone. He was happiest when he was alone."

Being alone was central to the Nixon personality and lifestyle. Nixon craved this privacy. Only known to the few around the Oval Office were the naps. Butterfield recalled, "At about 1 p.m. he disappeared and went into this little cubbyhole room, long and narrow, not more than about six feet wide, right off the Oval Office.

"There is a little hot plate and a little refrigerator. And you go back in, and there's a desk and a cot and a small bathroom. So he disappeared in there to eat his small curd cottage cheese, that's what he always had for lunch. Then he took a little nap. And that was never published that he took a nap." Butterfield said Nixon took off his jacket but normally left his necktie, shirt and trousers on when he lay down. "He slept for about an hour, got up and shaved. He had the heavy beard, so he always took the electric razor, then about ten of three got a cup of coffee and he came out and started a second day, clean shaven." He would work until 7 or 7:30 p.m.

"And that's when he left the Oval Office to either go back to the residence, but more often—more than 50 percent of the time—he went across the street to his EOB office. Like a man's library." It was a big office, and Nixon would relax, have a glass of wine or a Scotch, but usually a glass of red wine served by his personal butler. "Manolo Sanchez would fix him a nice dinner, and he'd sit there with his yellow pad. He wouldn't even take his jacket off until around 10:30 at night. And then he'd go home. Lonely existence, but I do believe he liked it."

Another time Nixon asked Butterfield, "Are these goddamn cabinet members that we invite to the various social functions at the White House, do they get around and talk to people?" There were usually a handful of cabinet members at state dinners, receptions or the Sunday worship service. "That should be one of their duties," Nixon said.

"Honestly, Mr. President," Butterfield replied, "no, they don't get around that much and I don't think they see making conversation with other guests is one of their duties."

"Well," Nixon said, "who does? Who's the best?"

"Oh, clearly the best is George Bush . . . I've heard him many times and I've watched him. 'Hi, I'm George Bush, our United Nations representative.' And he would chat with people."

"Oh, yeah, Bush. He would be good at that." Nixon then went into a thoughtful repose and added, "God knows I could never do that."

# 10

---

In December 1969, Nixon told Haldeman and Butterfield he wanted a new office arrangement. Haldeman was to move out of his large office adjoining the Oval Office and into a larger West Wing first-floor office in the southwest corner. Vice President Spiro Agnew, currently using that office, would have to be content with the office he had in the Executive Office Building. It was a pretty visible exile.

Bob, Nixon said, I want you to be able to think more, plan more, follow up on things more efficiently, be the assistant president. You get caught up in a lot of trivia here around the Oval Office, the day-to-day traffic.

Alex, the president said, you will move into Bob's office and handle the smaller matters, and the official schedule and official day. Though Nixon termed some of this work "trivia," Butterfield took the move as an endorsement of his efficiency and a sign of trust.

One result was that Butterfield did not get invited to all the meetings in Haldeman's new office that he used to attend. Butterfield was not happy about that, and was particularly upset he was not invited to one of Haldeman's political meetings for all senior Californians in the administration.

Butterfield's focus was now exclusively on the president, though

Haldeman clearly remained the top Nixon aide. He said that Haldeman and he gradually grew more distant once the move was made.

But as in real estate, West Wing power was connected to location, location, location. The direct access to the Oval Office and more control of paper flow and Nixon's day gave Butterfield more influence. He shadowed Nixon's life as no one else, plugged into nearly every aspect.

Though Nixon spent hours planning, thinking ahead and plotting, he could make instant decisions. And Butterfield was now positioned to be summoned to cater to his every impulse. He was also, along with Haldeman, someone who could authoritatively say no to unwanted intrusions from cabinet officers and others Nixon did not want to see.

According to a tape of a conversation between Nixon and Haldeman more than a year later, the switch in offices was a success.

"This thing is beginning to work out now?" the president inquired. "Alex is the perfect buffer."

"Yeah," Haldeman replied.

"Just let him do it."

Butterfield did become the principal intermediary between the president and his wife. He met with the first lady one or two mornings a week. He liked her. He believed she liked him.

"She never seemed especially cheerful," he recalled, "but she never did seem morose or down in her spirits. I felt sorry for her being married to this guy. I could see what she was going through."

He tried to get the first lady's views on the table. Before an upcoming state dinner, she told Butterfield, "I would so much like to have the Air Force Strolling Strings." The group of 20 airman musicians is a string ensemble that plays subdued show tunes and classical favorites while strolling around the audience. It was one of her favorites. "See if you can't talk to Dick."

When Butterfield had a chance he placed the Strolling Strings option before Nixon. It would be a little variety, something softer, more romantic than the jazz player Pete Fountain from New Orleans, the

Dixieland stuff Nixon wanted. "Mrs. Nixon has a point here, Mr. President," he said with a smile.

"No," Nixon said with finality. "I don't want the Goddamned Strolling Strings." But several times later she prevailed and the Strings played at state dinners.

Why didn't the president discuss these things with his wife? Butterfield wondered. Better not to ask.

When the president saw a nice article about Pat in the daily news summary he said, "Send Pat a copy of that," or "Let Pat see that," or "Tell Pat that."

The president and his wife did not stay together when they visited Key Biscayne. She had her own house on a cul-de-sac. "A lot of people didn't know that. On that same cul-de-sac the Secret Service had their place, the president had his, Bebe Rebozo, his longtime best friend, had his, Mrs. Nixon had hers. The pity of it. That's sad to me to even think of it. Because I cared so much for her. I really cared for her. There were times during our talks when I just wanted to put my arms around her."


One time as the Christmas season approached, Butterfield accompanied the president and the first lady in the helicopter. He was sitting across from them. The president was with his yellow pad.

"Dick," Mrs. Nixon said, "the girls and I were talking about going up to New York next week. Why don't you come along? It would be such fun, the whole family up there. And it's Christmas, and you know how New York is at Christmas. Why don't we all make a trip to New York City for the holidays?"

He didn't look up.

Get the girls and all go up, do some shopping, maybe see a play or musical, she continued.

He continued to write, not even looking at her.

We haven't done this for such a long time, she continued. It would be such fun. Fun, you know.

Nothing.

You son of a bitch, Butterfield thought. How can you treat her like that? Are you so inward? So self-absorbed? It was cruel, embarrassing for everyone but Nixon, who kept his head buried in his yellow pad. Butterfield wished he had the courage to grab the pad out of the president's hands, fling it down, and insist that Nixon answer his wife, even if it was just to say no.

"I heard every word she said," Butterfield recalled. Nixon's silence was inexcusable, hostile. "It hurt me. I shouldn't have let it affect me that much. I couldn't help but hear it, so I just sat there. And she knew that—had to embarrass her. She knew I heard. He never did answer. I wanted to reach over and—of course, I would never do it—and say, 'Answer her, God damn it! Answer her!' "

The helicopter flight continued in silence, interrupted only by the occasional shift in the tilt of the rotor blades—thwack, thwack, thwack—and the scratching of pen on yellow paper.

Butterfield concluded that Pat was what he called a "borderline abused" wife.

In late 1970, Butterfield's wife, Charlotte, and their daughter, Susan, were in a serious automobile accident. Susan had just gotten her driver's license and was driving with her mother on the freeway close to their house. A drunk driver came down the wrong side of the road and collided with their car. Charlotte went through the windshield on the passenger's side. Susan, who was shorter, got the steering wheel in her face and it knocked out a number of her front teeth. Both ended up in the hospital.

On November 21, 1970, Pat Nixon sent Butterfield a letter: "Dear Alex, . . . you are very much in our thoughts and prayers. This is a difficult time for all of you and we hope you will remember that we are among your many concerned friends who stand by to offer our encouragement and understanding. . . . Sincerely, Pat."

The Nixons sent flowers. Nixon ordered Butterfield to accompany Charlotte and Susan for a two-week rest and recuperation vacation in

Puerto Rico. When Susan, who was the more seriously injured, was released from the hospital, the president insisted that Butterfield bring her by the White House.

"You see those teeth right there," Nixon said to Susan when they met privately in the Oval Office as he pointed to and tapped his own front teeth. "They're not mine."

Butterfield had not known that Nixon's front teeth were not real. He was stunned by the way this usually awkward man gracefully empathized and put his daughter at ease, respecting and identifying with her condition.

"I loved Nixon for that," Butterfield recalled, shaking his head.

"Tricia and her date this afternoon evidently gave the Secret Service the slip," Butterfield reported to Nixon one weekend afternoon. The couple was out in a car being followed by Service agents assigned to her detail. "They turned down a road well ahead of them that led to a little airport." The agents think the date took Tricia up in an airplane. The Service was now doing all the checks at the airport and elsewhere. "They've got a plane in the air. They're terribly upset about it as you can imagine. They're doing everything right now they can do, and I'll keep you advised." They knew little about the young man. If they were airborne the situation was potentially dire.

"All right," Nixon said. "Yes, you keep me advised. I'm not to be disturbed by anyone else or any other business."

Butterfield had never seen Nixon so worried. His face seemed to fold inward.

There was no word all afternoon. Nixon was in agony but had to go into state dinner. Butterfield could see he was beside himself. The Secret Service soon reported to Butterfield that Tricia was safely back in the residence. He quickly scribbled a note for the president, who was about to be seated at the dinner.

"Mr. President, Tricia is back in the residence seemingly unaware of the concern she caused this afternoon. Alex."

He put the note on Nixon's dinner plate so he would see it when he sat down.

Nixon never said a word about the incident to Butterfield, who did not tell anyone, not even Pat Nixon or Haldeman. For Butterfield, however, the tense incident was important, representing what he called a "silent bonding" between two fathers.

# 11

---

"I'm fed up with these goddamned idiots who put their faces in mine after dinner and want to chitchat," Nixon told Butterfield about 90 minutes before the beginning of a state dinner in the spring of 1970. The president was leaning back in his chair, his feet on the desk and his legs crossed.

"Sit down, Alex," he said excitedly. "I'm getting sick and tired of all these bastards coming up and talking to me during that 30-minute coffee period after these state dinners."

The only chance guests had to talk to the president was the 30 minutes after the formal dinner when guests mingled in the Red, Blue and Green Rooms for coffee and cordials.

Nixon took out a typed list of the 108 expected guests and motioned for Butterfield to look. The president had put a check mark before five names and then read them aloud. Included were Arnold Palmer, the golf champion, and Clare Boothe Luce, a devout Republican, longtime Nixon friend, former congresswoman and ambassador. "Those are the only people I want to see during the coffee break," Nixon ordered. "Only those five! Not another goddamn soul. No one else. No congressmen. No senators. No nothing. Just those five people. You work it out, Alex."

Yes, sir. Butterfield realized his status with the president was more or less always on the line. This was going to be particularly tricky. The senior military aide and Butterfield normally stood near Nixon and introduced him to various guests as they mingled and roamed.

Now Nixon wanted not just protection from the "idiots" and the "bastards." He wanted an impenetrable shield. Each state dinner had its share of such people, dozens of guests, obligatory invitees, social hangers-on, foreign officials with their heads of state. Each would love to grab a moment with the president, and some were more determined than others. Attending a state dinner was a big deal. The guest list appeared in *The Washington Post* the next morning and it was scoured to see who had attended and who had not. But nothing compared to the chance to report to friends and colleagues the next day, "As the president told me last night . . ." Or "As I told the president . . ."

Time was short before that night's dinner, so before going down to shower and change into his formal wear, Butterfield called Lucy Winchester, the social secretary.

"Send me five of your most capable social aides," he said. These were generally attractive, young junior military officers assigned to the White House or elsewhere in Washington. When the five arrived all decked out in the formal uniform of their service, Butterfield explained.

"Listen carefully," he said, "we're going to execute a plan here, the president's plan and you must not fail me. This plan has to work."

Each would have a "designated" guest. During the pre-dinner cocktail hour they should track down his or her guest, talk to him or her, notice where they were sitting, and after dinner latch on to them before there were any distractions. They should bring their designated guest or couple to the Green Room (the smaller of the reception rooms where Nixon regularly stationed himself) and catch Butterfield's eye while keeping the conversation going with the guest and smoothly maneuvering to within 10 feet of the president.

Butterfield and the recently promoted General Don Hughes, the senior military assistant, would be hovering around the president, virtually guarding him, orchestrating the arrivals and departures of the "designated guests."

"If we're tied up, don't move in too fast but move towards me, and I will give you the sign."

Before dinner, Butterfield briefed General Hughes on the president's plan. About 9:20 p.m., after the formal dinner, it was showtime. Butterfield intercepted the president and General Hughes and slowed them down as they entered the Green Room. The first approved guest was nearby to be handed off to the president. As the president chatted with the guest, Butterfield spotted another of the military social aides with his guest in tow. He beckoned them over. Butterfield introduced himself and as they talked, he moved them slowly toward the president.

Had the guest had a chance to talk to the president? Butterfield inquired, knowing the guest had not. He then nodded to Hughes, who nodded back, grabbed the arm of the first guest and, with a smile, gently but firmly moved him or her out of the way and over to another group. Butterfield glided in and introduced the next guest to the president.

A couple of times Butterfield had to maneuver to cut off access or even throw a subtle body block against an invader, someone not on the list scrambling to get to the president. It was a rather smooth maneuver, the kind of precision, the seemingly effortless flying Butterfield liked.

Sometimes guests were in mid-sentence but there was no time to fool around, so Hughes took their arm and moved him or her on. "And so, Mr. President . . ." and he was hauled out. At times these exits were pretty rough. Maybe an arm or two got a minor bruise. No one seemed to mind. Each had had their less than five minutes with the president, and who else had? Only four others who didn't know they had been personally selected by the president.

The next day, Nixon had a brief dinner critique session with Butterfield.

"Did you have any trouble?" he asked.

No.

"Well, that's the plan from now on." He seemed elated.

Over the next months and years of state dinners, Butterfield and Hughes gained confidence and skill. It seemed that those who made the list never suspected they had been singled out by the president himself. Nixon always presented his list of about five.

"I want Pat to do this too," Nixon said before another dinner, suggesting she have a control list of about five people she might want to talk with.

So Butterfield took the proposal to Pat.

"Dick didn't . . ." she said laughing.

"Well," Butterfield said, "he thought you might want to consider it."

She laughed again. "Alex, you can't be serious?"

He indicated it was the president's wish.

"That's out of the question," the first lady said. "I like to talk to everyone."

Butterfield felt foolish asking. He had suspected she wouldn't try to insulate herself that way, and she continued to gut it out in the free-for-all with the state dinner crowd.

The procedure for the president, however, never changed, and he never said another word about it. Before each state dinner he routinely handed Butterfield a typed guest list with five check marks.

Butterfield was supposed to be Nixon's eyes and ears at these dinners. The next day the president wanted a detailed report when they met for their critique.

But Butterfield couldn't keep up. The president monitored the dinners like a catering manager. "Did you notice how long it took them to serve the salad?" he inquired after one dinner. "It took ten minutes to serve the salads."

Gosh, Butterfield thought, he had not been doing his job here. He recalled, "He's timing the waiters. The president of the United States, the host, sitting up next to the chief of state from someplace, is timing the waiters. So I thought, I may not be up to this observation part of my job."

•        •        •

Nixon set up nondenominational worship services at the White House on many Sundays. Billy Graham and other noted religious leaders would conduct them for about 300 specially invited guests.

"The basic purpose will be to use it as a political opportunity," Haldeman said in a November 13, 1970, memo to Butterfield. "We should invite potential candidates, finance people, new GOP-type leaders . . . and our other friends. . . .

"The president also feels that we should have guest lists developed so that once a church service is decided upon, we can go forth with the invitations with what few alterations might be necessary due to instructions from him."

Butterfield could see how important the services were as Nixon pored over the guest lists.

Six days later the New York *Daily News* ran a column noting that the guests seemed to be all Republicans. "The deliberate hand-picking of a congregation on the basis of political party affiliation cannot be considered either good manners or, for that matter, smart presidential politics," wrote Ted Lewis on November 19.

Four days later Haldeman shot Butterfield another memo that included a clipping of the column. "We should . . . be using these services as an opportunity to be nice to our enemies—and their families—as well as to reward our friends. Please be sure we always include Democrats and others known to be non-supporters of the Administration—but not to outright opponents."

The next summer Haldeman sent two memos to Butterfield about the White House services within nine days. On August 10, 1971, Haldeman said, "It's absolutely imperative that it clearly be understood by all concerned that Edward B. Fiske, the Religion Editor of the *New York Times*, is not to be invited to any White House Church Services again in the future under any circumstances whatsoever."

Fiske had just written an article saying the services were political and did not include "the poor and oppressed or minorities" but "the powerful in Washington and a healthy sprinkling of the people who put Mr. Nixon in office."

Then on August 19, 1971, Haldeman reminded Butterfield that the services were by invitation only. "There should be no press pool or any general press admission to these services.

"The *New York Times* and *New York Post* must never be invited to these services. No one from either of the papers—at any time."

Butterfield was shocked at the way Nixon used the popular services to humiliate Arthur Burns, a well-known economist and his counselor at the White House. In his memoir *RN*, Nixon wrote, "I created a new Cabinet-level position, Counselor to the President, for my old friend and adviser Arthur Burns." He underscored "my respect for his superior intellect." Burns, almost a decade older than Nixon, was considered the elder wise man on the staff in contrast to all the young beavers.

Burns was more conservative than Nixon, opposed some of his policies, but nonetheless wrote in his diary that his friendship with Nixon was "one of the three that has counted most in my life."

Butterfield was out at Rock Creek Park one Saturday afternoon when he was paged by the president through the White House switchboard.

"Tell Arthur he is not welcome at the worship service tomorrow morning," Nixon ordered. He was on the line only about 15 seconds. No discussion, no explanation, just the order and then the line went dead.

Nixon knew that Burns and his wife had said they really enjoyed the services. Butterfield was astonished that Nixon would use a withdrawn invitation so blatantly, but an order was an order.

"Arthur," he said in a call to Burns, "I hate to tell you this but the word is that you're not welcome tomorrow."

He did not know what else to say. Burns knew Butterfield was speaking with the authority of the president and the "word" could only be Nixon's.

Burns did not go to the service. Nixon, who continued to have some policy differences with Burns, did the same thing at least twice more, a last-minute Saturday call to Butterfield to cancel Burns's invitation.

A February 22, 1971, memo from Haldeman instructed Butterfield, "For the time being, hold up on Arthur Burns on any social invitations, just keep him off the list for a little while. Check with me in three or four weeks to see if he should be put back on for something or other. In the meantime keep him off of Church, etc."

Then there was the Kissinger problem. Nixon repeatedly voiced anger at the national security adviser's self-importance and self-centeredness.

When traveling on Marine One with the president, the official schedule and strict protocol required that each passenger be aboard the helicopter before the president so when the president arrived, Marine One could lift off immediately.

One time early on Nixon arrived and there was no Kissinger.

"Alex, go get him," Nixon ordered.

Butterfield left his seat and virtually ran from Marine One to Kissinger's office.

"Henry, for Christ's sweet sake," Butterfield said. "The president's out there waiting. We've got a schedule to make. Lots of people involved here."

Mimicking Kissinger's accent, Butterfield recalled the national security adviser saying, "All right, Alex, all right. I'm coming. I'm coming. I'll be there."

But Kissinger didn't quicken his pace as Butterfield escorted him to Marine One. Once onboard, Kissinger took his seat, but Nixon didn't say a word. Later on Kissinger kept the president waiting on Marine One a couple more times.

Kissinger was frequently late to state dinners, arriving up to eight minutes after everyone, including the president and the head of state guest of honor, was seated and eating. His arrival would create a stir, and Butterfield said, "It was as if he wanted people to think he'd been on the red phone, as if to say, 'I would've been here, but the Soviet Union called.' "

In 1970 Nixon finally called Butterfield in and said he wanted all of Kissinger's tardiness and self-inflated habits to stop.

According to Butterfield's notes on yellow legal paper, the president said:

"1. Too often says that he absolutely *must* get in to see the President. Frequently not all as urgent as K intimated, or stated. Like the boy who cried 'Wolf.'

"2. Enters President's office without checking. President may have sent for Henry, but Henry *must* check with Bull's office before going in. The President could be on the phone—etc.

"3. Late to meetings in the President's office—meetings in which he is to participate, etc.

"4. Slow to respond when called at odd time of day—unusually slow. Example 1: 20 minutes and 3 phone calls. Example 2: 22 minutes and 7 phone calls.

"5. Imprecise re amount of time he needs. Two minutes develops into 20 minutes. He should state time needed and try harder to follow that lead. Entire day's schedule is affected."

Nixon also complained about the briefing papers he received from Kissinger. They were often not timely, did not have an accurate list of participants or address the news or photo plan.

The president also said he did not like Kissinger's habit of gallivanting around Hollywood and Beverly Hills on weekends with movie stars. He seemed to enjoy being known as the "secret swinger."

Nixon ordered Butterfield to speak with Kissinger or to work through Haig to stop all these practices. "You do it your way," the president said.

Butterfield recalled he made several efforts with Kissinger directly or tried to use Haig as an intermediary. "But not much changed," Butterfield said, and Kissinger's habits were a continuing source of tension for Nixon.

On February 9, 1971, Haldeman sent a memo to Butterfield: "In seating at State Dinners, the President feels that Henry should not always be put next to the most glamorous woman present. . . . It's starting to cause unfavorable talk that serves no useful purpose."

Butterfield scribbled on his copy that he "relayed to Lucy personally." Lucy Winchester was the social secretary who did the seating arrangements.

# *12*

---

"The president wants a taping system installed," Higby said matter-of-factly on Wednesday, February 10, 1971. "And Bob wants you to take care of it."

Now at the beginning of the third year of Nixon's presidency, it was another of the instructions that flowed in a steady stream from Nixon to Haldeman and then often to Butterfield, though increasingly the orders were now coming to him directly from the president. Butterfield was glad to see how proximity brought him close to Nixon, who would just buzz or make a casual request as Butterfield hovered. If working for someone meant trying to alleviate their anxieties, Butterfield was very good. And Nixon had more than his share of anxieties.

Butterfield didn't think much about this latest order, knowing that Haldeman would soon pass through with details. Haldeman still used his old office as his route to the Oval Office because it was shorter than from his West Wing corner office.

When Haldeman later came dashing through Butterfield's office to the Oval Office with his yellow pad, Butterfield said, "When you come out, I'd like to talk to you about this taping system thing."

Okay, Haldeman said. When he emerged, Butterfield had some questions.

"Larry told me what the president wants. What are we talking about here? Just in the Oval?"

"He wants it in the Oval Office," Haldeman replied. "He wants it on the Oval Office telephones, in the Cabinet Room . . . and the Lincoln Sitting Room telephone. . . . We want a good system, we want something that works."

At times Haldeman and Butterfield would joke, wondering about the president's latest crazy idea. Or Nixon would order something and then change his mind. Butterfield thought someone, someday could write a book about the times Nixon changed his mind. These were the kinds of things that went down on their yellow pads and generated hundreds of memos.

Nixon first decreed, for example, that cabinet meetings should be action-oriented, but then ten months later he determined they should be more freewheeling with "no specific agenda" so he could lead "constructive discussion." The next month he determined that unstructured meetings weren't working and the agenda should be rigid with no discussion of politics and no "show and tell."

Though Nixon endlessly explored and sifted his options on most important matters, there was apparently no discussion about the merits or risks of such a taping system. Nixon and Haldeman's concern was that the memos prepared by senior staff who sat in on meetings were not that good or consistent. And Kissinger was hopelessly delinquent in turning in memos. So a taping system would be more reliable. The president wanted it. They were there to execute.

"Don't have the military do it," Haldeman said.

What was wrong with the White House Communications Agency, the military unit that oversaw communications for the White House?

"They're all dumb bastards," Haldeman said. "They'd find a way to fuck it up. The president doesn't want the military to have anything to do with this project."

The military personnel are transferred in and out, Butterfield noted. "If the recording system is really to be kept secret, I suppose I should go to the Secret Service."

"Probably," Haldeman replied. "But that's your decision. Just keep the military out of it and make sure as few people know about it as possible. Secrecy is key here. The only people on the staff who'll know about this are you, Higby and me."

That evening Butterfield called Al Wong, the head of the Secret Service Technical Security Division. He knew Wong well because the technical division regularly swept the Oval Office and other White House offices for electronic eavesdropping devices. They also swept hotel rooms when Nixon traveled and performed other technical chores to keep a bug-free environment around the president. Up until now, anyway. Butterfield dealt with Wong nearly every week.

"The president wants to install a taping system," Butterfield explained to Wong. "Listening devices in the Oval Office and on his phones."

"We've done this before," Wong confided and smiled, adding without explanation, "These things don't always work out as planned."

"Well," Butterfield said, "this will be different." The president wanted all conversations recorded.

Wong took this to mean a voice-activated system so nothing would be missed.

But Butterfield said they wanted a manually activated system in the Cabinet Room so the microphones could be activated and deactivated by a switch. "All your guys are trustworthy," Butterfield continued. "And that's a big part of this. When can you get it in?"

"When would you like it in?"

"How long would it take?"

"We can do it in a weekend if the president's not in town."

"He won't be in the next weekend, the one coming up."

"Then we'll have it in by Monday."

"Terrific."

Installation began Friday evening, February 12, after the president left for Key Biscayne and by Sunday evening the job was done.

"It's in," Wong said in a call to Butterfield on Monday. The president had not yet returned from Key Biscayne. "I'll come over and run you through it." Wong was soon there in the Oval Office.

"We've taken five microphones and drilled up from the bottom of the desk," Wong told Butterfield. "And the microphones are just barely along the surface. We've just put varnish over them."

"The microphones are right at the top of the desk?" Butterfield asked in mild astonishment. They were embedded and concealed with a thin coat of varnish? Five?

"That's right," Wong said, to ensure full coverage.

Pretty aggressive on the president's desk, thought Butterfield, even cheeky without asking for permission. Wong guided Butterfield over to the mantelpiece, where, he said, the microphones were in the lights resting on the mantel. This is where the president often took his guests, including heads of state. "This is all voice-activated," Wong added, referring to all the desk and lamp microphones.

"Meaning what exactly?"

Any speech or noise would trigger the tape recorder and capture it automatically when the Secret Service locator system showed the president was in the Oval Office. Wong then took Butterfield down to the basement level of the West Wing and showed him where the lines came into Sony 800B tape recorders. His technicians had broken through a brick wall at the end of a small locker room used by Secret Service agents. They had excavated space to house the tape recorders and covered the opening with a solid metal door.

How to explain all this to Nixon? Butterfield wondered. He believed that Nixon would be embarrassed and wouldn't want to talk about it. "If I said, 'The system's in, do you want me to brief you on it?' he would definitely say no."

"I think when the president comes in," he told Haldeman, "he ought to know a little bit about this system, so I'm going to tell him. . . . I'm going to brief him on the system."

"Yeah, good idea," Haldeman said.

"You want to be in on it?"

"No," Haldeman said, "I don't want to do that." As if distancing himself, he added, "I don't need to know that."

Butterfield knew that Haldeman avoided lots of things like this— things done, decided, finished and somewhat out of the mainstream.

One Watergate book on Nixon's tapes has a transcript of Butterfield briefing the president on the system. The tape is virtually inaudible, and Butterfield says he is convinced the transcript is inaccurate.

He said that he briefed Nixon at the end of the day on February 16, 1971, and that Nixon had very few questions.

He was uneasy and unusually quiet.

According to Butterfield, Haldeman and he were in the Oval Office with Nixon, who had his feet up on his desk.

"On this tapes thing," Nixon asked, addressing Haldeman, "who knows about that incidentally, Bob?"

"Just you, Alex and I and Higby and that's it."

"Rose doesn't know about it?" the president asked.

"No," Haldeman replied, and Nixon seemed to approve.

"Don't want Henry to know about it," the president said.

Haldeman indicated agreement.

"Ehrlichman?"

"No," Haldeman said, "absolutely not."

"This has got to be a well-kept secret," Nixon insisted. "And how many Secret Service people know?"

"Al Wong knows," Butterfield repeated, "and his technicians." Butterfield thought there were three technicians, but there had been four.

"Goddamn it," Nixon said, "this cannot get out. . . . Mum's the word," Nixon told them. According to an audible portion of the tape that day, this transpired. "I will not be transcribed."

"Correct," Butterfield replied. No one would listen and make transcripts.

"This is totally for, basically, to be put in the file. In my file. I won't want it in your file," he added indicating Butterfield, "or Bob's or anybody else's. MY FILE."

"Right," Haldeman said.

The purpose, Nixon said, is if they want to put out something positive or to correct the record.

Haldeman was already developing a cover story. "Anytime that anything gets used from it, it's on the basis of 'your notes' or 'the president's notes'—"

"That's right," Nixon said. "For example, you've got nothing to use from this today. Just forget it. File it. Everything today will be filed."

"I think it's gonna be a very fine system," Butterfield said.

Nixon later wrote in his memoir that he had the taping system installed because he wanted his administration to be "the best chronicled in history." Having an aide sit in on meetings, take notes and prepare a memo was not working, he said. The quality of the prose and perception varied radically.

Butterfield recalled that several times Nixon had lamented the absence of a perfect record of what had happened in the Oval Office. After the 1970, two-week postal strike was settled, Nixon said, "God damn it, we did pretty well. We brought everyone together. And we met there in the Oval Office and it took us a couple of weeks, but by golly, we settled the strike. I wish we had recorded exactly what went on."

Nixon had authorized a major military operation to cut the famous Ho Chi Minh Trail in Vietnam. It was a major supply route to the Vietcong. In Nixon's assessment, the operation turned out to be another "military success but a psychological defeat." He needed a dispassionate, factual record of his decision making.

Tapes could be used for his memoir or any other books he might author, he wrote. "Such an objective record might also be useful to the extent that any President feels vulnerable to revisionist histories— whether from within or without his administration—and particularly so when the issues are as controversial and the personalities as volatile as they were in my first term." He was obviously suspicious.

"Although I was not comfortable with the idea of taping people without their knowledge, I was at least confident that the secrecy of the system would protect their privacy," he wrote in his memoir.

Taping selected conversations or phone calls, as Kennedy and Johnson had done, would deprive Nixon of the total objective record, injecting "an obviously self-serving bias," he wrote.

"I did not want to have to calculate whom or what or when I would tape." So his system was voice-activated.

"Initially, I was conscious of the taping, but before long I accepted it as part of the surroundings."

"The interesting thing to me," Butterfield recalled, "was, about the tapes, he never seemed to be the least bit intimidated by their presence." The president seemed oblivious. No one would ever find out about them, and certainly no one would get their hands on them. "The White House is so powerful in many ways," Butterfield continued. "You've got too many things you can do. You don't think that the tapes are going to be in jeopardy. If there is a conflict about them, the White House will win.

"You get to feel," Butterfield recalled, "after a while, I think, that being president, you're going to win most of the battles just because of the power."

If Nixon thought of the taping as part of the surroundings and tuned out, I asked Butterfield, what about you? What was your level of awareness? Did you ever become numb or unmindful?

"No," Butterfield said. "No, I never did. No, I'm thinking of them all the time."

# 13

---

The saga of how Judge Warren E. Burger of the Court of Appeals in D.C. had campaigned for appointment to the Supreme Court fascinated Butterfield. The Burger approach included letters, notes, shared articles and at least one visit to Nixon at the White House.

Butterfield saved copies of the back-and-forth. It was part of his political education. One letter from Judge Burger shows the future chief justice as a clever and subtle player. He found the buttons on Nixon's console.

In his memoir, Nixon found it worth revealing how his connection with Burger went back to 1952, a crucial and perilous point in Nixon's career. During that year just before Nixon was to give his famous "Checkers" speech invoking the family dog and Pat's cloth coat to stay on the ticket as Ike's vice presidential running mate, Burger, then the Minnesota Republican leader, and his wife, Vera, sent Nixon a word of encouragement. According to Nixon's memoir they said, "Your Minnesota friends have complete confidence in your personal and political integrity. We are looking forward to your speech tonight. Please call if there is anything we can do."

In May 1969, the first months of Nixon's presidency, Washington exploded with the revelation by *Life* magazine that Supreme Court Justice Abe Fortas was to receive $20,000 a year from a foundation funded by millionaire industrialist Louis Wolfson. Wolfson had apparently bragged that his friend Fortas would help him with an investigation by the Securities and Exchange Commission. Initially, Nixon remained publicly silent.

With Fortas under fire, Burger sent a personal letter to Nixon along with a brief handwritten note to Ehrlichman asking him to give the letter to Nixon. "I am willing to risk annoying him for what I consider is important to the country—and to him."

"Dear Mr. President," Burger began in the letter dated May 8, 1969, "I had thought to write you Tuesday on what seemed to me an unwise course followed by some in contrast with the carefully correct course you followed in the Fortas matter. . . .

"The utterances from members of the Congress are, in my view, very damaging to the country, the courts generally and potentially to you.

"This week is a time for Republican leaders to 'view with dismay' and to 'be saddened' and 'disturbed' but largely silent. They should not 'attack.' First there is the matter of basic fairness. Second there are political consequences which will have an impact on the courts and the Supreme Court in particular and especially on the first nomination you send to the Senate.

"As to basic fairness: if the facts condemn the conduct of the Supreme Court Justice then let the *facts* do it in their own good time. . . .

"As to political consequences," he said, the Fortas supporters "are bound to be bitter over the harsh attacks. . . . As a consequence when your first nomination goes to the Senate, this suppressed rage will likely assert itself and your nominee may become *their* 'whipping boy.' That in turn will exacerbate the distressing situation in which the Court now finds itself; it will be very damaging to the country and it may be bad for your objective of restoring the Court to its former high standing."

Six days later, May 14, 1969, Fortas resigned from the Supreme Court. Since Chief Justice Earl Warren had already told Nixon he would resign the next month as chief, Nixon had two nominations. He hoped to change the direction of the court.

A week later, May 21, Nixon announced he was nominating Burger to the Supreme Court—but not to the Fortas vacancy. Instead he was going all the way and nominating Burger to be the new chief justice. The nomination to the chief justiceship was a surprise.

After hearings lasting less than two hours without a word of criticism, the Senate Judiciary Committee unanimously recommended Burger's confirmation to the Senate. Six days later the Senate did so by a vote of 74–3. The time from Nixon's announcement to confirmation was only 18 days.

It was almost as if Burger had appointed himself, Butterfield thought. The new Chief Justice Burger followed up with a series of fawning communications to Nixon.

Nixon appeared before the White House Correspondents' Association annual dinner on May 8, 1971. Many of the reporters received awards for minor exposés of the Nixon administration. There was lots of drinking, laughter and smirking. "I'm not a bit thin-skinned," Nixon wrote in a memo to Haldeman the next morning, "but I do have the responsibility and everybody on my staff has the responsibility to protect the office of the Presidency from such insulting incidents."

On Monday Burger wrote the president. "Your fortitude and forbearance in the face of gross rudeness by your hosts will always have my unbounded admiration. . . . To respond as you did with dignity and charity is a mark of your qualities and I suspect it was not lost on all those present.

"It is no comfort but it is perhaps instructive to remember how the press treated your predecessors, and particularly Washington and Lincoln. . . .

"I repeat that Saturday night marked a new measure of your capacities that will in time be recognized, and enlarged my respect and esteem."

On August 5, 1972, Burger wrote a two-page *CONFIDENTIAL* letter to Haldeman about his inability to get the White House to arrange military aircraft for his travel. Burger said that in 1969 the president himself had advised him on security and "to especially avoid use of commercial airlines" because of possible skyjackings.

It had been suggested, Burger wrote Haldeman, that he get the Justice Department to pay for the use of military aircraft. He was unwilling to do this. "I cannot be placed in that position with the principal litigants in the Federal courts. Neither am I willing to be placed in the position of a supplicant asking for a 'favor' since it is distinctly not my idea that I have government transportation." So he could find no alternative than to cease asking for government air transportation. "I want it to be clear that I am not ignoring the strong request of the President."

Burger's request was accommodated.

Butterfield closely monitored the rise of his old friend Colonel Haig. As Kissinger's deputy, Haig had been promoted to brigadier general in the fall of 1969. When Nixon wandered the West Wing after hours as he often did, nearly all offices were vacant. The staff had gone home—that is everyone except Haig, who was almost always there. Nixon frequently dropped in and found that Haig translated his slightest wish into action. Haig had quickly become a part of the president's inner circle. In a formal endorsement of an officer efficiency report in 1970 Nixon said that Haig should "be rapidly moved to the highest ranks of the Armed Forces." The next year Henry Kissinger said in his endorsement that Haig "is the most outstanding flag officer in the Armed Forces."

It is unusual for the national security adviser or the commander-in-chief to become so directly involved in an officer's formal evaluations.

On January 18, 1971, Nixon ordered the U.S. military to support an incursion by the South Vietnamese army into Laos. By February it was clearly a disaster. Haig sets the scene in his second memoir, *Inner Circles*. Over the years it became clear that he often exaggerated and provided dramatically self-serving accounts. But it is clear that Nixon was singularly impressed with Haig.

Haig wrote: "The president was in a cold rage. Without preamble he told me that he was relieving General [Creighton] Abrams of command in Vietnam immediately." Then the president told him: "Go home and pack a bag. Then get on the first available plane and fly to Saigon. You're taking command."

"Good God, Mr. President, you can't do that!"

"Why not? Lincoln fired McClellan for sitting on his ass in 1862. That's what I'm doing now. Abrams is the problem, and in situations like this one it's the president's job to remove the problem—the sooner the better."

Even the ambitious Haig, who had served in combat in Vietnam, saw the absurdity of a one-star brigadier general taking command in the major war theater from a four-star general who at the time was the most popular man in the Army, a hero of three wars. As Haig wrote, "I will not pretend that I was not tempted. I had no doubt that I could do the job; I knew the ground, I knew the enemy, and I knew what the President wanted. It is a very unimaginative soldier who has not dreamed of having supreme command thrust upon him in the hour of crisis."

Haig says he suggested that Nixon wait until the next day before making a final decision. In a calmer mood, Nixon ordered Haig to go to Vietnam not as a new commander but to make an in-depth assessment of conditions on the ground.

On March 1, 1972, Haig was promoted to major general, two-star rank. The next month Haldeman asked him to make an assessment and give recommendations for Nixon's campaign for a second term. This was pure politics and dangerous territory for an active duty military officer, clearly improper for an active duty two-star general working in the White House. Pentagon directives prohibit such participation in partisan politics by all military personnel. A more prudent officer might have found a way to sidestep the request. Haig took the view that he should obey the orders of the commander-in-chief. Period. Haldeman was the unassailable pipeline from the president.

Haig produced a four-page *EYES ONLY* memo to Haldeman that sounded unabashedly like a political consultant, passionate about his candidate.

"Many of our political strategists are taking for granted that McGovern will emerge as the Democratic candidate," Haig wrote.

"This was evident in the strategy discussions held in last week's Cabinet meeting." But Haig offered a different prognosis about the upcoming Democratic convention. "We must be prepared for an emotional convention consensus in favor of Teddy Kennedy. It is difficult to conceive of the old Democratic Party machinery, which relies essentially on a power base of Labor, Jewish money and nouveau riche resources, merging to support a candidate of McGovern's ilk since each of these sources of power could be seriously threatened by his stated policies."

Nixon's obsessions, Haig knew, included "Teddy Kennedy" and "Jewish money."

"Obviously McGovern is our most vulnerable opponent," he wrote. "The one theme which I believe is best stressed between now and the Democratic Convention is McGovern's irresponsible posture on the war in Vietnam in which we emphasize the fact that he is pushing a strategy which can only encourage the enemy not to negotiate and which in many respects is less stringent on Hanoi than even Moscow and Peking contemplate."

Haig also had views on domestic policy. "Concurrently, we should prepare, but not use, a host of themes which attack McGovern's strategy on domestic spending, inheritance, welfare programs, busing, aid to schools, national defense, etc., that can be used following the Republican Convention in August. The most important aspect of our anti-McGovern strategy should be to keep the homerun balls to the last phase of the campaign in a way which ensures that the President peaks off in the last three weeks of October" right before the election.

That Haig had these thoughts is perhaps not surprising. That he would commit them to a long memo is. Within the military officer corps there is both written and unwritten doctrine requiring political neutrality. It was the central reason Butterfield had resigned as an Air Force colonel before joining the Nixon White House staff. If the Haig memo were to leak, it would at minimum discredit him and brand him a sycophant. At the maximum, he could have been removed from the White House, tarnishing and likely ending his career.

Butterfield was surprised that Haig would take that risk, though it reflected the White House atmosphere of all-for-the-cause, the prevailing sense that the normal rules and restraints did not apply. There was an expectation that nothing so sensitive as *EYES ONLY* would get out.

Butterfield sent Haig a "Dear Al" letter on September 7, 1972, congratulating him on his promotion to general, four stars, and appointment as vice chief of staff of the Army. He noted that General Eisenhower had gone from two to four stars in 11 months. Haig had done it in six months, perhaps the most rapid rise in history, leapfrogging 182 more senior two-star generals, and all 46 three-star generals.

"Al, I couldn't be more pleased," Butterfield wrote. "The Vice Chief's slot and the four beanies that go with it are nothing more than just rewards for your years of dedication and labor above and beyond, and for your maintaining through it all a perfect balance. I feel good just knowing you."

# 14

Butterfield developed a close working relationship with Steve Bull, the president's personal staff assistant and aide-de-camp, the man responsible for keeping the president on schedule. Bull, a trim, athletic figure with a positive, can-do attitude, escorted the president's visitors and along with Butterfield moved Nixon through his official day.

Butterfield had a name for the president that he shared with Bull—Richard "I'll-Get-Those-Sons-of-Bitches" Nixon.

Bull, a stalwart Nixon defender, told me in a 2015 interview, "I think he carried some baggage from growing up a poor guy who had to overcome adversity and maybe he didn't know when he had to stop fighting."

In Butterfield's view, Nixon was controlled by "his various neurosis, the deep, deep, deep resentments and hatreds—he seemed to hate everybody. The resentments festered. And he never mellowed out."

From his early months and on, Butterfield carried enforcement directives from Nixon. Richard Dudman, who had written critically of the situation in Vietnam in the *St. Louis Post–Dispatch*, was a "violent leftist," and Ziegler had been ordered "not to permit our people to talk to the *Post-Dispatch*, the *New York Times*, or the *Washington Post* . . . all contacts with these news agencies (no matter how slight or how infrequent) be terminated immediately."

On the subject of public television, Butterfield reported, "The president wants to use every possible but discreet means to insure that public funds of this obviously leftist outfit are dried up."

Butterfield, on Nixon's orders, sent a memo to Attorney General Mitchell that the president wanted to "go after" the government's own eyewitness against Teamsters president Jimmy Hoffa. Nixon was trying to woo Hoffa to support him and in 1971 commuted his prison sentence.

To a report that the Nixon administration was not being as open as promised, the president ordered "ignore this kind of criticism. The fact of the matter is that we are far too open. If we treat the press with a little more contempt we'll probably get better treatment."

Even in moments of triumph, Nixon could not let go. His finest moment as president was surely the opening to China. Not only did he establish relations with the Chinese Communists but he leveraged the new relationship against the Soviet Union. It was a large global strategic move, and he was rightly pleased with himself. It should have been a moment of almost pure joy.

In his memoir *White House Years* Kissinger said the announcement of the trip by Nixon shook the world. "Not only was it a sensation for the media; overnight it transformed the structure of international politics." The president had been decisive, Kissinger said, noting that, "Nixon had an extraordinary instinct for the jugular."

During one planning meeting for the China trip with Haldeman and Butterfield, Nixon asked, "Who are the news guys going?" About 2,000 had applied to go and the list had been tentatively cut to about 100.

"I've got a list right here," Haldeman replied.

"Of news people?" Nixon said. "Good. Bring it in."

Haldeman brought in a long list that was typed on thin onionskin paper. The press was going to have its own plane. Lots of the bureau chiefs and television anchors were going. It was going to be a big deal for the newspeople who could say they went to China with the president.

Nixon read down the list.

"What is this son of a bitch doing here!" Nixon said as he got to about the 12th name. Not waiting for an answer, he violently crossed it out, tearing the thin paper. Haldeman came over to look at the name, which was barely legible because Nixon had obliterated it.

"Don't you remember that son of a bitch?" Nixon asked Haldeman. "The article he wrote after the '62 governor's race?" Nixon had lost that race and had declared to the media, "You won't have Nixon to kick around anymore because, gentlemen, this is my last press conference."

Haldeman had been the campaign manager.

"He's the assistant bureau chief someplace now," Haldeman said. "Do you really want to—"

"Yes, I do!" Nixon meticulously went down the list and crossed out another six or seven names. Stanley Karnow, *The Washington Post*'s veteran China watcher and Vietnam War expert, was excised. "Under *no* circumstances," Nixon wrote, indicating that only one newspaper from cities the size of Washington could send a correspondent. As a cover he said they could say a coin had been tossed, and *The Washington Star*, the afternoon rival of the *Post*, had won.

In all about 87 would go on the trip, including the TV stars Walter Cronkite, John Chancellor, Barbara Walters and Dan Rather.

Later, on April 3, 1972, for a Soviet Union trip to sign an important arms control agreement, Haldeman sent Ziegler a memo on the press contingent. He wanted some who had not gone to China. "If it is hard to go," he said reflecting Nixon, "it will mean more to be on the trip."

Referring to the upcoming presidential election, Haldeman directed that they should "first take the cities we need in the major states" such as New York, Chicago, Los Angles, Detroit, Cleveland, Cincinnati. "Then offer places to our good friends who missed the China trip" and "We should drop" several papers and columnists, including the conservative William F. Buckley.

Buckley had severely criticized the normalization of relations with China. Given the barbarity of the Chinese leaders, he had written, "We have lost—irretrievably—any remaining sense of moral mission in the world."

•   •   •

"Last weekend we put a naked girl in his bed," Bebe Rebozo told Butterfield

"A naked girl?"

"Well, it was a life-size blow-up doll," Rebozo said, smiling as he
recounted a prank he and Robert Abplanalp, the inventor of aerosol
spray and a wealthy Nixon friend, had played on Nixon down in the
Caribbean.

Perfect, thought Butterfield. "He'd be the guy you'd want to put the
naked woman in his bed. Because of the reaction you'd get. . . . Like a
bunch of high school boys."

Butterfield also thought it was good that Nixon had friends close
enough to him, confident enough to feel comfortable with such a
prank. Perhaps it provided a moment of comedy and much needed relief, though Rebozo never described Nixon's reaction to Butterfield.

Nixon had been pals with Rebozo, a Florida banker and businessman, since 1951. They traveled and vacationed together, watched
weekend sports on television, spent time just hanging out, apparently
not really talking much about politics.

Butterfield was frequently reminded that Nixon was awkward and
lonely, the real-life embodiment of the hunched, brooding figure of
cartoons. The Pulitzer Prize–winning *Washington Post* cartoonist Her-
block regularly portrayed Nixon as an isolated, devious loner.

For Butterfield, the quest for solitude made Nixon all the more impenetrable.

Haldeman wanted to spend time with his family and so he did not like
to go to Camp David with Nixon on the weekends. Butterfield drew
that duty. Nixon also wanted a secretary there in case he had dictation
or some other secretarial chore. Butterfield had a pool of five secretaries cleared for the task including Rose Mary Woods.

"He clearly liked one secretary better than the others," Butterfield
recalled. "And that was Nell Yates. But he didn't know how to say, have
Nell come up. . . . He wanted to say Nell." But he simply couldn't bring
himself to reveal his preference.

Imitating Nixon, Butterfield said, " 'Om, hmm, who's available again?' Nixon would stand there. It was painful. Eventually I just started using Nell almost all the time if she was available." And Nixon seemed to appreciate that.

Yates, 48, had worked in the White House since the end of Harry Truman's administration and knew the ropes as well as anyone. Slender, her hair in a tight bun, she was a fixture of quiet authority. Nell was Dwight Chapin's secretary and frequently was in and out of the Oval Office.

One Saturday night in May 1972 at Camp David, Butterfield recalled, "Well, he called her over. Called her on the telephone. She thought, well, I guess I'm going to go do some typing. 'No,' he said. 'I want you to come over and have dinner.' So she told Butterfield, 'I'm going over the president's to have dinner.' " That was in Aspen Lodge.

"She came back about three hours later. She was a pretty cool person to be really distraught, openly distraught, but said, 'Ugh, the most painful, uncomfortable evening of my life.' "

"What! Did he make a move or something?" Butterfield asked.

"An awful lot of starting to make moves and then withdrawing," he recalled her saying. "And not knowing what to say. I was just, every moment, I was alert to what was going to happen next. I was just very uncomfortable. And then he said, 'Let's go see my office.' So we walked back to see his office." It is behind the living room at his Aspen Lodge. "It was awful, and we stayed back there. I got the idea that when we went back to the office . . ." She said she was worried when they went back there because it's a little more isolated.

"Well, nothing happened," she said. "Nothing happened . . . it was awful, the conversation didn't flow well. He didn't know what to say."

Butterfield recalled, "He clearly had her over there for her company and I guess he got something from that. It was just another example of a lonely man. I don't know how else to interpret it. Nothing happened. She was just worn out when she came back from holding herself uptight for so long." She was afraid she was going to have to say no to the president. "It was traumatic in a way for her. She said it was the worst three hours of her life."

Yates declined to comment in 2015.

# 15

The morning of Wednesday, May 17, 1972, Nixon was at Camp David for talks with Kissinger and Soviet ambassador Anatoly Dobrynin.

Beverly Kaye, a 42-year-old White House secretary, had drawn duty for the brief trip there. She was one of the five in the Camp David secretarial pool.

Nixon showed an unusual, polite interest in her, according to a tape. Secret taping at Camp David had just been installed earlier in the month, Secret Service records show. A single microphone had been placed in Nixon's study plus two on his phones.

"Been here before?" Nixon inquired, according to the tape.

"No, sir," Kaye replied in a sweet, young voice.

"What cabin are you in?"

"Right up here in Maple," she answered.

"Did you come up last night?"

Yes, Kaye said, in a "helicopter from the Pentagon."

He had a memo to Haldeman he wanted typed and sent back to Washington. There was another project, he said. He had underlined portions of two briefing books and he wanted the underlines typed out.

"You just want plain paper, sir?"

"I just need the paragraphs that are underlined." Put the pages in a separate folder. "So I know what I have here. They're things I want to concentrate on."

"I see," Kaye replied.

"Just do it at your leisure. I don't need it today. . . . Walk around, see a little of the place."

"All right. I'll do that. Thank you."

"Take a swim," Nixon suggested.

Kaye laughed. "All right."

"All right," Nixon repeated. "Okay."

"Well, take care," she said.

"Bye," he said.

"Thank you."

"Bye," he repeated, and she left.

Nixon's daily records show that he went to Kaye's Maple Lodge at 4:08 p.m. and then he walked through the Camp David grounds until 4:20 p.m. (Butterfield did not know if Nixon took this walk with Kaye.)

The official records show that evening at 6:40 p.m. "The president had dinner with Beverly J. Kaye" until 7:33 p.m. The next morning, May 18, the president went to the Maple Lodge at 10 a.m. for five minutes.

At a later time Butterfield and Rebozo were also there at Camp David with Nixon, and boarded a helicopter for the return to the White House

"It was an awfully interesting 20 minutes," Butterfield recalled.

The trio were joined by three Secret Service agents, a military aide, the president's physician and Beverly Kaye.

Butterfield recalled, "We're in the Marine chopper. Bebe was with us. The president's in his very soft, cushioned chair. And he sees this miniskirted secretary, Beverly Kaye. The girls were wearing miniskirts then. And she is a little short. And she comes on to take her place back there and he sees her. And he says, 'Oh, um . . .' And I said 'Sir, her name's Beverly.' "

Nixon knew. "Beverly, why don't you sit up here with us?" he asked.

"He saw the miniskirt," Butterfield recalled. "It was very short. Her legs looked good I guess. So she came and I moved one way. So she sits between Bebe and me. And we strap in and off we go. And it's dark."

Butterfield makes helicopter noises. "You hear this thump, thump, thump. And we take off. And it's all dark around where Camp David is, and it's going to be dark for the next 20 minutes until we get into the Washington, D.C., area.

"But the way she's sitting, with a miniskirt—when you sit down, the miniskirt comes up." Her feet barely touched the floor.

Kaye was shy, quiet and known as a good worker. Wedged between Butterfield and Bebe, she seemed trapped. The helo lifted off smoothly and rotated to the right and headed south for the routine, 30-minute flight. No one spoke. Butterfield watched Nixon through the dim light. He could clearly see that Nixon was fascinated by the sight of her bare legs. He almost seemed excited by their proximity. Though, to Butterfield, the president seemed to be trying, he could not avert his gaze. He seemed transfixed.

The only sound was the whirring of the helo blades overhead. Still no one spoke. No one moved. A minute passed. It seemed to Butterfield that suddenly the darkness, the intense quiet, was an invitation for intimacy. A bond had formed. The normal rules did not apply. Nothing except the moment, a rare interlude, almost a space in time as they flew between Camp David and the White House.

"I can see him noticing her," Butterfield said. "It's very clear. And in truth, this is a natural reaction for a man. But to him, he was perhaps more fascinated than the average married man might be. He keeps looking over.

"And finally, just out of the blue sort of, he takes his hand . . . he takes his hand closest to the aisle and reaches over. And her legs are together, of course. And he starts patting her on the bare legs. Well, her legs are bare.

"In the manner of patting a young girl, like a four-year-old girl.

"And he said, 'Well, did you enjoy Camp David?' "

"Yes," she answered. Butterfield could feel her almost freeze up next to him. Nixon is still patting her legs.

"I guess there wasn't much to do," Nixon said. "We didn't have any work for you to do. I apologize for that. Because it can get boring up here."

"He was covering as much skin as he could with his hand." Butterfield and Bebe looked on silently. There was a power in the unspoken. Only one thing was going on, and no one spoke about it. "Bebe and I are just dying," Butterfield recalled.

Butterfield glanced down at Kaye. She seemed defenseless, and was trying to smile, but said nothing as the president continued to pat slowly.

Butterfield recalled, "And he's carrying on this small talk but still patting her. Because I can see now, Nixon being Nixon, he doesn't quite know how to stop. You know, to stop is an action in itself. So he's pat, pat, patting her. And looking at her. And feeling—I can see he's feeling more distressed all the time now about the situation he's got himself into.

"So he keeps trying to make this small talk, and I can see him saying [to himself], you know, when the small talk is over, what the hell am I going to do?" It was as if he took his hand away, that would draw attention to what he was doing.

"I can feel her shoulder right next—she has stiffened up like you can't believe. She's petrified. She's petrified. She's never had this happen before. The president of the United States is patting her bare legs."

For how long?

"It seems like half the way to Washington but I'd say a long time, minutes. And when he stopped, he broke the whole chain."

Finally, Nixon cleared his throat emphatically. "He stopped talking and he pulled his hand away, and turned his whole body toward the window and looked out into the darkness. And stayed in that position for quite a while."

Butterfield glanced sideways at Bebe. The shadows of the night flight passed over the face of the president's closest friend, and he looked pained.

"We were spectators," Butterfield said. "Who was going to do something?" Or joke, though it wasn't true, "Hey, Mr. President, that's my girlfriend."

Butterfield later tried to imagine what Nixon might be thinking: " 'Jesus, I shouldn't have done that.' Bebe and I are amazed. Watching that, we're sitting on either side of Beverly. I'm sure he could feel her stiffen up too. And this thing went on for a long time. And the poor man. I just thought, the poor, pitiful man. Yes, he was president of the United States." And yes, Butterfield had some respect and admiration for him at times. "But in this moment, I just thought, the poor, pitiful son of a bitch. The poor, pitiful son of a bitch.

"This was a yearning," Butterfield said, a longing for intimacy, his unrealized desire for contact. Perhaps the loneliness of command or the loneliness of his marriage. Butterfield added, "That part of it was obvious, and people should understand that. A good psychiatrist or a clinical psychologist or a mature person would see a lot and read a lot into that about Nixon himself. I mean, the average man would not do that.

"It was loneliness. Which hurt me, in a way, again for Pat. It was temptation there. I mean, he wasn't going to go any further than he did. I don't mean to imply that he would have. But it was interesting that the desire was so great that he actually made the initial move. It wasn't a caress. It was simply a pat, pat, pat."

I remarked that this would be considered wildly inappropriate in 2015.

"You could say it was inappropriate then," Butterfield said. "He made it seem like the grandfather, an elderly man to a niece or something like that—'There, there.' "

After the incident, Nixon displayed an awkward inquisitiveness about Kaye. According to the tape from the Oval Office on the morning of July 1, 1972, Nixon discussed plans to go to San Clemente, the Western White House, while Kaye was in the Oval Office.

"Are you going out this time?" the president asked.

"Yes," Kaye replied, not adding the formal "Mr. President."

"You like California?" the president asked.

"I like California very much."

"Where do you stay, you and the girls?"

The San Clemente Inn, which was the Western White House press center routinely used by staff and reporters.

"The Inn," Nixon said. "It's very nice . . . the man there, such a nice man. He's all for us. Takes care of all the girls."

Kaye agreed.

"Well, have fun," the president said.

"Thank you."

"Certainly," Nixon finally said, sounding on the tape a bit gallant.

Later, according to a tape of a November 20, 1972, conversation with Haldeman, Nixon was trying to determine which secretary could be trusted to transcribe some of his private dictations for his Daily Diary.

Of Beverly Kaye, Nixon voiced a note of suspicion. "Beverly I think, being single—if she's loyal. I don't know her loyalty. . . . That's the only thing. She's been in the State Department and all the rest. Has anybody ever checked the goddamned loyalty on this girl?"

"Oh, yeah," Haldeman reassured him. "We've checked, run tests. Done—"

"I can't use Rose on a lot of this stuff, Bob, because she'll try to get her own judgment involved in it. And she just got too sour.

"I'd like the most brilliant, loyal Nixon secretary. Preferably young, preferably single . . . very, very fast and loyal."

Nixon again mentioned Kaye. "We've had this little girl in the outside office for a long time," Nixon said. "I like this little girl. She's nice. Very good. Very smart. . . . This girl is awfully good."

"She is," Haldeman said.

"At the present time, she's better than Rose," Nixon said.

"Oh, there's no question."

Over the years Butterfield never spoke with Bebe, Nixon or nearly anyone else about Kaye or the incident on the helicopter. Kaye died in December of the next year from a stroke at the age of 43 while she was riding in a White House elevator.

Butterfield said he did not like talking about the helicopter incident, but he had included it in his book draft in the mid-1990s. As we discussed it two decades later, he tried to brush it off. "He's an older man," Butterfield told me. "Those legs looked inviting. They'd look good to anybody. We are men. There's something about a woman. We love them. In a nice way. They're great."

Was this the Nixon of Watergate—willing to cross boundaries? No, said Butterfield.

Was this an old man caught in an irresistible impulse to touch those legs? As if his helicopter was a penalty free zone. No, Butterfield said again. He did not see it that way. It was in no way a major or even visible part of Nixon's personality, but in that short, silent ride, Butterfield believed he glimpsed the unfulfilled, desperately human side of Richard Nixon. It was a side he imagined existed, but had never expected to see so vividly.

# 16

___

After nearly three and a half years in the job, Butterfield found that he could still be rebuked by Haldeman for a minor infraction—not of the rules but of Haldeman's expectation of total control.

This time it involved the attempted assassination of Alabama governor George Wallace, who was running as an independent for president. Wallace was seriously wounded as he campaigned in a Washington suburb the late afternoon of May 15, 1972. Wallace had received 10 million votes in 1968 and in a close race in 1972 he could siphon off enough Nixon votes to give the presidency to a Democrat.

Haldeman was furious with Butterfield that the president and he did not get prompt notification of the shooting.

Butterfield sent a two-page memo to Haldeman the next day trying to explain.

"You asked for particulars concerning my delay in getting word to you about the attempt on Governor Wallace's life yesterday afternoon. The answer, in a word, is that I had nothing but unconfirmed bits and pieces of information until 2–3 minutes before you called me on the telephone (4:19 or 4:20)." Butterfield said his secretary "was at the moment typing a very short paragraph of alleged facts which you were to receive . . . *before* anyone else . . ."

And he added, "so help me!" virtually swearing an oath.

In the memo, he gave an eight-point tick-tock on the information flow and his decisions over the 19 minutes. At 4:11 he approved a suggestion that the speechwriters be alerted to "the news and the possibility of the need rather quickly of a Presidential statement." Haldeman wrote in the margin, "First mistake."

Butterfield insisted that Haldeman was about to get a report. A hand-carried memo was only minutes away.

In closing, Butterfield wrote, "Every action that I took was premeditated."

At the bottom of Butterfield's memo with his blue felt pen, Haldeman said he wanted "immediate notification in the future—even if unconfirmed—and *no* notice to others until we decide on a procedure."

Clearly Nixon was unhappy. Wallace's candidacy was a sensitive issue. Any possible connection the would-be assassin might have to Nixon, the White House, the Nixon campaign, or any Nixon supporter could be a political disaster.

There was much attention on the would-be assassin, Arthur Bremer. Watergate break-in leader Howard Hunt later testified that Chuck Colson, Nixon's aggressive White House special counsel, ordered him to break into Bremer's apartment hours after the assassination attempt.

Carl Bernstein and I later reported this in *The Washington Post* and in our book *All the President's Men*. I met with Colson for the story, and he insisted he was pushing the FBI to get answers. In *All the President's Men*, we wrote:

" 'The President was agitated and wanted the political background on Bremer,' Colson said. Informed of the shooting, the President became deeply upset and voiced immediate concern that the assassin might have ties to the Republican Party or, even worse, the President's re-election committee. If that were the case, Colson noted, it would have cost the president the election."

There was, in fact, never any evidence that Bremer had any connection to Nixon. He was a loner. "It is my personal plan to assassinate by pistol either Richard Nixon or George Wallace," he had written in his diary two months earlier. He wanted to do "SOMETHING BOLD

AND DRAMATIC, FORCEFUL & DYNAMIC, A STATEMENT of my manhood for the world to see."

Bremer had stalked Nixon but found the Secret Service and police protection tight during an antiwar protest around Nixon's motorcade. So he was not able to get close enough to fire off a shot.

On the morning of June 17, 1972, Butterfield was listening to the radio as he drove to the White House. For Butterfield a presence at the West Wing on Saturday was routine, even though Nixon was in Key Biscayne. The news report caught his attention. In the early morning hours five men in business suits had been arrested with bugging equipment and sophisticated photographic equipment in the Democratic Party headquarters at the Watergate office building.

"Did you hear about this break-in?" he asked Nell Yates, when he got to his office.

"Yes," she said.

"You know," he said, "don't you, that we had to have done this?"

"Of course."

Butterfield was a bit surprised by the way she said it, no hint of doubt.

"Who else would it be breaking into the Democratic National Committee headquarters?" he asked. "Other Democrats? No, I don't think so. Probably Republicans. Which ones? The guys over in the White House with the Committee to Reelect the President." He paused. "But what made you say, 'Of course'? "

"Presidents know everything," Nell said. "I can't imagine anything happening in the Johnson era like that that President Johnson didn't know in advance."

"That's exactly the way I see it," Butterfield said. "It had to be us. We had to have done it. I can't imagine anything happening in this administration that the president and/or Haldeman haven't approved."

•     •     •

By the fall of 1972, Butterfield found himself stepping over the line into territory he never imagined he would visit, let alone become entangled in.

"Yes," Butterfield told the president and Haldeman in the late afternoon of Thursday, September 7, 1972. "It's all taken care of, sir."

Those seven words can be heard on a tape of the meeting in the Oval Office just two months before the presidential election. Butterfield remembers them well. Those words—*"YES. IT'S ALL TAKEN CARE OF, SIR"*—have haunted him for years, even up to 2015.

Haldeman had suggested that a spy be placed in a Secret Service detail to be assigned to Senator Ted Kennedy, the younger brother of the assassinated John F. and Robert Kennedy. Nixon liked the idea and had turned to Butterfield to ask, "Alex, can you do that?"

Rose Kennedy, Ted's 82-year-old mother, had personally asked Nixon for the protective detail as her sole surviving son was about to campaign aggressively for Nixon's opponent, the Democrat nominee for president, Senator George McGovern.

Butterfield knew that the order, which he had personally taken down the street to the Secret Service headquarters, was illegal. "I could have been indicted for that," he recalled. "I don't mind admitting it, but I'm admitting it because I thought I was too smart for that. Not too smart, that's the wrong word. But wise enough and old enough. But I'm almost glad to admit this, because when the president says, 'Alex, can you do that?' my immediate response was to say, 'Absolutely, yes sir!' "

If his role had been discovered, he was certain he would have gone to jail. But mostly he was surprised at himself, even astonished, for going along so quickly. "In a way, I was afraid of myself," he recalled.

I asked him why he didn't say, Hey let's wait a minute.

And he said, with a laugh, "It depends upon how you say, 'Hey, wait a minute.' "

It was expected, or you expected that you would move without thinking, no pause.

The tapes show that in the Nixon White House you said Hey wait a minute at your peril. The president's wish was an order—not reviewable, not to be reconsidered or doubted. Any questioning or hesitation would suggest softness, a fatal character flaw.

Nixon had been clear that Secret Service director James Rowley "was not to make the assignment" of who would be on the Kennedy detail or lead it. Nixon and Haldeman had their man: Robert Newbrand. As an active agent he had been on Nixon's detail when he was vice president. He had retired from the Service and was an odd-jobs, utility man in the West Wing used mostly by Rose Woods.

Butterfield, who had liaison responsibility with the Secret Service, got Newbrand reactivated as an agent and assigned to the Kennedy detail.

That's when Butterfield told Nixon, "Yes, it's all taken care of, sir." He added: "And we have a full force assigned, 40 men."

"One that can cover him around the clock, every place he goes," Nixon said.

The laughter that filled the Oval Office can be heard on the tape. This was going to be a big score.

Haldeman mentioned Amanda Burden, a 28-year-old New York socialite who had been linked romantically with Kennedy, who was married, in recent published reports.

Nixon noted the number of threats against Kennedy. The sheer number of Secret Service agents "builds the son of a bitch up," suggesting the increased visibility was the only downside.

Butterfield left the meeting at that point.

Now alone with Nixon, Haldeman, on the tape, continued, "Newbrand will do anything that I tell him to . . . he has come to me twice and absolutely, sincerely said, 'With what you've done for me and what the president's done for me, I just want you to know if you want someone killed, if you want anything, any way, any direction . . .' "

"We just might get lucky and catch this son of a bitch and ruin him for '76," Nixon said. "That's going to be fun."

"Newbrand will just love it," Haldeman said.

"I want you to tell Newbrand," the president instructed, "because he's a Catholic, sort of play it, he was for Jack Kennedy all the time. Play up to Kennedy, that 'I'm a great admirer of Jack Kennedy.' He is a member of the Holy Name Society. He wears a St. Christopher . . ."

Nixon's obsession with Ted Kennedy had been evident to Butterfield from the first months of the administration. On April 10, 1969, at the president's instruction, Butterfield fired off a two-paragraph "Action Item" memo to Ehrlichman from the president. It instructed Ehrlichman to get the so-called attack group in the White House to put Ted *"squarely* on the spot," and highlight his support for student demonstrations. The group was to mobilize the media so that "Teddy's support of all-out integration *and* bussing is widely publicized."

Two days later in another "Action Item" memo, Butterfield passed word to Ehrlichman about the president's concern with an article in *The New Republic*. At a recent Senate hearing, the liberal magazine said that Kennedy had been "cool and clever." Positive news about Kennedy roused Nixon.

The author of the magazine article said, "If we had been political scouts, and had never heard of his brothers, we'd have made note of him." The president suggested that Ehrlichman get the attack group to have something publicized about how "very amateurish" Kennedy had been at a recent briefing that Nixon had given.

Newbrand made weekly reports to Haldeman about Kennedy's activities but never documented anything untoward.

"I was an accomplice in an act of abusive government," Butterfield later said, shaking his head, "using a member of the Secret Service for some personal, petty purpose. We wanted to catch Kennedy in the act. If we could get Kennedy in bed with somebody . . . when he went to Paris, they were downright giddy. Hey, he's going to go to Paris. We'll nail him now."

Butterfield says he remains appalled at his behavior and weakness.

# 17

Sensitive and Top Secret CIA reports regularly passed through But-terfield. They showed, among other things, the extent to which Kissinger was excluded from some reports from sensitive Arab sources. In addition, some of the documents show how the United States intelligence agencies spied on its ally Israel.

On March 24, 1972, CIA director Richard Helms sent a SECRET/SENSITIVE memo to the president with several attachments. It showed that there were two channels feeding information to Nixon on the secret talks between Jordan's King Hussein and the Israeli leaders, most recently Prime Minister Golda Meir.

In one, Helms said that King Hussein had had "approximately fifty secret meetings with Israeli leaders."

King Hussein was the CIA's man. He had been on the CIA payroll since the Eisenhower years.

"You will recall," Helms reminded the president, "that early in this Administration, you told me to deal solely with the Secretary [of State William Rogers] on this issue of secret Israel/Jordan contacts. This I have done on all reports originating with the Jordanian side."

As for the Israeli version of the meetings, Helms said, "for the brief, recent accounts of the secret meetings from the Israelis, these have been sent to you via Dr. Kissinger at their request."

To assure the president that Kissinger was not getting the Hussein/Jordan intelligence, Helms said, "I am sending these two memoranda directly to you. No one on the White House staff has seen them or is familiar with their content."

Secretary of State Rogers was the point man for the Jordan side, but Helms said Rogers was away and would not be back in Washington before Nixon was scheduled to meet with King Hussein. "I thought it should be in your hands well in advance."

The source of one attachment from Helms is clearly a tape made of the Hussein-Meir meeting on March 21, 1972. The eight-page account contains several thousand words of verbatim quotes from the two leaders and their advisers.

Meir said that a peace plan proposed by King Hussein "would lead to the eventual liquidation of Israel."

She added, "Under no conditions will we return to the boundaries of 1967." Israel would not give up the occupied territory on the West Bank and in Gaza won during the Six Day War.

"No one wins in wars," Meir said.

"Our plan is to get the majority of Palestinians, who are moderate, into one block in order to isolate and destroy the extremists," Hussein said. "Do you object?"

"Yes," Meir said, "you will create more extremists. It is dangerous to call a people to a cause that cannot be implemented."


On September 26, 1972, Bruce Kehrli, the White House staff secretary, sent Butterfield a Top Secret memo about a potentially serious security violation. The most highly classified CIA Top Secret CIA Bulletin containing information on satellite imagery (codeword RUFF) and the most sensitive Category III communication intercepts (codeword UMBRA) had been found "between a couple of newspapers" in the office that produced the unclassified news summary for the president.

The document had been traced to the office of John Scali, a foreign affairs adviser to Nixon on the White House staff and later United Nations ambassador. Scali had become famous as an ABC news reporter during the 1962 Cuban Missile Crisis when he had claimed to be an intermediary between the United States and the Soviets.

"Suggest you reprimand Scali for the violation," Kehrli recommended. (Butterfield recalls he did not.)

The CIA Bulletin showed how the United States was spying on Israel by monitoring its missile development. A TOP SECRET RUFF report said: "*ISRAEL*: THE JERICHO SURFACE-TO-SURFACE MISSILE PROGRAM APPARENTLY IS NEARING THE TESTING PHASE.

"SATELLITE PHOTOGRAPHY OF THE YAVNE MISSILE TEST CENTER IN EARLY SEPTEMBER SHOWS WHAT APPEAR TO BE AT LEAST 11 MISSILE STAGE CANISTERS."

Israel, the Bulletin said, "HAS HAD THE INDUSTRIAL FACILITIES AND TECHNICAL EXPERTISE TO TURN OUT AT LEAST ONE JERICHO MISSILE A MONTH. IN ADDITION TO PRODUCTION FACILITIES AND A TEST RANGE, THE ISRAELIS ARE CONSTRUCTING WHAT IS BELIEVED TO BE AN OPERATIONAL SITE IN THE MOUNTAINS BETWEEN JERUSALEM AND TEL AVIV."

On the facing page the Bulletin had a detailed map of the Middle East showing the 260-nautical-mile range of the Jericho missile in a full circle. It demonstrated how the missile could reach Egypt (including Cairo), deep into Syria, all of Jordan and the outer edges of Iraq and Saudi Arabia.

An equivalent report and satellite photograph (TOP SECRET RUFF UMBRA) on China showed development of a new silo in the early stages of construction in the Wu-Chai missile test complex southwest of Peking.

Top Secret "intercepted messages" involving the Soviets and Japan were also detailed, as were communications involving China and Vietnam. "Peking is moving to make up part of Hanoi's fighter aircraft losses of the past few months. According to intercepts, 12 MiG-19s were scheduled to fly from China to North Vietnam."

In other words the same expensive, TOP SECRET intelligence technologies used on the most important targets such as China were being used to spy on Israel.

# 18

The Vietnam War inherited from the Kennedy and Johnson administrations was an ongoing nightmare.

As Butterfield was aware, the centerpiece of Nixon's strategy was the so-called Vietnamization of the war—withdraw U.S. troops as fast as possible so the South Vietnamese could take over the major share of their own defense. The other aim was Peace with Honor. The goal was to avoid anything that could be labeled defeat. Nearly all reports and classified memos on the war passed through Butterfield. "I had a good feel for the plan." At the same time he was not in the official loop for foreign, military and war policy, and he did not attend the endless meetings on the war—neither the small nor the large, the ultra top secret nor the routine.

"I read everything that went into him and that was sent out," Butterfield recalled. "I did not study every page."

One critical document that he kept has never been made public. As best I can tell, following a thorough search and discussion with archivists at the Nixon Library and elsewhere, the document does not exist in the official record, even among documents still considered classified. On May 15, 2015, I requested that Michael D. Ellzey, director of the Nixon Library, initiate a search for the memo. He forwarded an email on June 5, 2015, from Jason Schultz, his supervisory archivist, saying that the key locations had been searched and an archivist "was unable to find" the memo though it "is something that should be in our collection."

I also could not find the memo mentioned in any of the major books on the Vietnam War, including the memoirs of Nixon, Kissinger or other key players.

John Negroponte, a foreign service officer and specialist in Vietnam who was the National Security Council staffer most directly involved in Vietnam for Kissinger from June 1971 to early 1973, said he remembered nothing like it. "I never heard of the memo," he said when I described it to him.

It is an arresting document. In the president's own handwriting he makes an unambiguous declaration that a major and controversial part of his strategy—the intensive bombing for the first three years of his presidency and previous four years by Johnson—had achieved "zilch" and was a "failure."

This is the background. On January 2, 1972, five days before he would formally declare that he would run for reelection, Nixon gave an hour-long, prime-time television interview to Dan Rather of CBS News.

"On everyone's mind is the resumption of the widespread bombing of North Vietnam," Rather said. "Could you assess the military benefits of that?"

"The results have been very, very effective," Nixon replied, "and I think that their effectiveness will be demonstrated by the statement I am now going to make." He said that he soon would announce a withdrawal of more U.S. troops.

It was an unqualified endorsement of the bombing as a successful strategy and its positive military impact. Up to that point, Nixon had ordered the U.S. military to drop more than 2.9 million tons of bombs in Laos, South Vietnam, North Vietnam and Cambodia, according to a 2013 study, "Electronic Records of the Air War Over Southeast Asia."

That staggering number of 2.9 million tons of bombs exceeds the 1.7 million tons dropped by President Johnson in those same countries from 1965 to 1968 during his presidency.

The day after the Rather interview, January 3, 1972, Kissinger sent a one-page memo to the president that was a routine update on the war. It was classified TOP SECRET—SENSITIVE, CONTAINS CODEWORD.

The memo said, "The Communists have launched heavy artillery attacks" in Laos and "Heavy cloud cover and haze have hampered U.S. air strikes." In addition, a force of 1,000 irregular Vietcong guerrilla forces had arrived. "The irregulars . . . have been highly effective." There also have been "continued reports of sizeable Communist troop movements" in two other regions of Laos. Da Nang Air Base also had been struck with rockets, causing minor damage. The printed contents from Kissinger are part of a routine update but what happened next is anything but routine.

Nixon took the update memo, tilted it sideways and in pen wrote in longhand to Kissinger: "K. We have had 10 years of *total* control of the air in Laos and V.Nam. The result=Zilch. There is something wrong with the strategy *or* the Air Force. I want a 'bark off' study—no snow job—on my desk in 2 weeks as to what the reason for the failure is. Otherwise continued air operations make no sense in Cambodia, Laos etc. after we complete withdrawal."

And then at the bottom, he scrawled: "Shake them up!!"

A copy of the memo with Nixon's handwritten note to Kissinger is reproduced on page 116.

The commander-in-chief who had directed the bombing in Southeast Asia for nearly three years was declaring that the result was "zilch" and a "failure." That 2.9 million tons translates into more than 5 billion pounds of explosives. Nixon was acknowledging no strategic gain. He asked for a new "bark off," "no snow job" review. I could find no evidence that one was done.

I reached Kissinger by phone Monday, June 29, 2015, as he traveled on the Amtrak train for a meeting in Washington, D.C. I summarized the orders Nixon wrote to him on the January 3, 1972, memo.

Kissinger said he didn't remember that specific memo from 43 years ago. But he was not at all surprised by such an order from Nixon. "Periodically things would come in from him and sometimes they were meaningful," Kissinger said, "and sometimes you would just wait and see."

Had there been 10 years of bombing failure, as Nixon maintained? I asked.

"That is true," Kissinger said. I was utterly surprised at his candor so I asked it again. "Almost certainly that is true," he said.

Kissinger said Nixon usually wanted to intensify the bombing. "He was in the habit of wanting more bombing . . . his instructions most often were for more bombing."

But Nixon wrote to you that it wasn't working, that something was wrong with the strategy or the air force? "I could find you fifty memos that said the opposite," Kissinger responded.

But didn't Nixon sound frustrated and angry? "It is true he was frustrated," Kissinger said. He said he recalled that no study was done in response to Nixon's order for one that was "bark off" and "no snow job."

He said the Nixon Library should have this memo as should the Library of Congress, which he complained has been too slow to release his documents. I said I would continue to seek out a copy from the archival records and that I would enlist the assistance of one of Kissinger's former aides.

"Now, you're not going to quote me on this, are you?"

Yes, I said I would.

It is significant to see what happened after Nixon declared that the bombing had achieved "zilch." In 1972, he ordered increased bombing and the U.S. military dropped 1.1 million tons in that year alone— more than in any single year of the Johnson presidency. Included in the 1.1 million tons was 207,000 tons in North Vietnam alone. The most Johnson had dropped on North Vietnam was 198,000 tons and that was in 1968. In 1973, Nixon dropped 440,000 tons in the four countries.

Rather than forsaking bombing, Nixon once again embraced it.

The opponents of the war probably could not have imagined such a clear condemnation of Nixon's policy written in his own hand. The bombing had achieved "zilch." This is not a stray comment on one

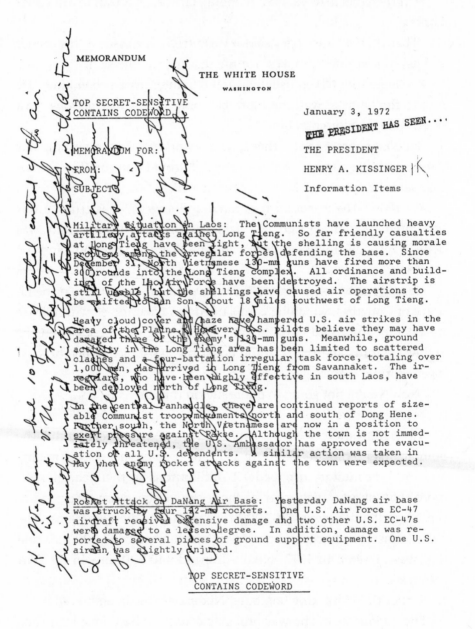

MEMORANDUM

THE WHITE HOUSE
WASHINGTON

TOP SECRET-SENSITIVE
CONTAINS CODEWORD.

January 3, 1972

THE PRESIDENT HAS SEEN....

MEMORANDUM FOR:        THE PRESIDENT

FROM:                  HENRY A. KISSINGER

SUBJECT:               Information Items

Military Situation in Laos:  The Communists have launched heavy
artillery attacks against Long Tieng.  So far friendly casualties
at Long Tieng have been light, but the shelling is causing morale
problems among the irregular forces defending the base.  Since
December 31, North Vietnamese 130-mm guns have fired more than
300 rounds into the Long Tieng complex.  All ordinance and buildings of the Lao Air Force have been destroyed.  The airstrip is
still usable, but the shellings have caused air operations to
be shifted to Ban Son, about 18 miles southwest of Long Tieng.

Heavy cloud cover and haze have hampered U.S. air strikes in the
area of the Plaine.  However, U.S. pilots believe they may have
damaged three of the enemy's 130-mm guns.  Meanwhile, ground
activity in the Long Tieng area has been limited to scattered
clashes and a four-battalion irregular task force, totaling over
1,000 men, has arrived in Long Tieng from Savannaket.  The irregulars, who have been highly effective in south Laos, have
been deployed north of Long Tieng.

In the central Panhandle, there are continued reports of sizeable Communist troop movements north and south of Dong Hene.
Further south, the North Vietnamese are now in a position to
exert pressure against Pakse.  Although the town is not immediately threatened, the U.S. Ambassador has approved the evacu-
ation of all U.S. dependents.  A similar action was taken in
May when enemy rocket attacks against the town were expected.

Rocket Attack on DaNang Air Base:  Yesterday DaNang air base
was struck by four 142-mm rockets.  One U.S. Air Force EC-47
aircraft received extensive damage and two other U.S. EC-47s
were damaged to a lesser degree.  In addition, damage was reported to several pieces of ground support equipment.  One U.S.
airman was slightly injured.

TOP SECRET-SENSITIVE
CONTAINS CODEWORD

of his taped conversations. The language is plain and direct from the commander-in-chief.

When I went over the copy of the memo with Butterfield in his apartment in La Jolla, California, he confirmed it was Nixon's handwriting. Without question. He had seen thousands of examples in notes and marginal comments.

"I can tell by the way he writes here that he's upset," Butterfield added. At my request, Butterfield then read the memo aloud before a camera filming him.

He noted that "Shake them up!!" was underlined twice. "I'm sure he pressed into the paper on that. He's furious. And that is an amazing memo."

As I think the history of the Vietnam War shows, Nixon's "zilch" memo was accurate. The bombing was not working. It was a failure, and certainly not "very effective" as he had assured Dan Rather.

"We're going back to *The Best and the Brightest*," Butterfield said, referring to David Halberstam's landmark book that excoriated the architects of the Vietnam War. "We're in something that we never had any business getting involved in."

"Now we've been doing this for three years and what is the result?" Butterfield asked. "Zilch."

"But," I said, "here's the commander-in-chief saying it's a failure."

"Yes," Butterfield replied.

"We've achieved zilch," I said.

"Yeah," he replied.

"And hundreds of thousands of [tons] have been dropped."

"Hundreds of thousands," Butterfield repeated, "that's right."

"In Vietnam," I said, "and he's saying it's done nothing."

"The air operations are making no sense," he said.

"What gives here?" I asked. "What is somebody to make of this? It's 'very, very effective' publicly, and then on a top secret memo he says we're achieving zilch and it's a failure."

Butterfield said he could not explain. "I can't put it together. I didn't have a very optimistic view of how it would end even when I was over there flying [in the early 1960s]. And prior to that, for three years, I was working for General O'Donnell, who was the commander-in-chief of all air forces in the Pacific Theater. When we would go over there, we went over about once a month and we would always meet with [South Vietnamese] President Diem. It was always worse than it had been on the previous visit. There was no reason to be very optimistic. And you know, the Vietcong and the North Vietnamese were 20 times more persistent than we anticipated. We always thought we could do this easily, with one hand tied behind our back. And they continued to wear us down."

Suppose, I asked Butterfield, that a reporter for *The Washington Post* in January 1972 had obtained a copy of the memo with Nixon's declaration of "zilch" and "failure." Suppose it had been published then with his handwritten conclusions, what would have happened?

The reporter would have been made editor of *The Washington Post*, Butterfield said facetiously, been given Ben Bradlee's job. It would have been a real exposé.

What is so crucial about Nixon's scrawled declaration is that it could not have been something that dawned on him on January 3, 1972.

The "zilch" conclusion had grown over three years. In what way and when did he realize this? History may never know. Maybe Nixon never knew, never grasped the full weight of his own conclusion. What gives that assessment credibility is that it was not Nixon's alone. Read and sort through all the documents, tapes, books, speeches and histories on Vietnam and it leads to that conclusion. It was "zilch." It was not working. There is a note of panic in the note in his demand for a "bark off" study, "no snow job," on his desk in two weeks. As if two weeks of honest study could somehow remedy three years.

What is to be said about a wartime leader who goes on with war knowing a key part of the strategy is not working? The memo bolsters the conclusion about the senselessness of the war. How much anguish had been inflicted on Americans, Vietnamese, Cambodians, Laotians and others? How could the devastation and human suffering be measured?

Neil Sheehan in his Pulitzer Prize–winning book perhaps says it best with his title, *A Bright Shining Lie*. It was a lie, and here Nixon made clear that he knew it.

"When you're in the White House," Butterfield said, "everyone lies. You can sort of get feeling immune."

There remains the question of what did Kissinger know?

The real psychological study of the Nixon-Kissinger relationship may never be done. It is often described as a partnership, but it was marked by deep distrust, rivalry and self-protection.

The only hint I could find in the rest of the Vietnam record that Nixon had some second thoughts in January 1972 was in Haldeman's diary. In an entry for Saturday, January 1, 1972—two days before the "Zilch" memo—Haldeman wrote:

"K [Kissinger] called from New York all disturbed because he felt someone had been getting to the P [President] on Vietnam. . . . Henry's concerned that the P's looking for a way to bug out and he thinks that would be a disaster now."

# *19*

Nixon did not ease his way into more bombing after the "Zilch" memo. The next month, February 1972, according to a TOP SECRET/SENSITIVE/EXCLUSIVELY EYES ONLY memo from Kissinger to the secretary of defense, Melvin Laird, Nixon ordered a dramatic bombing escalation. It was in anticipation of a large North Vietnam offensive.*

Kissinger wrote Laird that as a result of a National Security Council meeting on February 2, a month after the "Zilch" memo, Nixon had made the following decisions.

According to Kissinger's memo, "the President has directed that the Secretary of Defense undertake the following actions. . . . Add, as soon as possible, one additional [aircraft] carrier to the three currently available for operation in Southeast Asia. . . . Deploy additional B-52s to permit a sustained sortie rate of about 1500 per month. . . . Deploy additional fighter bomber squadrons to Southeast Asian bases. . . . Remove all existing sortie restrictions for both B-52 and tactical air missions during the current dry season in South Vietnam. . . . You should authorize air strikes into the northern portion of the DMZ

---

*I did not find a copy of this two-page memo in Butterfield's files, but it was declassified in 2007.

whenever the field commander determines that the enemy is using the area in preparation for attack in the south."

This memo is not referred to in either Nixon's or Kissinger's memoirs.


Nixon was very worried about what Kissinger might have in his files, according to a taped November 20, 1972, conversation with Haldeman.

"Now another thing that I desperately need something on is this: I've got to get from Henry's office, get to my library file, all of my memoranda and his memorandums. Now, he doesn't know, as you know, that we've got the recorder in there." Kissinger was not aware of the secret taping system. Nixon also reminded Haldeman that "None of those should be transcribed; don't want them transcribed.

"Mine. Mine," he declared. "I have got to get Henry's stuff . . . and I want the original. I don't want copies. You understand?

"I've got to get his memoranda to me. Every memorandum he's written to me, and everything I've written to him, has got to be put in that file now. . . . How are you going to get it?"

"Easily," Haldeman assured him. "Because he's assured me all along that's exactly the case. I now say we're at the end of the first term, and we've told the whole staff, so it's not singling him out, all the first-term papers have got to be moved over now. And physically, and I'll take possession of them. And put them in your box."


On May 9, 1972, Nixon dictated a TOP SECRET—EYES ONLY memo to Kissinger that Butterfield has in his files. It was declassified in 2010, years after most major Vietnam War histories were published.

Nixon quotes seven paragraphs from the 20-paragraph memo in his 1978 memoir. The selection illustrates the point Nixon frequently made—it depends who writes the history. It also depends on who selects the documents and what portions to make public.

In total, it is a revealing stream-of-consciousness document. The day before, May 8, Nixon had ordered the mining of Haiphong Harbor and the bombing of key military targets in North Vietnam. It was again a significant escalation, in part, the kind of bombing that five months earlier he claimed had achieved "zilch." He also seemed to realize fully that he was playing a mind game with the North Vietnamese.

The seven paragraphs that Nixon uses in his memoir include the following strong assertions of his determination: (All the emphasis is Nixon's.) "I cannot emphasize too strongly that I have determined that we should go for broke. . . . We must *punish* the enemy in ways that he will really hurt at this time. . . . I intend to stop at nothing to bring the enemy to his knees. . . .

"We have the power to destroy his war making capacity. The only question is whether we have the *will* to use that power. What distinguishes me from Johnson is that I have the *will* in spades."

What he left out of his memoir was a description of the means.

The full memo in Butterfield's files adds this dimension:

". . . over the next few days I also want some targets hit which will have maximum psychological effect on morale in North Vietnam. That is why it is so important to take out the power plants. If your operational group thinks of any other targets of this type hit them and hit them hard."

Nixon also says that he will circumvent the chain of command, which by law runs from the president to the secretary of defense and to the military commanders. Because Laird opposed the mining and bombing, Nixon said he would deal with General Creighton Abrams, the commander in Vietnam. "I intend to give the directive directly to Abrams in the field and I will inform Laird and bring him into line. . . .

"Over a longer period of time we can be more methodical in directing our air strikes to two specific targets—the rail lines, highways and POL [petroleum] supply areas. . . .

"Needless to say, indiscriminate bombing of civilian areas is not what I have in mind. On the other hand, *if the target is important enough,* I will approve a plan that goes after it even if there is a risk of some civilian casualties."

He also left out the following: "I want as part of the plan this week, on an urgent basis, making strikes on all air fields in North Vietnam, particularly in the Hanoi-Haiphong area. I realize that they can be put back into operation a few days after a strike, but the psychological effect could be considerable. On this score, I particularly want to hit the international airfield where civilian planes land."

He had one more thought to offer in this long monologue.

"Also, this week I want *one major strike*. Get Abrams to collect his assets and have one 500 plane strike by Thursday or Friday of this week so the enemy will know that we mean business all the way."

At the top Nixon appended a handwritten note to Rose Woods that she should file in "RN personal," and issued this order: "K reread and Haig also before filing."

When the State Department declassified its version of the memo in 2010, it said in a footnote that nearly a month later Haig forwarded the memo to Kissinger with the notation, "Henry—the president sent this via Alex Butterfield this morning and asked that we both reread it. I am afraid that Rebozo will rekindle the fire over the weekend and we must all be ready for the ritual."

Butterfield said he does not know what this meant.


Though not aware of Nixon's "Zilch" memo, Ken Hughes, a researcher at the University of Virginia's Miller Center, and an expert on Nixon's tapes, has found significant new evidence about Nixon's actions in the Vietnam War. In his 2015 book, *Fatal Politics: The Nixon Tapes, the Vietnam War, and the Casualties of Reelection*, Hughes shows that Nixon was aware that the massive bombing did not do the job militarily but it was politically popular. Hughes argues with a great deal of evidence that the bombing was chiefly designed so Nixon would win reelection.

On the day after Nixon resigned, papers were removed from the desk in his hideaway office. Included was a 79-page "Confidential Survey" done for the Republican National Committee three years earlier at the end of July 1969. The survey is in the Nixon Presidential Library now. It stated that 66 percent of those polled would favor bombing and blockading North Vietnam for six months. On May 8, 1972—six months before the election—that was precisely what Nixon did when he ordered the new bombing of the North and the mining of Haiphong.

Nixon would later claim in his 1985 book, *No More Vietnams*, that the bombing and mining "succeeded in crippling North Vietnam's military effort." Hughes cites CIA, DIA and Pentagon memos showing that bombing was not that effective because the North was getting more supplies than it needed to fight the ground war in the South and could last for two more years even if the bombing and mining continued. *The Official History of the People's Army of Vietnam, 1954–1975*, first published in Vietnam in 1988 and translated into English in 2002, states: "The volume of supplies shipped from the North to South Vietnam in 1972 was almost double that shipped in 1971." This claim and others in the *Official History* could not be verified.

According to a September 8, 1972, tape recording, Nixon reported to Kissinger that the poll numbers favored bombing. "Just got Harris's data," the president said. "It's two-to-one for bombing. Two-and-a-half-to-one for bombing. They want us to be very, very tough." Nixon wrote that his popularity in 1972 was often attributed to his China opening, but "what really sent it up was the bombing and mining of Haiphong."

According to the tape of an October 6, 1972, meeting, Nixon disparaged the bombing, telling Kissinger, "We've never done anything militarily that's worth a shit in North Vietnam except the mining."

Nixon did voice concern at one point about the human impact of the bombing. "I see those poor North Vietnamese kids burning with napalm, and it burns my heart," he said, according to an October 12 tape. Three days later, Nixon was basking in the prospect of election victory in three weeks. "We're not going to lose. Haha. Okay," he said according to an October 15 tape.

The next day, October 16, according to the tape of the discussion, Nixon harked back to the day he ordered new bombing and the Haiphong mining, telling Kissinger:

"May 8 was the acid test. And how it's prepared us for all these things. The election, for example."

"I think you won the election on May 8th," Kissinger said.

# 20

It is, of course, impossible to review all of the Nixon-Kissinger actions and memos on Vietnam here. But some of the Butterfield documents raise questions about the public record, particularly the selection of information on Vietnam in both Nixon's and Kissinger's memoirs. Crucial parts of memos have been omitted from their memoirs, altering the historical record in significant ways.

For example, Kissinger, who was in South Vietnam for meetings with South Vietnamese president Nguyen Van Thieu, sent a Top Secret Flash, Sensitive, Exclusive Eyes Only two-page memo dated October 22, 1972, to the White House. This was just two weeks before the U.S. presidential election.

It also contains Nixon's handwritten note at the top to "File RN personal," meaning it should go only to Nixon's personal file. The same dark ink appears to be Nixon's underlines on key passages.

In Kissinger's memo he proposes that Nixon send a letter to Soviet leader Leonid Brezhnev, who was acting as an intermediary with the North Vietnamese on peace negotiations. The national security adviser recommends saying that Nixon "would be prepared to work out a bilateral arrangement" with the North. This would exclude South Vietnam, the U.S. ally in the war.

"We have always said that we would not impose a solution on our allies," Kissinger said. But that was what he was proposing and he added, "obviously I favor" this option.

In his memoir, Nixon does not even acknowledge that Kissinger made a proposal for such a "bilateral arrangement," and writes that he categorically rejected such a concept and would not even entertain the thought.

"I did not feel that I could let this happen. . . . If we abandoned him [Thieu] South Vietnam would fall to the Communists within a matter of months and our entire effort there would have been for naught."

On the very next page Nixon quotes the first line of Kissinger's cable of October 22, 1972: "It is hard to exaggerate the toughness of Thieu's position. His demands verge on insanity." But Nixon leaves out the rest including Kissinger's favored course of a "bilateral arrangement" with the North.

In his memoir, Nixon writes, "I immediately sent a message to [Premier] Pham Van Dong through the North Vietnamese delegation in Paris, reminding Hanoi that we had always taken the position that we could not proceed unilaterally" without the participation of South Vietnam.

Of course this was contrary to Kissinger's favored course—"a bilateral arrangement"—as outlined in the portion of the cable that Nixon did not acknowledge.

In his memoir, Kissinger also does not mention or acknowledge his favored course. He mentions the cable and says, "We wanted Soviet assistance to keep Hanoi on a restrained course." But he makes no mention of his willingness to make "a bilateral arrangement" with the North—something both Nixon and he assured the South Vietnamese president would never happen.

Neither Nixon nor Kissinger uses the line from the cable in which Kissinger recommends that more should be done than just a letter to Brezhnev. "Here you would add orally that, of course, the November 7 considerations must weigh very heavily," Kissinger said. November 7 was the date of the upcoming presidential election.

A full copy of this Top Secret memo was released publicly in 2010 when it was declassified and published by the State Department Office of the Historian. It was among more than 4,000 pages of documents released in four volumes from the Vietnam era. This was more than three decades after the Nixon and Kissinger memoirs were published. The failure to tell the whole story suggests it may be time for a fresh examination of the entire Vietnam record in light of Nixon and Kissinger's substantial efforts to distort the record and not explain what they were really doing.

The next day, Monday, October 23, Kissinger met with Thieu for two and one quarter hours and in his memoir he calls the session "a melancholy encounter" and quotes some benign exchanges with the South Vietnam president.

But a five-page TOP SECRET/SENSITIVE EXCLUSIVELY EYES ONLY cable back to Nixon and Haig that is in the Butterfield files shows the extent to which Kissinger did not tell Thieu much of the truth, insisting he would not do precisely what he had proposed to Nixon a day earlier.

"First," Kissinger reports on what he told Thieu, "I want to make it clear there never have been talks or communications with the other side which have not been communicated to you. You have been apprised fully of every development as it has occurred and have been consulted on every move we have made with the single exception of the meeting on September 15 when we believed it was necessary to move before we had heard from you.

"The U.S. will never sacrifice a trusted friend. We will not deal with anyone but the President of Vietnam and will have no communication with anyone but the president of Vietnam."

Kissinger added, "We do not consider President Thieu's demands unreasonable."

In the notetaker's summary, the cable continued, "Dr. Kissinger said that he would probably have a press conference when he returned to the U.S. He will give the impression that progress is being made. . . .

"When he returned to the U.S., he will consider himself President Thieu's comrade in arms," adding ambiguously but more truthfully, "warning, however, that we may not face the ideal way in which we can continue together.

"Dr. Kissinger . . . assured Thieu that nothing would be done behind his back and that consultation would continue."

In his memoir Kissinger goes further. "Outrageous as Thieu's conduct had been, our struggle had been over a principle: that America did not betray its friends. I agreed with Nixon that turning on Thieu would be incompatible with our sacrifice."

It would be naive in the extreme not to realize that this is the way diplomacy is often conducted, but in his memoir published five years after Nixon's resignation, Kissinger masks the truth by selective use of his cables. Both he and Nixon leave out any reference to a separate "bilateral" arrangement with the North that would be a sellout of their longtime ally.

By December the Peace Talks had broken down and on December 18 Nixon began the so-called Christmas bombing of the North, unleashing massive B-52 Stratofortress raids on Hanoi and Haiphong. Code-named Operation Linebacker II it was the largest heavy bomber strike launched by the United Sates since the end of World War II.

The North called this "extermination bombing," but as Nixon said in *RN*, "they did not require that the bombing be stopped as a precondition to their agreeing to another meeting" for peace talks.

If the bombing was effective and having such an impact, why did the North not require or even request that it be halted? Part of the answer may be provided by the official North Vietnamese history, which says that they were able to use the massive American bombing raids for propaganda purposes and to boost morale.

This history also suggests that contrary to U.S. claims much of the bombing was not effective and did minimal damage—in other words "zilch" as Nixon had written earlier in the year.

It portrays the Christmas bombing as brutal but claimed the bombing served to rally the people and military. The first night of bombing, December 18, 1972, the history says the North shot down three B-52s. This is confirmed by U.S. records.

"This glorious victory in our initial battle strongly encouraged the fighting resolve and will to win of the soldiers and civilians of the entire nation," the Vietnamese history says.

After 12 days the Christmas bombing was halted. "The enemy's massive strategic offensive using B-52s against Hanoi and Haiphong had been crushed," the Vietnamese book says. "Nixon's dream of negotiating from a position of strength had ended in total failure." The history claimed the North had shot down 34 B-52s. The U.S. said it was only 15, though another nine suffered medium to heavy damage.

In the midst of the new bombing and with the reelection behind him, Nixon wrote in his memoir that he sent "the strongest letter I had yet written to Thieu." Nixon then bluntly surfaced the idea that he would make a bilateral agreement with the North if necessary. It was, he told Thieu, "my irrevocable intention to proceed, preferably with your cooperation but, if necessary, alone."

Thieu finally went along and the Paris peace treaty was signed January 27, 1973, but the war did not end until April 1975 when the United States evacuated all its forces.

# *21*

Watergate and Vietnam will be Nixon's chief legacies. There was, however, another side to Nixon. Why does he retain a small, though diminishing number of admirers? The answer, I think, is his mind. It was remarkable in many ways. He had the gift, misused so unfortunately in Watergate and Vietnam, of a strategic mind—the capacity to lay out general principles, and also the small and large steps needed to achieve a big goal. He faltered tragically in his chief legacies. But he was capable of determining where he wanted to be in a year or two and taking the actions to get there.

The Butterfield files contain some memos and dictations from Nixon that illustrate this. Extreme critics of Nixon tend to discount this side but it existed. He knew how to mobilize others, especially when it was in his political interest. This applies, most dramatically, to 1972 when he was campaigning for reelection. His maneuvers were often tinged with duplicity and ardent self-promotion. They also show his single-mindedness and his capacity to wring the maximum political advantage out of a situation. He possessed the capacity to plot. It helps explain how he rose to the presidency, and once in the White House achieved some genuine successes in foreign and domestic policy. He also knew how to appeal to the ego of others, and to use humor.

On April 8, 1972, Nixon dictated a four-page memo to John Ehrlichman, then his chief domestic adviser. With the reelection campaign in full swing, Nixon knew that the main job was no longer governing but selling his case for reelection.

"Over the past week-end I have had some opportunity to evaluate the activities we will be engaging in for the next seven months before the election. I have concluded that, at this point, your assignment should be substantially changed in substance while remaining the same insofar as title and format are concerned. In essence I want you to become the man in charge of selling our domestic programs and answering attacks on them, rather than the man in charge of developing these programs, and riding herd on them within the Administration to see that everybody follows the line in executing them."

Ehrlichman was to become the campaign manager for Nixon's domestic programs but Nixon didn't want to say so since "title and format" would not change.

"You have handled the development of the programs with superb organizational ability and substantively have seen to it that they have come out along the lines of my own thinking."

It may not be possible for a presidential aide to receive greater praise.

"This task, however, is now completed and what remains to be done—modification, implementation, etc.—can be done by others, whom I will mention in a moment in this memorandum. They may not be able to do the job you have been doing quite as well as you are doing it, but that will not matter much. What is important is that you will be released to do something that they either cannot do at all or which you can do far better—selling the programs personally and through directing others."

Nixon suggested that Ehrlichman get George Shultz, then the director of the Office of Management and Budget (OMB), to bring to life "the management side of OMB which has been somewhat dormant." He suggested that Ehrlichman stay out of "conflicts" between cabinet officers so he could focus on selling.

"In any event, the players who will take your old assignments will be a matter for you to decide," Nixon continued. "I am simply suggesting the line of my thinking and will abide by any recommendations you make and any decisions you make."

Nixon was expressing total trust.

The issues to address included busing, taxes, drug abuse and the high cost of living, he said. "As I run down these items, I know that the automatic reaction of the White House staff will be—why doesn't the President go on television and make a fireside chat—or why doesn't he engage in some kind of a gimmick which will spotlight the particular issue. I am perfectly willing to do anything or say anything that will help us get across our points in these areas.

"However, as I look back over the past three years, our great failing, particularly in the domestic area, has been that once the President shoots the big gun the infantry doesn't follow in adequately to clean up and to hold the territory. . . . There are always the issues where the opposition is on the attack. The Administration's closeness to big business, its support of the big man as against the little man, etc. . . .

"But we have to face the fact that in the domestic area, except for [Treasury Secretary John] Connally in these cases where he wants to go to bat, we do not have powerful enough spokesmen." He cited the "failure" of Shultz and Health, Education and Welfare Secretary Elliot Richardson during a recent meeting on busing.

"You are the best all-around spokesman for the Administration's domestic programs. You have an orderly mind, you are convincing, you are tough and you are very effective on television. I know that you have been reluctant to be a public spokesman for the reason that sensitivities of Cabinet officers might be irritated—bruised. . . . But from now until election we can't be concerned about whether Cabinet officers have bruised feelings."

This role as the front person was only half the job. "The other half is for you to organize the appearances by others just like you were running a campaign."

Adopting the language of combat, Nixon said, "What we need is a commander who will organize and direct the troops to follow up once the President makes a statement or to counterattack when the enemy levels with an attack against us. This is the task I would like for you to undertake."

He added, "In the foreign policy field, I pretty much have to do this job myself. The impossible relationship between [Secretary of State] Rogers and Kissinger is such that we find it very difficult of course to get followup of my foreign policy initiatives by Rogers unless he feels it is a pretty sure thing insofar as public approval is concerned. . . .

"I want you to do what I would do in the domestic front if I had the time to spend on that as well. . . .

"Much of the reason for our doing a poor job of selling them is that we don't have a very good cast of characters. . . .

"Great ideas that are conceived and not sold are like babies that are stillborn. We need some deliveries within the next few months, even if they have to be cesarian. I will approve any programs you have to bring about those deliveries," and he added with a touch of humor, "provided of course you recognize my total opposition to any abortions." Signed, THE PRESIDENT.

After belittling Rogers, Shultz and the cabinet in general, Nixon then four months later to the day orchestrated one of the supreme presidential stroking sessions. It was a cabinet dinner at Camp David on August 8, 1972.

A tape of a discussion Nixon had with Butterfield the day before the dinner illustrates how he carefully calculated, and understood the importance of who was invited and who was excluded.

For 12 minutes Nixon conducted a person-by-person review of who to have and the importance of trying to eliminate senior White House people. That way, Nixon said, "the cabinet feels they're getting special attention." By reducing the list an invitation would become "a greater compliment to those who are there," he said.

That afternoon he spent another 10 minutes calibrating the list with Butterfield.

"We ought to cut it more," Nixon said. He wanted to drop several senior counselors and Ehrlichman. "You have Haldeman there, because he is basically a political man. Ehrlichman is not political." This was a preposterous statement given that four months earlier he had ordered Ehrlichman to devote all his time to selling the administration's domestic policies politically.

Ehrlichman stayed on the list, however, as did 16 others from the White House staff, including Butterfield, who took attendance. The dinner included 14 cabinet members and five from Nixon's reelection committee.

A 17-page transcript of Nixon's after-dinner speech is among Butterfield's papers. The president at first mentioned Clark MacGregor, the former Minnesota congressman and the current head of the Committee for the Re-election of the President, often abbreviated as CREEP.

"We are very proud of this campaign team, except for MacGregor, they are young and vigorous," Nixon joked. Of Maury Stans, the chief fundraiser, Nixon said, "The lousiest job in campaigning is raising money, particularly after we have already sold the ambassadorships several times." Laughter. "He is accused of things that all finance chairmen are accused of. He is not guilty of many of them." Laughter.

He praised the wives, but said there was not enough room to invite them to the dinner at Camp David "even with this big facility which Laird says he has worked into the Vietnam budget." Laughter again.

A recent public opinion poll showed that "only 15 percent of college youth say that they are Republicans." Why is Treasury Secretary Connally's Democrats for Nixon so important? he asked. "Because getting Democrats is the name of the game." So talk about nonpartisan principles, he said.

"In campaigning for the United States Senate in California in 1950, in campaigning for the House of Representatives in 1946, I never once mentioned the word, 'Republican.' Never.

"But if you just go in and make that hard-hitting 'Republicans are good and Democrats are a bunch of devils,' it makes it so difficult for them to come over. So let them come over. Let them come over easy."

He turned to his opponent. "A vote for McGovern is a vote to add

80 million people to the welfare rolls, that a vote for McGovern is a vote to add $140 billion to the budget."

He summarized, "But attack. Always attack."

"The war, a terribly difficult issue for us. We don't have an easy answer. We have, however, a very outstanding record.

"This Administration—and I am not overstating it—we have really changed the post-war world. It will never be the same again."

He said he had read some staff papers about what to do in the campaign and they recommended, "Don't mention foreign policy because people already know about China and Russia." He begged to differ.

"Forget it! Remind them of it! Hit it over and over again. That is where we are strong. That is where they are weak." Raise the issue of competence, experience and the high caliber of his advisers.

"But the main thing for us to remember is to keep emphasis on the big game," he said.

He praised all of them for their political experience. "What we have going for us is not only a candidate for President and Vice President but we have, from the Secretary of State [Rogers] right up and down the line in this cabinet, a group of politicians. For that reason we will beat the hell out of them.

"Well, they have four helicopters out there. These are the only ones that were not shot down in Vietnam. So you had better take a ride." There was laughter. "We wish you well."


Nixon also knew the importance of passing out compliments to his staff. On October 25, 1972, certain he was going to win reelection in two weeks, he wrote a personal note to Pat Buchanan, who was in charge of compiling the daily news summary. On the first page of that day's summary, he penned in his own handwriting, "I am constantly amazed at the brilliant work done in . . . the News Summary. It is invaluable for all of us." Signed RN.

# 22

---

Butterfield wanted out. Anticipating reelection, he heard Nixon tell Haldeman on several occasions that it would be, more than ever, a time for vengeance.

"Now, we're going to get them, Bob," Nixon said. "Now we're going to nail those sons of bitches." The atmosphere of retribution aimed at Democrats, the media, the antiwar movement and any perceived Nixon opponent was pervasive.

Butterfield was almost permanently distressed by his own acquiescence to Nixon's request that they use a Secret Service agent as a planted spy in Kennedy's security detail. He kept bringing it up in our discussions. "I was affected by how easily I said yes, sir. Couldn't believe it, really, afterwards. But it was so natural to say, yes, sir."

He added, "I had seen myself and heard myself get caught up in this thing and be anxious and ready to facilitate an abusive government." Many times—though, he said, not at all times—he felt about the Nixon White House: "The whole thing was a cesspool."

On the other hand, "It was such a good job, in so many ways. It was prestigious. I knew everybody." He was treated like one of the most senior Nixon aides. For example, there is a picture of an elegant,

intimate, black-tie eight-person dinner party hanging on a wall in Butterfield's La Jolla penthouse condo. It was taken in 1971 at the Watergate apartment of then Attorney General John Mitchell and his wife,
Martha. Treasury Secretary John Connally is seated between Martha
Mitchell and Charlotte Butterfield. Butterfield is in the seat of honor
on John Mitchell's right. Mitchell knew the importance of Butterfield
to the Nixon White House.

"I knew my job well," Butterfield said. "I could do it." He was at the
center of part of the Nixon universe, with only a thin wall, 20 steps
from his desk to Nixon's in the Oval for more than three years. He was
not in the endless Watergate meetings and was not aware of and did
not participate in various conspiracies. "I wasn't the guy working on
the cover-up," he said. Because of the hammerlock control exercised by
Nixon and Haldeman on all matters, he was certain they were aware of
the Watergate crimes and were covering them up.

On November 7, 1972, Nixon won a historic landslide, capturing 49
states and 61 percent of the vote. That day Butterfield and all appointees in the executive office of the president received a confidential,
one-page memo from Haldeman requesting that in the next three
days they list preferences for possible service in the next administration. "This should accompany your pro forma letter of resignation to
become effective at the pleasure of the President." He wasn't being
singled out. All White House staff and other presidentially appointed
officials were asked to submit resignation letters. When this became
public, Nixon was almost universally seen as ungrateful—thank you
for your service, now please resign.

In his memoir, Kissinger calls the resignation-now demand
"appalling . . . degrading . . . frenzied, almost maniacal . . . political
butchery . . . wounding and humiliating . . . conveying in his hour of
triumph an impression of such total vindictiveness and insensitivity to
those who were basically well-disposed to him."

Haldeman asked for "a basic book about your current assignment."

Butterfield, like many, frequently felt underappreciated, as if no one understood the breadth of his vast responsibilities. He compiled a 16-page memo listing what he saw as his 26 primary duties.*

Item 26 was, "Attend to special classified and/or highly sensitive projects of particular interest to the president."

Foremost of these was the secret taping system, which, of course, he did not list.

On November 10, Butterfield dictated a confidential response to Haldeman.

"Dear Bob: I know that you are confronted with a gigantic reorganization task, so despite the importance of this letter to me personally, and to my family, I will be as brief as possible." He then went on, as was his habit, not being very brief at all.

"Hoping, of course, that you will read between the lines and understand many of the whys and wherefores. . . .

"First let me say in all sincerity that in no way will I ever be able to repay *you* for taking the chance you did with me and my abilities. You alone gave me the honor and opportunity of a life-time. . . . I must tell you that I will be forever grateful. . . .

"I will serve *either* of you in *any* capacity whatever."

---

*Included were: alternate to Haldeman; supervise staff secretary and everything "destined for the President's desk"; supervise the security office and security clearances for all nominations for presidential appointments; supervise offices of Presidential Papers, Special Files, presidential receptionists, the president's daily schedule, the Secret Service, the ushers, the military assistants, the Office of White House Visitors; serve as single point of contact for cabinet members' foreign travel, significant presidential ceremonies; supervise or coordinate the president's exchanges of gifts; principal coordinator of decision on when to lower the U.S. flag over federal buildings and when to close federal buildings; coordinate use of presidential aircraft or for "White-House directed" missions; coordinate all recommendations for telephone calls the president should make; principal adviser to White House telephone switchboard operators; secretarial support for the president at Camp David or Key Biscayne; "special liaison between the president and the First Lady"; maintain inventory of the president's personal wines; maintain master record of the president's contacts with "distinguished foreign personages"; maintain a master record of all the president's contacts with cabinet and sub-cabinet officials; function as secretary to the cabinet.

Butterfield later told me that offer to do anything was "probably not too sincere."

He continued, "I seek a change. I am anxious to find something which will give me greater challenge, greater responsibility, a somewhat higher salary, and more and better employment opportunities" after the second term.

He compared himself to Jack Valenti, President Johnson's yes-man, cheerleader and odd-jobs attendant, and allowed some bitterness to show.

"I fear being 'typed,' especially in my current Valenti-like role. . . . But my guess is that he [Nixon] considers the good, fairly efficient, man-servant in the outer office akin to the village idiot— one without mind or opinion. Yet I have done many other things in my lifetime, more by far than most people, and proved to myself and others."

He complained that he had been harnessed and limited. "Prospective employers, however, will have no idea of what I might be able to offer if I remain here on the White House Staff, so 'contained.'

"This is not to say I want to be in the limelight. I am not built that way." Because he was not a lawyer and had not been a businessman or "advertising executive" (like Haldeman), he said, "I must *now*, during this next 2–4 year period, surface sufficiently to make contact with the outside world."

In order of preference, he would first like to be appointed secretary of the Air Force. Then he listed secretary of the Navy in deference to his father, a retired rear admiral, and then several undersecretary positions.

"This seems a helluva presumptuous note on which to close, but then you *did* ask."


"That wasn't the plan," Haldeman told Butterfield after reading the memo. "The plan was that you would stay on," adding, "The president now knows you very well" and noting that Butterfield had worked very closely and effectively with Nixon—not an easy task. "I would like to think about this a little bit," Haldeman added, meaning he was going to consult Nixon.

"Bob tells me you really want to leave," the president said to Butterfield a short time later after coming into Butterfield's office and taking a seat near his desk.

"It isn't so much that I want to," Butterfield replied. "It's just that I've been here four years and I've loved every minute of it, Mr. President. I just thought it might be good to get out to one of the departments."

"Well," Nixon said, "if you're going, I'd like you to consider the State Department, deputy secretary of state for political affairs." State was the liberal-leftist hangout, Nixon had repeatedly said.

Butterfield did not feel guilty proposing a change. He felt he and Nixon worked well together, but the distance between them was ever present, as it seemed for everyone working for Nixon. The president was so withdrawn, isolated, lonely. They were never close. They had almost complete proximity but little intimacy. "I don't think that he went home and wept when at the end of the first term I'm one of the first guys who wants to get out of there."

Butterfield had concluded that Nixon developed real admiration, what he termed love affairs—what might now be called man-crushes— with four people: Secretary of the Treasury John Connally, special counsel and tough guy Charles Colson, deputy national security adviser Alexander Haig, and counselor Patrick Moynihan.

"I might put myself in there as perhaps a half love affair," Butterfield later said with a chuckle.

The job of finding a new assignment for Butterfield was passed to John Ehrlichman. Because of Butterfield's Air Force and vast piloting experience, Ehrlichman suggested that Butterfield become the head of the Federal Aviation Administration. The FAA oversees and enforces civil aviation regulations and air safety. The current FAA chief was having trouble because he was in the newspapers for his extensive travels to play golf, Ehrlichman said. So he was out.

"If you want, you can go to the FAA and then in a year you can go be secretary of the Navy."

Butterfield liked the idea of the FAA. "I felt well suited for that because I had broken so many FAA regulations in my time."

Nixon later told him he liked the idea because then Butterfield would be one of "our guys" in the Transportation Department along with Bud Krogh, who was nominated to be deputy transportation secretary. The president wanted at least one senior key person in each department and agency, saying they were a team and their home base was the White House.


Some leaders build personal bonds that extend way beyond the office. Nixon had never built the bond that would create that do-or-die loyalty in Butterfield.

"I had come to like him," Butterfield said in one of our interviews. "We had tacitly kissed and made up" from the early days in 1969. "But he was rude to me. He was clearly rude, but I softened." Still Butterfield always remembered. "Two or three times he was rude to me," he recalled, his eyes narrowing as he thought back. There had never been an apology. They had never closed the deal. Some experiences were indelible and could not be forgotten or erased.

Butterfield took snubs very personally, and by his own account they tended to almost live within him for years, even decades afterward. One enduring snub occurred when he worked for McNamara in the 1960s, and he wrote about it in his book draft. Wearing civilian clothes, not his uniform, Butterfield was at a reception at the Johnson White House and a powerful congressman, Wayne Hays, approached him. Hays would later become famous for putting his mistress Elizabeth Ray, who could not even type, file or answer the phone, on his House payroll.

"Hi! Wayne Hays, Ohio," he said extending his hand.

"I'm Colonel Butterfield," he replied, shaking Hays's hand firmly. "I'm here with Mr. McNamara."

Hays scowled, quickly pulled his hand away, and without a word spun around and walked away.

A full 39 years later Butterfield wrote this of the Hays incident:

"I was dumbfounded . . . incredulous. . . . Who the hell did he think he was? I remember feeling warm, flush, then furious. It couldn't have been my name, I thought to myself. It's the military thing again. Goddamn it! I thought of seeking him out, confronting him right there and challenging him point blank to tell me what it was he didn't like about me." In his imagination, he wrote that he wanted to say *Are you one of those arrogant bastards who looks down his nose at the military? Is that it, you half-pint son of bitch?* "But I was so full of rage, I doubted I could keep myself under control. The hell with it! I put my drink on an empty tray, retrieved the chart kit [of Vietnam maps] and returned at once to the Pentagon. In the days that followed, I thought of little else. I worked. I did what I had to do, but the incident with Wayne Hays never left my mind."

It was 50 years later when I asked Butterfield about the encounter with Hays and the memory still triggered an outpouring.

Another apparent snub that stuck with Butterfield also dated back to the Johnson White House. During a routine meeting with McGeorge Bundy, Johnson's national security adviser, a secretary came in to say there was a call for "Colonel Butterfield." Apparently Bundy, who had seen him often and always been friendly, didn't know that Butterfield was in the military.

He wrote, "As I excused myself and got up to leave, I looked over at Bundy for a nod or sign of consent. He appeared at once startled, or so it seemed. Then he gave me a hard cold stare. It was part scowl, a mean look; and because the others saw it, and he knew that, it was unforgivably rude."

Two other times, Butterfield wrote that Bundy did not speak to him and on another occasion, "I felt his failure to at least make eye contact and say hello was purposeful." This, he wrote, "was devastating to me . . . the truth was that I'd been deeply hurt."


So in mid-February 1973 Butterfield moved to an office in the Executive Office Building to prepare for his Senate confirmation hearings as head of the FAA.

After four years of such proximity, what was the good-bye session with Nixon?

There was none, Butterfield said.

"You don't remember a kind of good-bye?"

"No, no, no."

Butterfield just cleaned out some personal books. Left the large color picture of Nixon and the first lady that was hanging above the fireplace. He also left four large pictures of Nixon on the far wall. It was a set he had personally selected from White House Photographer Ollie Atkins—head shots of Nixon. In one Nixon was sipping coffee, in another he had his hand on his chin, in a third he looked thoughtful, and in the last he looked almost impish.

"I liked them. They're interesting pictures. And I had them nicely arranged on the wall in my office, prominently displayed."

So you left them?

"I left everything as it was." Having stood by as Nixon signed his signature hundreds of times over the four years, he never asked the president to sign a picture or memento to him.

There was no good-bye at all, no drop in to his office, no good luck, Alex, at the FAA, no party?

"No muss, no fuss. We just didn't have ceremonies. To suggest a farewell session would have put pressure on Nixon. It really would have. He didn't want that and I didn't need it."

As the person who was supposed to make sure departing White House aides left their official papers behind, Butterfield had witnessed many senior aides taking dozens of boxes. There was no good way to tell what was personal and what was technically official. He had seen Arthur Burns, the Nixon counselor, leaving in 1970 to become chairman of the Federal Reserve. Burns had packed up boxes equivalent to a small library.

So when it was his turn, Butterfield too carted off boxes of files and documents. "I just took my boxes of stuff and left," he recalled. "I had my car there. Charlotte had her car . . . and I took them straight to the FAA and put them in a storage room next to my office."

•        •        •

The importance of the tapes to Nixon is illustrated by a recorded conversation he had with Haldeman on his 60th birthday, January 9, 1973, as Butterfield was winding down his time in the White House.

"I want control of these," Nixon said again, reminding Haldeman, "I want nothing ever transcribed out of this."

"You have total control," Haldeman said. "Nobody knows it exists except Alex and me and one guy, one technician." Higby and at least three Secret Service agents, however, also knew.

Nixon said that someday he "would get somebody to write a history" using the tapes.

They could expand verbatim coverage, Haldeman suggested. "With that little Sony [recorder] . . . we could use those in places where you could just keep it inside a drawer or something, you know?"

"I don't know whether it'd pick up," Nixon said.

"We could run some tests," Haldeman said. "It's a damn sensitive mic."

"We'll see."

Haldeman said the secret, voice-activated tapes were beyond anyone's reach. "The point of these tapes that are locked in a vault that nobody knows what they are or anything else, and they—I don't think Rose or anybody else knows about them."

"Don't tell them," Nixon said. "Don't tell them."

"That kind of thing," Haldeman said sounding a note of comfort, "that's yours."

# 23

During the nine months following the Watergate burglary, the White House cover-up seemed to be working.

I asked Butterfield about stories that Carl Bernstein and I had written in *The Washington Post* tying Watergate to a larger illegal effort, a massive campaign of political spying and sabotage run by the Nixon White House and reelection campaign.

"That didn't scare me at all," Butterfield said. "Because of the power of the White House, even if we do get in trouble, we'll pull out. The White House would never really go down."

That was a widely held view. Conventional wisdom was that Nixon was too smart to be involved. Interest in the scandal was low—with two important exceptions. One came from the legislative branch, and the other from the judicial. The first was Senator Sam Ervin, the North Carolina Democrat. He called me to his office on January 11, 1973, to say he was going to chair a full-scale investigation by a Senate committee that would have full subpoena power to get documents and call all and any of Nixon's White House and campaign aides. Ervin said he had read our stories in the *Post* about the involvement of higher-ups. "Any leads or sources of information you might be willing to share with us, it certainly would be appreciated and held in the strictest of confidence."

I said that a reporter could not share that information with the government. Ervin said he understood but they were going ahead with a full-fledged investigation. "Now," he said, "I believe that everyone mentioned in your and Mr. Bernstein's accounts should be given an opportunity to come down and exonerate himself. And if they decline, we'll subpoena them to ensure they have a chance to clear their names." He smiled, barely able to contain himself as his bushy eyebrows danced.

Including Haldeman? I asked.

"Mr. Haldeman or Mr. Whomever," Ervin said.

The second person who took an unusual interest in our *Post* stories was Judge John Sirica, who oversaw the trial of the five Watergate burglars and their supervisors, G. Gordon Liddy, a former FBI agent, and E. Howard Hunt, a former CIA man. All either pleaded guilty or were found guilty. I ran into Sirica at a reception at the time and he told me he was deeply troubled by the inconsistency between the government's case and the *Post* stories. The government had alleged in his courtroom that Gordon Liddy was boss and mastermind of Watergate. Our stories said that Watergate was a massive spying and sabotage operation aimed at the Democrats and run and funded by the White House (Haldeman and others) and the reelection committee (Mitchell and others).

Bernstein and I had written about a $25,000 campaign check that had been deposited in the bank account of one of the Watergate burglars, Bernard Barker.

At the trial, Sirica asked the government prosecutor, Earl Silbert, "Are you going to offer any evidence in this case on the question of how the $25,000 check got into the possession of Mr. Barker?"

Silbert wanted to convict the seven defendants, wasn't focused on any higher-ups, and didn't have a good answer for Sirica, who was interested in tracing the money and a wider conspiracy.

At a court hearing three days after the verdict, Sirica publicly criticized the government. "I have not been satisfied, and I am still not satisfied that all the pertinent facts that might be available—I say *might* be available—have been produced before an American jury. . . .

"Everyone knows that there's going to be a congressional investigation in this case. I would frankly hope, not only as a judge but as a citizen of a great country and one of millions of Americans who are looking for certain answers, I would hope that the Senate committee is granted the power by Congress by a broad enough resolution to try to get to the bottom of what happened in this case. I hope so. That is all I have to say."

The next month the Senate voted 77–0 to set up the Watergate committee. The unanimity was almost unheard of. Even Republicans smelled something.

In March, James McCord, the leader of the five-man Watergate burglary team, sent a letter to Judge Sirica, who read it in open court. McCord said that he and others were under "political pressure" to plead guilty and remain silent, that perjury had been committed at the trial and that higher-ups had approved the Watergate operations. By the end of April, Haldeman and Ehrlichman had been forced to resign, and Mitchell was poised to testify before the Senate Watergate committee about what he later called the "White House horrors."

For four days in June 1973, former White House counsel John Dean transfixed the country—and much of the world—with his sworn, televised testimony before the Senate Watergate Committee. In stunning detail, Dean described meetings with Nixon that showed the president was deeply involved in the Watergate cover-up and running the illegal effort to obstruct justice. After the last day of Dean's testimony, *The New York Times* front-page headline said: "Dean Ends Testimony, Story Unshaken."

From the 10th floor of the FAA Building on Independence Avenue in downtown Washington Butterfield tuned in on his office TV.

"One who knew about the tapes," he recalled, "could not help but think about the tapes all through the Dean testimony." The absolute secret of the tapes was still holding. "But Dean was saying for the first time anyone ever uttered the words, that the president is guilty of complicity in the cover-up."

From his four years at the center of the Nixon-Haldeman operation, Butterfield was certain Dean's charges were true. "The president
is the choreographer of the cover-up," Butterfield said later. "He's the
director of all activity."

The tapes, he believed with certainty, would be the needed proof
and settle the question. The public opinion polls at the time showed
that about two thirds of the country believed the president's denials.
And Dean was seen as a young, ambitious lawyer out of his depth, desperate to keep himself out of jail.

"I was thinking of the tapes the whole time," Butterfield recalled.
"God, if they only knew. If they only knew. In a way I wanted it to be
known. In the deep recesses of my brain, I was eager to tell.

"It isn't that I wanted to shout out, 'There are tapes out there!' But
I thought that would settle everything. I can settle everything."

What was his obligation and to whom? At times he said he thought
he might have no choice. If he were interested in the truth, the real
truth—"there is only one kind of truth," he once told me—then he
should come forward. "To get it out," he said later. "Get it over."

But he did not want to volunteer. That would mean crossing the political divide in America. You were either with Nixon or against him.

I asked at one point, "Don't we go through our lives—in part—
seeking cover for our best instincts?"

"Sure," he answered. Yet the questions remained: What was his
best instinct? And what might be the best cover? So he stewed over his
dilemma and did what a cautious person often does—nothing.


One day, as Butterfield watched, Dean was testifying about an April 15
meeting with Nixon:

"The most interesting thing that happened during the conversation was very near the end. He [Nixon] got up out of his chair, went
behind his chair to the corner of the Executive Office Building office and in a barely audible tone said to me he was probably foolish
to have discussed" executive clemency for one of the Watergate co-
conspirators, Howard Hunt. Dean said he thought the room might

have been bugged and Nixon knew, thus accounting for his actions to move and speak so softly.

There it was! Butterfield realized, but no one seemed curious and there was no follow-up. He found that hard to believe. Dean later wrote in his memoir, *Blind Ambition*, that he too was surprised there was no follow-up.

About Dean, Butterfield recalled, "I was sure he didn't know about the tapes, and I was sure that in his mind, he was thinking of a little handheld set that you could put in a desk drawer."

In *All the President's Men*, the 1974 book that Carl Bernstein and I co-authored, we wrote the following about this period, "There was, however, one unchecked entry on both lists (of possible sources)— presidential aide Alexander P. Butterfield. Both Deep Throat [later revealed as FBI deputy director Mark Felt] and Hugh Sloan (the Nixon campaign treasurer) had mentioned him, and Sloan had said, almost in passing, that he was in charge of 'internal security.' "

The phrase "internal security" was often a term for wiretapping. In January 1973 I drove to Butterfield's house in Virginia with no appointment hoping he would be there and I could interview him. I recall that someone peeked out from behind the drapes or curtains, but no one came to the door. I did not go back later, though I should have. Butterfield was a prospect that was unexplored.

After Dean's testimony, Senate Watergate staffers compiled a list of so-called satellite witnesses from the White House to be interviewed to see if they would refute or support any of Dean's testimony about Nixon's involvement.

Even before Dean's testimony I had asked a committee staff member if Butterfield had been interviewed.

"No, we're too busy."

Some weeks later I asked another staffer if the committee knew why Butterfield's duties in Haldeman's office were defined as "internal security."

As we wrote in *All the President's Men*:

"The staff member said the committee didn't know, and maybe it would be a good idea to interview Butterfield. He would ask Sam Dash, the committee's chief counsel. Dash put the matter off. The staff member told Woodward he would push Dash again."

It is unclear if the committee would have decided to interview Butterfield without this push. Butterfield thinks not—and claims that I fingered him. "They never would have called me in a million years," he said. "I was an unknown."

"I know what was behind it. You were."

On July 10 or 11, Butterfield received a call from Eugene Boyce of the Senate Watergate Committee requesting a "routine interview."

"I wanted to help them if I could," Butterfield recalled. "They said, 'Can you come up for an interview?' It's just to learn some administrative stuff about the White House, how the paper flowed. And I said, I guess I could do that Friday."

"Perfect," said Boyce.

Several months before, on April 27, the U.S. attorney investigating Watergate and his key assistants had interviewed Butterfield. They wanted to know about White House procedures, paper flow, reporting channels and other administrative and organizational matters. Never once did they get close to asking about a tape recording system.

The only person outside the White House or the Secret Service Butterfield had told about the secret taping system was Charlotte, his wife of 24 years.

"Well, just like before," he said to her the morning of his Senate interview Friday, July 13, "I know they won't mention tapes. But if tapes are brought up, I think the best thing for me to do is wing it if I can, if the question is oblique or vague. If it's a direct question, and I hope that doesn't happen, but if it's a direct question, I think I'm going to have to say, 'Yes, there are tapes.' I can't get caught up in this thing."

"That's a good idea," Charlotte said. He was glad she agreed. Her commonsense approach, he believed, balanced his more impulsive nature.

Watergate was exploding now and many of the big names—Haldeman, Ehrlichman, Mitchell—were being called to testify. "I'm ready," he told her. He felt confident he could deal with the committee interview. He believed he was skilled at answering questions vaguely. He felt there was only one chance in a million that any interrogator would ask about listening devices in the White House. He would have bet money that nothing about audiotapes would come up.

When I interviewed Charlotte in 2014, Alex Butterfield was present. I asked her if she thought the secret of the taping system was going to get out.

"I knew he was going to tell them," she said with confidence.

That created a bit of commotion.

"I'll let that stand," Butterfield said from across the room. "I'll let that stand. That's interesting."

"You were confident he was going to tell?" I asked her.

"He told me he was," she replied laughing.

"Do you think he wanted to tell?" I asked.

"Yes."

"Why?"

Butterfield interrupted, saying to her, "That's all right. Say that."

"Why do you think he wanted to tell?" I asked again.

Now apparently released by her ex-husband to answer, she said, "I think he had that much dislike for the president at the time."

"Mm-hmm" was all Butterfield said.

I had for a long time thought that one of Butterfield's motives was payback to Nixon, though he downplayed it.

He then mentioned that soon before his testimony in 1973 he had told his closest friend, Bill Lilly, without giving any details, "You won't believe this, but I do believe that I could bring down the president."

"And I do think you wanted to," Charlotte said, staring at him from across the room.

*"I'm giving some credence to what you say,"* Butterfield said to her.

# 24

In July, a woman from the Senate Watergate secretarial pool pulled aside Scott Armstrong, a 27-year-old committee investigator for the Democratic majority.

"I've got something you might be interested in," she said quietly laying out a multipage document. It was a summary of Nixon-Dean meetings that Fred Buzhardt, Nixon's White House Watergate lawyer, had provided exclusively to the committee minority counsel Fred Thompson. Armstrong was astonished because the document included verbatim quotes. Under an uneasy truce between the majority and minority staff, everything was supposed to be shared. And he had not seen this important document as he was preparing to lead the Butterfield interview.

Armstrong was a friend from Wheaton, Illinois, where we had both been raised. He had been hired by Sam Dash, the committee's chief counsel, based on my recommendation. Dash had tried to recruit me to work for the committee and when I declined, he asked who I thought he should hire. The smartest person you can find, I said. Who is the smartest person you know? he asked. I mentioned Armstrong, a Yale graduate who had spent a year at Harvard Law School.

Dash and Armstrong had been working together closely during the early months of the committee investigation. They had been gathering evidence that Senator Howard Baker, the committee vice chairman, and his counsel, Thompson, had been trying to help Nixon. In executive sessions with the Democratic majority staff, which included Dash and Armstrong, John Dean had revealed that Senator Baker had "secret dealings with the White House" and had met privately with Nixon.

A tape of a February 22, 1973, meeting would later show that Baker told Nixon, "I'm your friend. I'm going to see that your interests are protected."

After this both the majority Democrats and minority Republicans agreed to share all information. There would be no private meetings or discussions with the White House.

Then in early July, Baker brought legislative aide Jim Jordan to a closed door committee meeting. Dash, suspicious, ordered Armstrong to follow Jordan. Outside the Senate, Jordan got a cab. Armstrong caught another cab and followed Jordan to the Executive Office Building next to the White House. When Armstrong returned to Dash's office, he called Buzhardt's White House office. Is Jim Jordan there? Armstrong asked. Jordan came to the phone. The back-channel subterfuge was ongoing.

Armstrong told Dash about the White House version of the Nixon-Dean meetings that included some selected verbatim quotes clearly designed to impeach Dean.

Dash was able to get a copy of the document, and he gave it to Armstrong who planned to spring it on Butterfield at the end of the committee staff interview. Armstrong thought he might have a possible "Perry Mason" moment.

On Friday afternoon, July 13, Butterfield was being driven to the Senate. It was a hot, muggy Washington summer day, temperatures in the 90s. Room G-334, in the New Senate Office Building, was grubby. The chairs were stained with spills from fast food, and the wastebaskets overflowed with cigarette butts and sandwich wrappings. The faded green carpet was filthy. No one, including janitors, had been allowed in the room for fear someone might plant an eavesdropping device.

The session was attended only by committee staff. No senator was present. It was not thought to be that important.

Armstrong spent nearly three hours asking Butterfield detailed questions about White House operations and the information systems Nixon used. At that point, he handed the Buzhardt document to Butterfield, who had never seen it before.

Where did it come from? Armstrong asked him.

"Somebody probably got the information from the chron-file and jotted it down," Butterfield replied.

As he read from the White House document, Butterfield expressed surprise that it contained a direct quote from Nixon at a meeting dealing with the paying of blackmail money to Howard Hunt. The president was quoted: "How could it possibly be paid? What makes you think he would be satisfied with that?"

"Where did you get this?" Butterfield asked.

Armstrong said the document had come from Buzhardt. "Could it have come from someone's notes of a meeting?"

"No," Butterfield said, "it seems too detailed."

"Was the president's recollection of meetings good?

"Was he as precise as the summary?"

"Well, no, but he would sometimes dictate his thoughts after a meeting."

"How often did he do so?"

"Very rarely."

"Were his memos this detailed?"

"I don't think so."

"Where else might this have come from?" Armstrong pressed.

Butterfield stared at the document, and then slowly lifted it an inch off the table. "I don't know," he said.

"I'm minimally panicking," Butterfield recalled. "I'm stalling for time."

"Well, let me think about this awhile," he told Armstrong. He pushed the document toward the center of the green felt table. He was clearly troubled.

Armstrong surmised that Butterfield was reluctant to reveal a White House filing system that the committee did not know about. In an account of the session written in 1989 for *The Journal of American*

*History*, Armstrong wrote this about his next move: "I began drafting up sample subpoena language for these newly revealed systems."

Armstrong had come within a hair of asking the direct question. His question, "Where else might this have come from?" was really close. A lawyer might bend the question to suggest Armstrong was asking if it might have come from someone other than Buzhardt. That was far-fetched, Butterfield knew. That's why he asked for time to think. He was relieved when Armstrong dropped the subject and indicated he had no further questions.

Donald G. Sanders, a former FBI agent, was the deputy Republican counsel, sitting in to represent the minority. In his version for the 1989 history journal, called "Watergate Reminiscences," he wrote, "One did not then lightly contemplate serious battle with the White House. There was a very different aura about the infallibility and inaccessibility of the White House. The balloon had yet to be punctured."

As Armstrong's questions went on, Sanders was more and more focused on the White House document. It was so specific, stated with such precision, that it had to come from verbatim recordings. He was mystified why Armstrong had not asked about possible tape recordings.

When his turn came, Sanders's heart was pounding and his breath short. During the hours of listening, he had found Butterfield quite cagey, outwardly responsive but providing narrow, carefully constructed answers. After a few preliminaries, Sanders reminded Butterfield of John Dean's testimony when the president had taken Dean to a corner of the room to whisper. It suggested that their conversation was being taped and that the president was trying to avoid being recorded.

Is it possible Dean knew what he was talking about? Sanders asked.

"John Dean didn't know about it," Butterfield answered. He picked up the Buzhardt memo. "But this is where this must have come from."

Sanders noted that Butterfield had earlier mentioned that Nixon had a machine with "Dictabelts" on which he made dictations for his personal diary. "Was there ever any other kind of taping system in the president's office?" Sanders asked.

Instantly, Butterfield recognized that it was as clear and direct a

question as he might get. He paused. "There were always options,"
he later told me. He could not see a safety play. He had made his own
ground rules. The question had been asked. He chose to plow forward,
whether by clear intent, momentum, or a mix of both.

"I was hoping you all wouldn't ask that question," Butterfield recalled saying. "I've been wondering how I'd respond if you did. I'm
concerned about the effect my answer will have on national security,
on our relations with foreign governments. But I suppose I have to assume that this interview is as formal and official as one would be before the full committee?"

"Yes, that's right," Sanders answered.

"Yes," Butterfield said. "There was a taping system at the White
House." The look on Butterfield's face was both consternation and relief. "The White House system was fairly elaborate."

Armstrong and Sanders were stunned as Butterfield went on for
about 45 minutes answering their questions about the vast network of
taping, how it operated and who knew of its existence.

Butterfield said that for all he knew Haldeman or Larry Higby
had revealed the secret system. That was not honest. He knew better.
Whatever the circumstances, he was certain, as well as he knew his
own name, he later said, that neither would break the unspoken oath
of silence to protect the president and his secret taping system at all
costs. They would go to their deaths before revealing it.

"Look," Butterfield said, "this information about the tapes is dynamite." He urged them to keep it confidential.

Abruptly they all left, and he was alone. At home he told Charlotte what had occurred. She gave a kind of physical shudder. I have a
strange foreboding, she said.

The White House strategy of attempting to discredit John Dean by
supplying selected quotes of his meetings with the president had back-
fired spectacularly, leading Armstrong to focus on the Buzhardt memo
and Sanders to ask the direct question.

# 25

—————

"I was pretty aware that that moment could change my life," Butterfield recalled. "I thought I could be drummed out of the Nixon administration immediately. I might have been shot. A lot of people loved Nixon. I'm getting him into trouble. I'm thinking how much time do I have to pack a bag and leave town." And he added half facetiously, "Maybe time to get a face-lift."

But the answer to why Butterfield revealed the taping system has layers.

He later recalled for the history journal article for the issue of March 1989, "I answered truthfully because I am a truthful person. I used to play that down to some considerable extent, but I see no reason to invent other reasons for having been open and honest and direct once the sixty-four-dollar question was put to me." He added, "I'm as sure as I know I'm sitting here that if he hadn't asked, I would never have volunteered."

He told me in 2015, "I'm not trying to be like a Boy Scout and tell you I did it because it was the right thing to do."

When we discussed this all those years later, he said he actually thought Nixon had been good for the country in many ways. At a few other times he said the Nixon White House had been no less than a "cesspool." He added, "This isn't a contradiction. A person can easily be good for the country while operating a cesspool."

Such is the state of our politics, I thought.

It is still not that simple. David Thelen, the editor of *The Journal of American History* who interviewed Butterfield in 1988, sent the transcript of his interview about the tape disclosure to him. Butterfield wanted to include more and added: "I was, at times, impatient for the truth . . . and in some strange, deep-down, almost subconscious way was relieved by having the direct question asked of me by Mr. Sanders."

I asked Butterfield if he subconsciously thought Nixon had it coming?

"Did I feel that the truth should come out?" he said, rephrasing the question. "Yes I did."

"Did you have the sense you'd lit the fuse that would be the end of the Nixon presidency?"

"Mm-hmm," he responded. "Yeah. Yeah, yeah. I had the sense before I did it that I have here the fuse and the match. . . . Dynamite tends to explode when somebody sets the timer on it." At the same time, he insisted, "There wasn't a burning desire. It wasn't a mission."

Everyone, of course, does things, even important things, that are not a mission. Butterfield was initially intrigued as I tried to unearth his precise motive or motives.

He was emphatic that he didn't feel he had an obligation to protect Nixon. But as we delved further, he said, "I don't feel I had a motive. I'm not sure I like the term 'motive.' I was just the guy who happened to know all this stuff and I had a bad start with Nixon."

He came to like parts of Nixon's personality—his drive, focus and energy. Other parts, not so much. But it is clear that the "bad start" had never left him. Nixon's rebuffs—his rudeness, as Butterfield repeatedly calls it—set the conditions for him so he could step away and not feel the intense loyalty of other presidential intimates who had attached themselves, their careers and future to Nixon.

Butterfield was untethered.

"I really was sorry," he told me at another point. "On the other hand, there was this disinterested citizen in me, this is going to be kind of a service to the country in a way."

And there were practical considerations. He was thinking in part, he said, "It'd sure be great if this information were out. We would save a lot of—how long is this nation going to do this? We can settle all of this real fast if you guys just listen to me." He added, "Anyone who knew would feel the same and have the same thoughts." At least anyone who did not want to conceal the truth.

He also said he did not fear Nixon. "I thought, Jesus, you know I hate the idea of Nixon hating me."

So his were a jumble of thoughts and emotions that would remain with him for decades. Nonetheless, he said, there was a bottom line. "I was open and honest and straightforward."


But I pushed him on the question of motive. The mystery of human motivation looms as a big, central question, I said, particularly when so much consequence attaches to what he did. I noted that Graham Greene, the celebrated novelist, wrote of "those interior courts where our true decisions are made."

Often real motives are hard to discern, I told Butterfield. Maybe they are so deep and tangled that we cannot know ourselves, and they remain concealed in that interior court. Maybe there is a cover story. Can it be penetrated or is the road too long and fraught with uncomfortable introspection? This suggests there is some limit to understanding, and the path there is not only foggy but endless.

Butterfield said he agreed.

Immanuel Kant, the German philosopher, wrote, "We can never, even by strict examination, get completely behind the secret springs of action."

Are these "secret springs" like the "interior courts"?

In 1961, my freshman year in college, I remember coming upon a much more simple explanation in a short novel that was all the rage, J.D. Salinger's *The Catcher in the Rye*. Here the young protagonist,

Holden Caulfield, full of angst over the phonies of the world, declares, "I mean how do you know what you're going to do till you *do* it?"

John le Carré, the great spy novelist, had another take. He wrote in his 1979 spy thriller, *Smiley's People*, about the floor at headquarters where the bosses had their offices, "Why did the fifth floor always think people had to have one motive only."

Much later I came upon Joseph Conrad's novel *Lord Jim* and these lines: "They wanted facts. Facts! They demanded facts from him, as if facts could explain anything!" If facts could not get you there, what could?

When I pressed Butterfield for more, further contemplation about his motive, he insisted, "I can assure you I don't feel that I had a motive. I just don't think I had a motive—like I'm going to tell eventually, I'll find a way to tell." He said he had wanted to avoid a legal trap in which he said something that was not true and perjured himself. "But I do believe that in the interest of justice, it had to come out. I mean, I'm not in favor of people getting away with something."

Yet, he stated flatly, he did not see himself as the dispenser of justice. "I got caught up in this wave," he said. "In a wave, and I was riding this wave." There was a momentum that pointed toward disclosure. Yes, he said, that was the wave.

Nixon could have invoked executive privilege for you, I said, as he eventually did with the Secret Service technical agents who installed the taping system. Could that conceivably have prevented you from appearing at the Ervin committee staff interview? Nixon could have said you were so intimately involved in his presidency, and had such a unique view and were so close to him that he could not permit that you testify. He could have argued that you were like a psychiatrist, a lawyer or even a spouse. And that he, as president, was deserving of a special privilege and protection from your testimony. That would have resulted in a long delay in the courts for months if not more. The Senate Ervin committee, the House Judiciary Committee investigating possible impeachment, the Watergate special prosecutor, the media and the public might have grown tired of Watergate and turned to other matters.

"Yeah," Butterfield said, clearly tiring of the discussion of motives. "It could have been different. Could've been different."

The day after his closed-door testimony, Saturday, Butterfield went to his office as was his habit. He was an administrator and the comforting routine of paper and small decisions filled the morning. In the afternoon he flew up to New Hampshire to dedicate a new air control tower. The audience for the speech and ribbon-cutting ceremony consisted of about 100 people, including state and local aviation officials. In the back of his mind, he was worrying that he might soon be addressing a larger audience.

He arrived back home to Admiral Drive in Alexandria by 6 p.m.

"You've had calls all afternoon," Charlotte said. "One person, Scott Armstrong." And he wanted the name of your former White House secretary.

The web was expanding, Butterfield realized. Investigations have an insidious quality, moving in an ever-widening circle. The president's staff and now the secretaries to the staff. He called Armstrong, who said the Watergate Committee was going to tie him to the revelation of the tapes. Armstrong was recommending that Butterfield be called as a public witness before the whole committee.

"Surely, you can keep the tapes' existence under wraps," Butterfield pleaded. At least for two weeks until Haldeman was scheduled to testify before the committee.

"Impossible!" Armstrong said. "It's going to leak for sure!"

Armstrong seemed in a frenzy to Butterfield, almost out of control. Butterfield felt sick and realized he needed to get advice. But from whom? He called Senator Howard Baker of Tennessee. Baker was the senior Republican on the Watergate Committee and its vice chairman. Butterfield knew him casually from times when Baker visited the White House. He wanted to discuss in person some major, fast-moving developments, he said. Baker agreed to see Butterfield at his home the next afternoon, Sunday.

Butterfield, worried about his FAA duties, didn't want Watergate to interfere with his important trip to the Soviet Union. He was supposed to negotiate some critical aviation and trade issues beginning Tuesday.

The next afternoon, in Howard Baker's living room, he unloaded the whole story of the secret taping system. "You know me, it took me an hour and a half to tell him," he said later.

When he finished, Baker said that he already knew the whole story. He had just been briefed by his own staff. "I've got the whole file upstairs," he said, smiling the Baker smile, friendly but sly.

Jesus! Butterfield thought. He looked for some nuance in Baker's grin. But there was none. "I want to be certain," Butterfield told Baker, "that mature and senior people were considering the ramifications of the release of this information . . ."

"Alex," Senator Baker said in a tone that suggested he was going to share the secrets of the ways of the world. "*Everything* leaks! I don't like to admit it, but *everything leaks.*" He would be surprised if it kept for another day.

"So what's the plan?" Butterfield asked. "I was on the sidelines where Watergate was concerned. And my business now is aviation safety." He was going to Moscow in two days. "We're kicking off what amounts to a new era of trade between the U.S. and the U.S.S.R. It's called Aeronautica '73 and involves hundreds of government and industry leaders."

If a look could convey "I don't give a shit about Aeronautica '73" it was on Baker's face. "I'd say there's as much chance you won't have to testify as there is that you will." It was the classic Baker line. Whatever the outcome, he'd be right. Baker was well known in the Nixon White House for trying to have it both ways, raising the strategy to an art form. Nonetheless, he went further and indicated he would do what he could to quell any effort to put Butterfield on the witness stand before the cameras.

Butterfield was at the door feeling that he would not have to testify publicly. After all, Baker was now in his corner.

"Does the president know about this yet?" Baker asked, one Republican to another. "Hadn't you better inform Haig or someone over there that the committee has had this information since Friday?" Having been summoned out of the Army, Haig was now in Haldeman's old position as White House chief of staff.

Butterfield thanked Baker for his time, and support. On the way home he had his driver stop at the Windsor Park Hotel. He jumped out of the car, found a pay phone, and left a message for Len Garment, the White House lawyer who was his designated contact at the White House.

Garment called him at home about 9 p.m. Butterfield unloaded his story.

"Jesus Christ!" Garment almost shouted. It seemed an involuntary and uncharacteristic bark of surprise. Butterfield understood, and could sympathize. Garment hung up without another word.

# 26

"There is little I don't remember about July 16," Butterfield wrote two decades later. He came in early to the office that Monday to get a head start on his inbox, normally the soothing—even addicting—chore to prepare for a 9 a.m. staff meeting. Time flies at a staff meeting when you are the one in charge. As the leader of the U.S. delegation for Aeronautica '73, he was preparing for a two-week trip.

Still no call from Howard Baker or anyone on the Watergate Committee to confirm that he would not have to appear.

He kept an 11 a.m. appointment to have his hair cut at the Carlton Hotel, a few blocks north of the White House. The barber was Milton Pitts, whom Butterfield had personally recruited several years earlier to cut President Nixon's hair. Chuck Colson, one of Nixon's hatchet men, had recommended Pitts. After a security check Pitts became the official Nixon barber installed one day a week in the one-chair barbershop in the West Wing basement. Pitts was a stylist. He shampooed Nixon's hair, blended the cut with a razor, and then used a blow-dryer. The simple routine transformed Nixon's steely-gray, oily and curly hair into a softer, fuller, more natural and modern look.

It was such a change that *Time* magazine sent a reporter to investigate and Pitts was publicly proclaimed a hero.

Butterfield was a regular with Pitts at his shop in the Carlton.

While waiting his turn this morning, he almost fell asleep before being called.

Nearly every TV set in the nation, certainly in Washington, was turned to the live hearing of the Senate Watergate Committee. A set in the corner of the barbershop had it on.

Keep your eye on your work, Mr. Pitts, Butterfield said, and I will follow the hearings and promise to alert you to anything extraordinary. The White House witness, Dick Moore, a special presidential counsel and a public relations image expert, was testifying. He sounded befuddled as if he were trying to confuse whatever issue came up. It was a circus, comical, Butterfield thought. As Moore veered further and further from any question, Butterfield's mind drifted and his eyelids drooped as Pitts snipped and chatted away.

"It's for you!" the receptionist called, handing Butterfield the phone, breaking his reverie. He had not even heard the phone ring.

Jim Hamilton, an assistant chief counsel for the Watergate Committee, introduced himself. The decision had been made that Butterfield would appear publicly before the committee at the beginning of the afternoon session that day at 2 p.m.

What! Butterfield was steaming mad. This was not right or fair. What about Howard Baker? What about Butterfield's schedule? He told Hamilton he would not appear.

"Very well," Hamilton replied coolly, "but I'll have to report to the chairman your refusal to appear."

"Fine," Butterfield snapped. "You do that, because I mean what I say. I'll be goddamned if I'm going to jump through a hoop for the mere convenience of your committee. I think all of you are moving much too fast on a matter that I consider to be both sensitive and delicate in the extreme." Butterfield realized he was so tightly wound that he was practically shouting.

Hamilton said he had not known that Butterfield would be so upset. He apologized and hung up.

Butterfield immediately realized that he should have been the one apologizing. Hamilton was just relaying a message. Where the hell was Senator Baker, his ally?

Even in 1973 there were what seemed to be the wonders of modern communications. Butterfield now noticed on the TV screen that a young man with a full head of hair was bending over Senator Ervin, then age 76, whispering in his ear. Ervin couldn't turn around very well, so Butterfield could see the young man fully. Could that be Hamilton?

"There's the fellow I was just talking to," Butterfield said to Pitts, surmising what might have happened, "the one whispering to Senator Ervin."

Ervin's famous bushy eyebrows rose and fell—a distinctive, almost trademark whoop, whoop, whoop—suggesting that he had just heard unexpected and surprising news. He turned and whispered something back.

"I just talked to Senator Ervin," Hamilton said in his second call to Butterfield.

"I know. I think I saw you on the tube."

"Well," Hamilton said, "the senator told me to tell you that if you're not in his office by 12:30 he'll have federal marshals pick you up on the street."

Improbable, Butterfield thought. But it was time to calm down, smooth it over if he could. Chuckling, he apologized for his earlier outburst and said he would need some more time, but promised to be in Ervin's office by 1 p.m.

After his haircut, he went straight to a phone booth and called home.

"Susan," he said, fortunately reaching his daughter, who had just completed her sophomore year at the University of Virginia. Get one of my clean white button-down shirts, and the dark suit and my favorite tie, the bluish one with diagonal stripes. Bring them to the Howard Johnson's restaurant at the north end of Alexandria. I will meet you there in 20 minutes. No time to explain, he said.

He called Len Garment at the White House to alert him. "Len, the Ervin committee just called. They want me to testify today, this afternoon at two o'clock."

"You'll have to get your own lawyer!" Garment said with uncharacteristic sharpness. And *bang* down went the phone.

Butterfield realized that he probably should have been seeking legal advice. But he had an attitude about lawyers. They tended to muck things up. Though of two minds about lawyers—it never hurts to ask for legal advice at least informally—he felt he would proceed on the track he was on.

Soon he was in a meeting with Ervin, Baker and their counsels in the same messy, windowless conference Room G-334 where he had first been questioned.

Butterfield began by apologizing for his earlier outburst to Jim Hamilton. Then speaking directly to Senator Ervin he argued that it would be "inappropriate" for him to be the one to testify in public. Let someone more involved like Haldeman do it. "I'm completely on the periphery here," Butterfield said. This was a weak argument, he quickly realized.

Ervin displayed his Southern understanding. To have someone else reveal the taping system would be "inappropriate," he countered, implying that Butterfield should get the credit.

Butterfield felt the meeting was "relaxed, friendly and unhurried," as he later wrote. Of course, if he had insisted on having a lawyer, there was no way the four lawyers in the room could deny him. Everyone who appeared before the committee was granted the right to counsel.

But Butterfield made no demands, no requests. If he had, it almost certainly would not have changed history. But a delay would have given Nixon and the White House time to plan a strategy. Butterfield felt he was riding this wave and part of him did want the credit. He was going along with their process and procedures.

"It's getting late," Ervin said. He and Baker showered him with compliments. He was their witness now.

Butterfield went to the washroom. He had not brought a toothbrush or his gargle. But he had a comb to run through his hair. He leaned forward on the sink and stared into the mirror. He bit hard on his lower lip and tried to picture the future. Suddenly the names of several world leaders, Golda Meir and British prime minister Harold Wilson, came to mind. What were they and other world leaders going to think about being secretly taped? Or everyone or every group that had had what they thought were private meetings with Nixon in the White House?

The afternoon news had a report headlined: MYSTERY WITNESS NEXT.

Butterfield had a moment to call Charlotte.

"Don't tell me you're the Mystery Witness?" she said.


Then eight uniformed Capitol Hill police arrived to take him up to testify. Clomp, clomp, clomp through the marble corridors. Two in front waving people out of their path. Two others in tandem on each side, and two behind. There was something overbearing about it, a Roman parade, clearing the way to the elevator.

As the phalanx entered the Senate Caucus Room, a large, ornate famous hearing room, they bulled their way down the far aisle to the witness table maintaining a furious momentum through the jam-packed interior that was alive with sound and cameras clicking.

Butterfield was sworn in. Fred Thompson, the minority counsel and Baker's right-hand man, began the questioning because Sanders, also a minority staff member, had elicited the information of primary interest.

Butterfield sat erect, looking hesitant with his fingers interlocked. He felt relaxed, however, because he knew what would be asked and what he would answer. Thompson, who later became a movie actor and senator himself, spoke in his confident voice. He had long side-burns and longish hair in the style of the time.

This was it, Butterfield said to himself. After a few preliminary questions, Thompson asked: "Are you aware of the installation of any listening devices in the Oval Office?"

Butterfield paused. Thompson had used the present tense.

"I *was* aware of listening devices, yes, sir," he said, correcting to past tense.

Eight words that shook the world. It seemed to Butterfield there was absolute silence and no one moved. They were still and quiet as if they were witnessing a hinge of history slowly swinging open—way open. Then after a few seconds, came a stirring and sudden rush of comment. It was as if a bare 10,000 volt cable was running through the room, and suddenly everyone touched it at once.

Butterfield could see that those in the room were momentarily stunned. Listening devices in the Oval Office! Tapes! The intensity was immediate. White House tapes! Butterfield could see it in their faces, hear it in the voices. The secret was out: Nixon Bugged Himself. Not at random but continually. It was baffling that the president had turned over the secret record of his presidency to machines. Even to Butterfield, who had known the secret for years, it was nothing less than incredible. "Wonders of Watergate do not cease," William Greider of the *Post* wrote on the front page.


During his testimony he was asked about his reluctance to disclose. Yes, he said, he was worried that he might be preempting the president. "But obviously not so reluctant that I failed to answer."

He closed with words that for the rest of his life he wished he had not uttered: "This matter which we have discussed here today, I think, is precisely the substance on which the president plans to present his defense. I believe, of course, that the president is innocent"—and he looked up at the senators—"of any crime or wrongdoing, that he is innocent likewise of any complicity."

More than 40 years later, Butterfield found it difficult to review his testimony. We had just spent some time concentrating on how honest he had been when he disclosed the taping system.

"I've just sat here telling you about how I don't lie," he said to me in 2015, "and wouldn't lie, but that is a white lie. I did not believe the president was innocent. So I have to admit that."

Butterfield said he was playing both roles—riding both horses—one of the aggressive, truth-telling citizen and the other of a former, loyal member of the Nixon team. "I got one leg in the stirrup of the other horse," he said.

At that moment years before, he said, he was confused, disoriented. "I was being put through a wringer there, and I wasn't sure how I felt. But I like to think what I did was the right thing to do."

At the same time, he was full of mixed emotions. "I felt confused, conflicted and regretful," he told me in 2015.

He exited the Caucus Room at 3:20 p.m. He walked alone down the empty corridor, not a soul in sight. The reporters were all filing bulletins or putting together stories. He likened it, in his own mind, to leaving the Rose Bowl at the end of the first quarter. But he had no idea where he was. He didn't know how to get out. He finally found an office and paged his driver, who had been driving around in circles. Finally Butterfield found him, and they went back to the FAA.

Lou Churchville, Butterfield's public relations officer, ran into his office ecstatic. For months, Churchville had been working to get Butterfield known in the aviation community and Washington. "I don't have anything to do now!" he said. "You're known. They know who you are now."

Butterfield didn't look at television that night since he had to pack for the long trip to the Soviet Union and get to bed.

# 27

The next morning, Tuesday, July 17, he rose early to make sure he was at the FAA hangar at Washington National Airport at 5:40 a.m. His plane was a four-engine, eight-passenger JetStar. He took the left seat, the pilot's. The copilot took the right. The plane was airborne at 6 a.m. "I love making takeoffs right on time," he recalled later. He took the JetStar to 8,000 feet, rolled left and swung around through the sun. Shortly they were passing over Washington, and he looked down wondering. He had been in too much of a rush to look at the morning's *Washington Post* or tune into the radio. He was in a bubble.

As he took the plane through 16,000 feet, his copilot took over, apparently aware of and sympathetic to Butterfield's distraction and momentary inattention.

Butterfield could imagine the stir now, the chatter, the excitement, the sense that the mystery of Nixon might be solved. "Goddamnit!" he thought. Part of him wished he hadn't gotten himself involved. He had inflicted the major blow on Nixon, probably more than major.

A great part of the Nixon presidency was designed to keep the outside world from seeing the real Nixon, from intruding into the inner sanctum. And here was the possibility of the biggest exposure of all time, ripping open the curtain, peeling off the masks.

For a moment Butterfield wanted to blame Senator Baker for not

rescuing him from being the agent of public disclosure. Slippery Howard Baker.

Then, in a moment of clarity, Butterfield realized it was not Baker's
fault. The senator had promised nothing.

As the plane headed for the first fuel stop in Newfoundland, he developed another line. He couldn't have done anything differently, he
reasoned, ticking off the forces and circumstances. The Senate committee was legal, they had come to him, they had asked the questions,
he had only answered them. Nixon had said in a major speech in May
that all his aides were free to testify and that he would not invoke executive privilege.

Butterfield had protected the tapes for years. He was no blabber-
mouth, no leaker. He was only testifying in the spirit of cooperation
urged by Nixon. Why had the White House lawyers given Nixon's direct quotes to the Senate Watergate Committee? Without those, almost
certainly, there would have been no such question from Sanders, "Was
there ever any other kind of taping system in the president's office?"

No question, no need to answer. But he caught himself. This was
all supposition. Why did all this sound so defensive, he wondered?
Why the feeling of hopelessness? Why the despair? No, it was not
that he regretted his decision, only that the duty—if that was the right
word—had fallen to him. It was so personal now. He had crossed to
the other side of the political divide.

As he gazed out the window he tried to think of other things but
couldn't come close. What would Nixon do? What would his response
be? What could it be? Having been there, so up close, Butterfield knew
there would be a scramble.

Butterfield dwelled for a moment on the man on the street, the
average American. What would he or she think? What would they be
saying around the water cooler? This would be big, big news. High
drama indeed, the roiling, snowballing scandal.

For Butterfield, it was not a happy time. "I know I'm toast. I'm on
my way out. I'm sorry that the task has fallen to me."

•     •     •

He saw the first newspaper about the disclosure when they arrived in Great Britain. An article in *The New York Times* quoted his mother. "He always stood for moral integrity and straightforwardness. He doesn't like me to talk this way, but he was an Eagle Scout and carried the cross in church." Oh, my God, Butterfield thought. She added that he "was brought up very strictly by a Navy father, who's trying to get me off the phone right now."

Too late.

Nixon later wrote in his memoir, "I was shocked by this news. As impossible as it must seem now, I had believed that the existence of the White House taping system would never be revealed. I thought at least executive privilege would have been raised by any staff member before verifying its existence." He also said he wrote a note on his bedside notepad: "Tapes—once start, no stopping."

Al Haig, who had taken over as Nixon's chief of staff just two months earlier, said in his overlooked 1992 memoir, *Inner Circles*, that he knew some tapes were made in the Nixon White House but Butterfield's testimony came as an unimaginable surprise.

"This was the first I had heard of the existence of an eavesdropping system that recorded every word uttered in the presence of Nixon, and it came as a total surprise to me," Haig wrote. "I had no foreknowledge of Butterfield's appearance, let alone the nature of his testimony."

Haig, who was predisposed to let loose with his inner feelings, added (and Nixon was still alive when this was published): "It never occurred to me that anyone in his right mind would install anything so Orwellian as a system that never shut off, that preserved every word, every joke, every curse, every tantrum, every flight of presidential paranoia, every bit of flattery and bad advice and tattling by his advisers."

That pretty much said it all. On his own, without consulting the president, Haig ordered the system dismantled. "Tear it out," he directed.

Nixon was in Bethesda Naval Hospital for viral pneumonia and Haig went out to see him because he believed the Butterfield revelation was too sensitive to discuss over the phone. Always the options man, Haig said Nixon had two—keep the tapes or destroy them.

The White House Watergate lawyers accompanied Haig to see Nixon. They were divided. Fred Buzhardt, the West Point graduate, Southerner, former Pentagon general counsel and Haig's good friend, said, "Destroy the tapes."

Leonard Garment, the New York intellectual, excitable and a Democrat at heart, issued a warning rather than advice after hearing Buzhardt's bottom line.

"Mr. President," he told Nixon, "that would be an intolerable act. If you were to do such a thing, I must tell you that I would feel obligated to resign in protest and publicly explain the reasons for my resignation."

"Get out of here," Nixon ordered both lawyers. "Al, you stay."

There was no decision that night, and Haig returned to the hospital the next morning.

"Al, I've thought about this all night long," Nixon said. "Maybe Alex Butterfield has done us a favor. These tapes will be exculpatory. I know I never said anything to anybody that could be interpreted as encouragement to cover things up. Just the opposite."

The president continued, according to Haig, "Al, we know that Dean lied and the tapes proved that. We don't know what other lies may be told by people who are trying to save themselves." His suspicion extended to his closest former aides. "Who knows what Ehrlichman might say, or even Bob Haldeman. The tapes are my best insurance against perjury. I can't destroy them."

It was unclear if this was an all-consuming case of denial or whether it was a way of enlisting Haig further into another round of the cover-up. Maybe it was the viral pneumonia that was causing him to hallucinate.

One immediate consequence, as Haig wrote, was that the tapes made Nixon a "laughingstock. All over the country, his supporters and enemies were asking the same question: How could he, of all people, have been so dumb as to install such a system?"

•    •    •

The disclosure of the tapes launched a political fight, a legal fight, a character fight, and a moral fight that strained the constitutional system for over a year. That story of dramatic struggle has been told elsewhere. There was the Saturday Night Massacre when Nixon fired Special Prosecutor Archibald Cox, the disclosure of a mysterious 18½ minute gap on one of the tapes, endless hearings, the House impeachment investigation, the backdating of the deed to Nixon's vice presidential papers to claim a $500,000 tax deduction, the use of government funds to vastly improve his estates in Key Biscayne and San Clemente, and more questionable or illegal campaign contributions.

Butterfield often thought of the fate of the Nixon aides who were involved in Watergate crimes and did jail time. "Disciples of the president," Butterfield called them. There was Bud Krogh, one of the supervisors of the Plumbers break-in team who did four and one half months in prison. Dwight Chapin, the Nixon appointments secretary and White House political spying and espionage contact, did eight months. Jeb Magruder, the deputy Nixon campaign manager, spent seven months in prison.

"These guys," Butterfield said, "young, bright and full of enthusiasm, were ensnared by the glitter and deceit of the presidency. Their loyalties were used and exploited by Nixon." It was particularly repugnant to Butterfield that these enthusiastic Nixon disciples and their families were left to pay the price.

A year after he disclosed the taping system, Butterfield was called before the House Judiciary Committee investigating the impeachment of Nixon. It was July 1974. Butterfield had gone through a sea change. Any redeeming characteristics in Nixon had been overshadowed by the extent of the lies and the crimes. Butterfield cooperated fully with John Doar, the chief counsel of the impeachment investigation. Butterfield's essential point in his testimony was that though he had no personal knowledge of the Watergate cover-up and other abuses and crimes, he did know how the White House worked. Nixon was obsessively a detail person, he said, and Haldeman was a pure extension of

Nixon. And it was inconceivable, Butterfield testified, that Haldeman would have done anything without Nixon's knowledge and approval. Butterfield consciously decided to tell it all—and to contradict the president's claim that he did not know about the Watergate cover-up. Butterfield said he was certain that Nixon not only knew but was in charge of all Watergate-related activity.*

After the testimony on July 2, 1974, which was closed to the public, word quickly got back to the White House that Butterfield had been excessively cooperative and was openly anti-Nixon. He was clearly no Nixon supporter, as if anyone needed more evidence.

"You're destroying the greatest leader this country ever had!" Rose Mary Woods declared loudly in an evening phone call to his home one night that month. She sounded highly intoxicated.

Butterfield defended himself and his actions. "Rose, don't say that," he insisted. "That's simply not true."

He received about five similar calls at home from Woods that month.

"You're on the other side," she said in one call. "You always were."

•       •       •

---

*Under oath Butterfield told the House Judiciary Committee that Haldeman had initially approached him for the White House job out of the blue. Butterfield omitted that he had written Haldeman to request a meeting about working in the administration. Butterfield told me that he had asked Haldeman to omit that part of the story. Haldeman, however, confirms that Butterfield wrote him.

"I had virtually forgotten his existence," Haldeman wrote in his 1978 memoir, *The Ends of Power*. "Then a letter from Australia arrived at our New York headquarters. . . . I had not seen nor heard of him in twenty years. . . .

"Remembering him as a nice guy, and impressed with his record, I ran some additional checks and found he was highly recommended. In his letter, he had urged that I let him fly to New York to meet with me personally. I called him in Australia . . . and told him to come on. At that stage I was still impressed with the thought of someone hopping on an airplane and flying himself around the world for a job interview.

"We had a good talk, and I felt he would be an excellent choice for the job of my deputy."

Haldeman speculates that it is possible Butterfield was a "plant" but offers no evidence. "Whatever Butterfield's motivations, his answer to a Senate staffer's questions about a taping system triggered Nixon's downfall." Haldeman adds generously, "I still consider him a personal friend." (*The Ends of Power* [New York: Times Books, 1978], p. 204.)

On July 24, 1974, the Supreme Court in a unanimous decision ordered Nixon to turn over the tapes to the Watergate prosecutor. This included the so-called smoking-gun tape that established that Nixon was actively in charge of the cover-up, directing that the CIA move to limit the investigation. The tape proved in detailed, vivid back-and-forth conversations between Nixon and Haldeman that Butterfield was right about how the president controlled the Watergate decisions and actions.

Just 15 days later, on the evening of August 8, Nixon announced in a live national television address that he would resign the presidency the following day at noon.

That day Butterfield was alone in his FAA office. He tuned into the TV set to watch Nixon's farewell address to cabinet, staff and friends in the East Room of the White House. Butterfield could see it was a talk without text or order. Perspiring, Nixon talked about his father, mother, money, brothers and death.

Nixon put on his eyeglasses and read from Theodore Roosevelt's diary about the loss of his first wife: "And when my heart's dearest died, the light went from my life forever."

Nixon waved his hand as if to urge that his final point not be lost: "Always remember, others may hate you—but those who hate you don't win unless you hate them, and then you destroy yourself."

It was as if Nixon finally unraveled the essence of himself. He had witnessed the awful destructive power of hate. Instead of getting the others, it had eaten and doomed him.

That was it, Butterfield realized. The hating was at Nixon's center, the driving force to get the "sons of bitches," to settle all the scores for all the slights and snubs and opposition. This hate, the duplicity, the incessant plotting had become the engine of his presidency.

Butterfield almost couldn't absorb it. The East Room was full of sobbing, the clear sound of weeping. Some held handkerchiefs to their faces, squeezed their arms to contain themselves, and a few held hands. "I could not believe that people were crying in that room," he said. "It was sad, yes. But justice had prevailed. Inside I was cheering. That's what I was doing. I was cheering."

# EPILOGUE

"What extraordinary vehicles destiny selects to accomplish its design," Kissinger writes near the end of his memoir *White House Years*. It is a thought worth pondering.

For a long time, Butterfield could see that people from the Nixon administration avoided him. Often it wasn't subtle. Old friends would walk right by him. But it was seldom rude. There were a few whispered signs of approval, "Hey, Alex, nice going. We were proud of you." But not many, maybe not enough.

One incident in 1986, a dozen years after Nixon's resignation, particularly bothered him. His 86-year-old father, retired Rear Admiral Horace Butterfield, had a heart attack in Alaska. His mother, who had dementia, was traveling with her husband and was left in a small motel 100 miles away when his father was flown to a hospital in Anchorage.

Butterfield flew immediately to the remote outpost to care for his mother, then phoned to get assistance from a general in the Alaskan Air Command. Years earlier, as lieutenant colonels, they had been friends in the Pentagon. "I don't want to talk to him," Butterfield could hear the general speaking to an assistant. "Tell him I'm not in."

He was sure it was because of his role in the demise of Nixon. "Military friends were the last to understand," he told me. "They could not possibly know what I knew about Nixon and various facets of his personality and White House operation. There is the commander-in-chief thing. They can't easily rationalize his taking a hit, much less a major blow from a former member of the club."

Over the decades Butterfield wondered why he had to be the one to disclose the tapes. "Why me? Why did fate play this dirty trick on me?

"It never did make me doubt that I had made the right decisions once put in that situation," he said again. "But it would have been nice if more people had understood what was really going on."

To get rid of the FAA administrator generally requires an airplane crash. On December 1, 1974, a TWA 727 jet went down some 40 miles west of Dulles Airport, killing 92. It was pilot error, but as always the FAA had a role to play as some investigators faulted an air controller.

Claude Brinegar, the secretary of transportation and Butterfield's nominal boss, was not pleased when Butterfield had been selected to run his department's largest organization. Throughout Butterfield's tenure the two had been at each other's throat. And at one point Butterfield had a minor run-in with Gerald Ford before he became vice president, and now Ford was president. "Alex," White House chief of staff Donald Rumsfeld called in early 1975, "the president wants you to go now."

Butterfield submitted his resignation and his last day at the FAA was March 31, 1975. He stayed on as a paid consultant to the new secretary of transportation, William Coleman, for 60 days and then went on a one-year speaking tour. He recalls that he received $2,500 for each of 13 speeches, mostly on government ethics.

In July 1975, Fletcher Prouty, a retired Air Force colonel and discredited JFK assassination conspiracy theorist, went on television to allege that Butterfield had been working as the CIA "contact man" in the Nixon White House.

"It's Watergate all over again," Charlotte reported to her husband over the phone. "The lawn is full of journalists."

CBS *60 Minutes* correspondent Mike Wallace put Butterfield on the air to categorically deny the charges. "Not a shred of truth," Butterfield said of the charge. "Absolutely false."

"I talked tough on that program," Butterfield recalled, "or tried to." No evidence to support the claim was ever provided. Prouty said the source was Howard Hunt, who denied that he had made such a charge.

Charles B. Seib, the ombudsman for *The Washington Post*, investigated and wrote in a column July 22, 1975, that the charge had "fizzled" and the leaders of the congressional investigations found zero support for the charges.

Because of the tapes disclosure, Butterfield was radioactive. He sent out résumés to 88 firms, and finally got a job as chief operating officer of International Air Service Company in San Francisco. The firm was one of the largest flight-crew leasing and pilot-training agencies in the world. The company paid him $65,000 a year, and in addition provided the use of a beautiful home outside San Francisco and a new Jaguar sedan.

"I had this little spot in the drive I took from where I lived up to work where I could go 100 mph safely."

In 1979 he moved to Los Angeles as president and chief operating officer of California Life Corporation, a financial holding company, at $150,000 a year. He joined the Bel-Air Country Club and felt financially secure for the first time since leaving government.

In 1980 George Herbert Walker Bush, after being elected Ronald Reagan's vice president, fought hard to get Butterfield appointed ambassador to NATO. But Haig, who had been selected as Reagan's secretary of state, blocked the appointment. "Haig wouldn't even see me," Butterfield said.

From 1984 to 1994 Butterfield started and ran Armistead & Alexander, an international consulting company that specialized in improving productivity in businesses. He and Charlotte were divorced in 1985. In 1988–89 he returned to Washington briefly as a volunteer on the Inaugural Committee of President-elect Bush. He wrote a 100-page paper on White House administration and served for seven weeks running the volunteer desk at Inaugural Committee headquarters.

Butterfield effectively retired by 2000, when he started taking Italian courses at the University of California, San Diego. He earned a master's degree in American history and even now is working on a PhD dissertation on the president's pardoning power. He lectures once a year at Oxford University in England and serves on several boards, including Dr. Seuss Enterprises.

On several of my visits to his penthouse in California, I walked along a hallway 20 feet long where he had hung 30 framed photographs. To my surprise they were almost exclusively from his Nixon White House days—Nixon with his family; Butterfield with Nixon outside on the White House grounds; Butterfield's family with Nixon; Butterfield in numerous Nixon White House meetings, large and small; Butterfield with Nixon in the Oval Office; Nixon with Sammy Davis Jr.; Butterfield testifying and disclosing the secret taping system to the Senate Watergate Committee; Nixon's resignation-day farewell address when he was sweating and overwrought with emotion.

Another was a cartoon of Nixon waking up in bed with a smile telling Pat, "I just had the most beautiful dream—that Alexander Butterfield didn't reveal that conversations in the Oval Office were taped!"

One photograph was inscribed, "To Alex Butterfield, With deep gratitude for your outstanding contribution to the success of the 1972 Republican National Convention." Signed in Richard Nixon's autopen.

I asked him why put all the photographs up? Why such a large gallery?

Well, I have them, he said, and I thought I ought to put them up.

We lingered over them.

Here was the paradox on the wall. On one hand, the photographs were there to remind visitors, and perhaps himself, that he had been there at the center of things and been an intimate witness to it all. On the other hand, they were there to show he was the one who testified about the secret taping system, and lit a fuse that helped bring it all down.

The last photograph shows a formal receiving line. Butterfield is shaking hands with Nixon's successor, Gerald Ford. They are staring wordlessly into each other's eyes.


In 2015, Butterfield told me of his 40 years since Nixon, "it wasn't really a happy time. However, I don't think I did any moping.

"I thought at times what could have been, had I remained in the Air Force and become a general officer.

"No regrets. If I had to do it over again, I figure I'd do the very same thing." Life in California is so different from Washington, he said. He found contentment on the West Coast, and says he is at peace with himself. If he had not disclosed the tapes, he said, it is likely he would have fit eventually into the California Republican business world and been welcomed into its upper echelons. He likely would have gone to the Bohemian Grove, a private men's club that meets in the summer for a three-week encampment with some of the most powerful political and business figures in the world. "In another life, I probably would've been going to those things." Instead he found anonymity, and basked in it.

"Nobody knew, you know, my name. Back East a waiter in a New York restaurant might know from a credit card. But out here, no way. You could spell it out, and you could even tell them you had a key role in Watergate. They'd say, Water-what?"

# SOURCE NOTES

I conducted the following taped interviews with Alexander Butterfield that totaled more than 46 hours:

| Date | Location | Duration |
|---|---|---|
| **2011** | | |
| July 18 | Edgewater, MD | 5 hours |
| **2014** | | |
| June 22 | Washington, DC | 2 hours, 25 minutes |
| June 23 | Washington, DC | 5 hours, 5 minutes |
| July 22 | La Jolla, CA | 7 hours, 3 minutes |
| July 23 | La Jolla, CA | 2 hours, 21 minutes |
| December 5 | La Jolla, CA | 2 hours, 17 minutes |
| December 6 | La Jolla, CA | 3 hours, 37 minutes |
| December 7 | La Jolla, CA | 4 hours, 9 minutes |
| December 8 | Coronado, CA | 1 hour, 21 minutes |
| **2015** | | |
| January 20 | La Jolla, CA | 6 hours, 2 minutes |
| January 21–22 | La Jolla, CA | 7 hours, 6 minutes of videotaped interviews over two days |
| April 15 | Phone interview | 1 hour, 32 minutes |
| May 4 | La Jolla, CA | 27 minutes |

On September 10, 2014, my assistant, Evelyn Duffy, interviewed Butterfield on tape in La Jolla for 2 hours and 15 minutes.

I have quoted throughout the book from Butterfield's book proposal and his unpublished book draft, bearing the working title "Fellow Countrymen." Several chapters are missing.

## PROLOGUE

4  *"I had believed"*: Richard Nixon, *RN: The Memoirs of Richard Nixon* (New York: Grosset & Dunlap, 1978), p. 900.

## CHAPTER 1

6  *"He was drop-dead handsome"*: Interview with Charlotte and Alexander Butterfield, December 8, 2014.

9  *Butterfield would later write*: Alexander Butterfield, Unpublished book draft.

## CHAPTER 2

16  *"He was a golden boy"*: Interview with Charlotte and Alexander Butterfield, December 8, 2014.

18  *White House aide Egil "Bud" Krogh would later call it*: Egil "Bud" Krogh with Matthew Krogh, *Integrity: Good People, Bad Choices and Life Lessons from the White House* (New York: PublicAffairs, 2007), p. 41.

## CHAPTER 3

20  *"If they are away after midnight"*: Richard Nixon, "Remarks at the Swearing In of New Members of the White House Staff," January 21, 1969. Online by Gerhard Peters and John T. Wooley, *The American Presidency Project,* http://www.presidency.ucsb.edu /ws/?pid=2163.

23  *During these early days:* President Nixon's Daily Diary suggests this dinner took place on January 30, 1969, http://www.nixonlibrary.gov /virtuallibrary/documents/dailydiary.php.

## CHAPTER 4

25  *One subject was Nixon's bedside table:* Alexander Butterfield, Unpublished book draft.

28  *On February 18, Haldeman came racing in:* See H.R. Haldeman, *The Ends of Power* (New York: Times Books, 1978), p. xix. In his memoir, Haldeman says he went back for his 20th wedding anniversary, which

was the 19th of February, and he was going to celebrate with Jo and a few close friends.

## CHAPTER 5

34 *At 8:10 a.m. Butterfield hurriedly put together a memo:* Memo from Alexander Butterfield to President Nixon, Subject: Wire from the Virgin Islands Legislature, February 19, 1969, 8:10 a.m. See pp. 203–204 in Appendix.

35 *"Feeling duty-bound":* Alexander Butterfield, Unpublished book draft.

36 *"My mind was made up":* Ibid.

## CHAPTER 6

37 *"On the way to the White House":* Alexander Butterfield, Unpublished book draft.

39 *"The president was an actor":* Alexander Butterfield, Unpublished book draft.

40 *"I had never, in 21 years":* Ibid.

40 *On February 22, 1969, his memo:* Ibid.

41 *"The President has directed that the religious inscription":* Ibid.

42 *Nixon's appearance drew lots of attention:* See Noel Murray, "Nixon Gets Socked in Laugh-In's Most Famous, and Influential, Five Seconds," *A.V. Club,* September 13, 2012, http://www.avclub.com/r/84881tsd.

42 *Keyes had met Nixon in the 1960s:* Interview with Steve Bull, March 12, 2015.

## CHAPTER 7

48 *Butterfield took a sheet of White House stationery:* Memo from Alexander Butterfield to President Nixon, June 19, 1969. See p. 205 in Appendix.

48 *At one point, Nixon referred:* "The president's news conference," June 19, 1969. Online by Gerhard Peters and John T. Wooley, The American Presidency Project, http://www.presidency.ucsb.edu/ws/?pid=2106.

## CHAPTER 8

50 *a series of press reports by journalist Seymour M. Hersh:* See Hersh's articles reprinted in: *Reporting Vietnam Part Two: American Journalism, 1969–1975,* ed. Milton J. Bates et al. (New York: Library of America, 1998), pp. 13–27.

50 *Secretary of Defense Laird had laid it out:* Memo from Melvin Laird to President Nixon, Subject: The My Lai Atrocity, September 3, 1969.

51 *Haig, Kissinger's deputy, sent internal:* Memo from Al Haig to Alexander Butterfield, Subject: Additional Information on My Lai Incident, December 3, 1969, with attachment.

51  *His first article*: *Reporting Vietnam Part Two*, p. 13.

51  *Sergeant Michael Bernhardt was quoted*: Ibid., p. 18.

52  *Another witness, Michael Terry, said*: Ibid., p. 21.

52  *In his November 25 story*: Ibid., p. 22.

52  *"Do you ever dream about this?"*: "Transcript of Interview of Vietnam War Veteran on His Role in Alleged Massacre of Civilians at Songmy," *New York Times*, November 24, 1969, p. 16, http://archive.org/details /MeadloWallaceInterviewNov241969.

52  *Stephen Ambrose, a leading military historian, said*: Robert Miraldi, *Seymour Hersh Scoop Artist* (Lincoln: Potomac Books, 2013), p. 27.

53  *Across three pages of notes*: Handwritten notes of Alexander Butterfield, November 27, 1969. See pp. 206–208 in Appendix.

54  *In a* SECRET *memo to the president*: Memo from Alexander Butterfield to President Nixon, Subject: Ronald Lee Ridenhour (And Other Information re My Lai), December 17, 1969. See pp. 209–213 in Appendix.

55  *In his memoir Nixon wrote, "Calley's crime"*: Richard Nixon, *RN: The Memoirs of Richard Nixon* (New York: Grosset & Dunlap, 1978), p. 499.

55  *He said that "maintaining public support"*: Ibid., p. 500.

55  *"The whole tragic episode"*: Ibid.

55  *Hersh visited it in early 2015*: Seymour M. Hersh, "The Scene of the Crime," March 30, 2015, *The New Yorker*, pp. 53–61.

### CHAPTER 9

56  *According to his daily log*: "The president toured the ground floor offices in the EOB building to wish employees a merry Christmas," Nixon's Daily Diary for December 24, 1969, http://www.nixonlibrary.gov /virtualibrary/documents/dailydiary.php.

57  *Haldeman weighed in*: Memo from H.R. Haldeman to Alexander Butterfield, January 14, 1970. See p. 214 in Appendix.

58  *Butterfield checked her personnel file*: Memo from Alexander Butterfield to President Nixon, Subject: Sanitization of the EOB, January 16, 1970. See pp. 217–218 in Appendix. See also: Memo from Alexander Butterfield to H.R. Haldeman, January 16, 1970. See pp. 215–216 in Appendix.

58  *So on January 16, Butterfield outlined*: Ibid.

### CHAPTER 10

64  *According to a tape of a conversation*: OVAL 455-1; February 22, 1971; White House Tapes; Richard Nixon Presidential Library and Museum,

Yorba Linda, California. This conversation took place just 10 days after the taping system was installed and working.

66 *On November 21, 1970, Pat Nixon sent Butterfield:* Pat Nixon handwritten note to Alexander Butterfield, November 21, 1970.

67 *When Susan, who was the more seriously injured:* The president's schedule for December 4, 1970, indicates that Susan Butterfield was scheduled to meet with Nixon at 3:15. See also President's Daily Diary for December 4, 1970, http://www.nixonlibrary.gov/virtualibrary /documents/dailydiary.php.

### CHAPTER 11

73 *"The basic purpose will be":* Memo from H.R. Haldeman to Alexander Butterfield, Subject: Church Services, November 13, 1970. See p. 219 in Appendix.

73 *Six days later:* Ted Lewis, "Praise Him from Whom the GOP's Blessings Flow," "Capitol Stuff," New York *Daily News,* November 19, 1970.

73 *Four days later Haldeman shot Butterfield another memo:* Memo from H.R. Haldeman to Alexander Butterfield and Charles Colson, November 23, 1970. See p. 220 in Appendix.

73 *On August 10, 1971, Haldeman said:* Memo from H.R. Haldeman to Alexander Butterfield, August 10, 1971. See p. 221 in Appendix.

73 *Fiske had just written an article:* Edward B. Fiske, "Praying with the President in the White House," *New York Times,* August 8, 1971.

74 *Then on August 19, 1971:* Memo from H.R. Haldeman to Alexander Butterfield, August 19, 1971. See p. 222 in Appendix.

74 *"I created a new Cabinet-level position":* Richard Nixon, *RN: The Memoirs of Richard Nixon* (New York: Grosset & Dunlap, 1978), p. 342.

74 *He underscored "my respect for":* Ibid., p. 519.

74 *"one of the three that has counted":* Robert H. Ferrell, ed., *Inside the Nixon Administration: The Secret Diary of Arthur Burns, 1969–1974* (Lawrence: University Press of Kansas, 2010), p. 39.

74 *A February 22, 1971, memo from Haldeman:* Memo from H.R. Haldeman to Alexander Butterfield, February 22, 1971. See p. 223 in Appendix.

75 *According to Butterfield's notes:* Handwritten notes of Alexander Butterfield, undated. See p. 224 in the Appendix.

76 *He seemed to enjoy:* Jerry Schecter, "Parting Shots: Henry Kissinger, Not-So-Secret Swinger," *Life,* January 28, 1972, pp. 70B–71.

76 *On February 9, 1971, Haldeman sent a memo:* Memo from H.R. Haldeman to Alexander Butterfield, February 9, 1971. See p. 225 in the Appendix.

## CHAPTER 12

78  *Nixon first decreed:* Typed notes of Alexander Butterfield on H.R. Haldeman memos to Alexander Butterfield dated April 13, 1970, and February 18, 1971.

78  *The next month he determined:* Typed notes of Alexander Butterfield on an H.R. Haldeman memo to Alexander Butterfield dated March 22, 1971.

79  *That evening Butterfield called Al Wong:* A November 19, 1973, account by Supervisory Security Specialist Raymond C. Zumwalt of the United States Secret Service Technical Security Division provides additional details.

80  *One Watergate book on Nixon's tapes:* OVAL 450-1 and 450-10(cl); February 16, 1971; White House Tapes; Richard Nixon Presidential Library and Museum, Yorba Linda, California. See also Douglas Brinkley and Luke A. Nichter, *The Nixon Tapes* (Boston: Houghton Mifflin Harcourt, 2014), pp. 3–5. Digital audio and transcripts of these conversations may also be found at http://www.nixontapes .org/origin.html.

82  *"the best chronicled in history":* Richard Nixon, *RN: The Memoirs of Richard Nixon* (New York: Grosset & Dunlap, 1978), p. 500.

82  *In Nixon's assessment, the operation:* Ibid., p. 499.

82  *"Such an objective record":* Ibid., p. 501.

82  *"Although I was not comfortable":* Ibid., pp. 501–2.

82  *Taping selected conversations or phone calls:* Ibid., p. 502.

82  *"I did not want to have to calculate":* Ibid.

83  *"Initially, I was conscious of the taping":* Ibid.

## CHAPTER 13

84  *"Your Minnesota friends":* Richard Nixon, *RN: The Memoirs of Richard Nixon* (New York: Grosset & Dunlap, 1978), p. 102.

84  *In May 1969, the first months:* See Bob Woodward and Scott Armstrong, *The Brethren* (New York: Simon & Schuster, 2005), pp. 14–15.

85  *"I am willing to risk annoying him":* Handwritten cover note from Warren Burger to John Ehrlichman, May 8, 1969. See p. 226 in Appendix.

85  *"Dear Mr. President," Burger began:* Letter from Warren Burger to President Nixon, May 8, 1969. See pp. 227–228 in Appendix.

86  *After hearings lasting:* "Senate Committee Okays Burger Court Appointment," United Press International, June 4, 1969.

86 *Six days later the Senate did so:* Supreme Court Nominations, Present–1789, http://www.senate.gov/pargelayout/reference/nominations/Nominations.htm.

86 *"I'm not a bit thin-skinned":* Memo from President Nixon to H.R. Haldeman, May 9, 1971, as quoted in Stanley Kutler, ed., *Watergate: A Brief History with Documents* (Hoboken: Wiley-Blackwell, 2009), p. 16.

86 *"Your fortitude and forbearance":* Letter from Warren Burger to President Nixon, May 10, 1971. See p. 229 in Appendix.

86 *Burger said that in 1969 the president:* Letter from Warren Burger to H.R. Haldeman, August 5, 1972. See pp. 230–231 in Appendix.

87 *In a formal endorsement:* Alexander M. Haig, Jr. with Charles McCarry, *Inner Circles* (New York: Warner Books, 1992), p. 271.

87 *The next year Henry Kissinger said:* Ibid., p. 272.

87 *"The president was in a cold rage":* Ibid., p. 275.

88 *"I will not pretend":* Ibid.

88 *Haig produced a four-page:* Memo from Al Haig to H.R. Haldeman, June 20, 1972. See pp. 232–235 in Appendix.

90 *Butterfield sent Haig a "Dear Al" letter:* Letter from Alexander Butterfield to Al Haig, September 7, 1972. See p. 236 in Appendix.

### CHAPTER 14

91 *Bull, a stalwart Nixon defender, told me:* Interview with Steve Bull, March 12, 2015.

91 *Richard Dudman, who had written critically:* Memo from Alexander Butterfield to Henry Kissinger, July 14, 1969, and Memo from Alexander Butterfield to H.R. Haldeman, May 19, 1969.

92 *On the subject of public television:* Memo from Alexander Butterfield to H.R. Haldeman, July 16, 1969.

92 *Butterfield, on Nixon's orders:* Memo from Alexander Butterfield to John Mitchell, June 20, 1969.

92 *To a report that the Nixon administration:* Memo from Alexander Butterfield to John Ehrlichman, June 10, 1969. See p. 237 in Appendix.

92 *"Not only was it a sensation for the media":* Henry Kissinger, *White House Years* (Boston: Little, Brown, 1979), p. 163.

92 *"Nixon had an extraordinary instinct":* Ibid.

93 *"Under no circumstances":* Bernard Kalb, "Why They Mattered: Stanley Karnow, 1925–2013," *Politico Magazine*, December 22, 2013.

93 *"If it is hard to go," he said:* Memo from H.R. Haldeman to Ron Ziegler, subject: Press for the Russian trip, April 3, 1972.

93   *"We have lost"*: William Buckley, Jr., " 'Week Changes World,' But
     to What Extent?," *Lawrence Daily Journal-World*, March 2, 1972,
     p. 4.

94   *"He clearly liked one secretary better"*: Reached at her home in North
     Carolina on June 24, 2015, Nell Yates declined to comment. "I don't
     see any reason to drag all this out," she said. "It is overkill if you ask
     me. I think I'll hang up now."

### CHAPTER 15

96   *Secret taping at Camp David:* Account by Supervisory Security Specialist
     Raymond C. Zumwalt of the United States Secret Service Technical
     Security Division, November 19, 1973.

96   *"Been here before?":* CDHW 189-9; May 17, 1972; White House Tapes;
     Richard Nixon Presidential Library and Museum, Yorba Linda,
     California.

97   *Nixon's daily records show:* President's Daily Diary for May 17, 1972,
     http://www.nixonlibrary.gov/virtuallibrary/documents/dailydiary
     .php.

97   *The next morning, May 18:* President's Daily Diary for May 18, 1972,
     http://www.nixonlibrary.gov/virtuallibrary/documents/dailydiary.php.

100  *"Are you going out this time?":* OVAL 746-12; July 1, 1972; White House
     Tapes; Richard Nixon Presidential Library and Museum, Yorba Linda,
     California.

101  *Later, according to a tape:* OVAL 228-1; November 20 1972; White
     House Tapes; http://www.nixontapes.org.

### CHAPTER 16

103  *"You asked for particulars":* Memo from Alexander Butterfield to
     H.R. Haldeman, subject: Notification of Wallace Shooting, May 16,
     1972. See pp. 238–239 in Appendix.

104  *"'The President was agitated and wanted'":* Carl Bernstein and Bob
     Woodward, *All the President's Men* (New York: Simon & Schuster,
     1974), p. 329.

104  *"It is my personal plan to assassinate by pistol":* Arthur Bremer,
     *An Assassin's Diary* (New York: Harper Magazine Press, 1973).

106  *Those seven words can be heard:* OVAL 772-015; September 7, 1972;
     Presidential Records Program, The Miller Center, University of
     Virginia, http://www.whitehousetapes.net/transcript/Nixon
     /772-015-0 (Webpage no longer active).

107  *Nixon had been clear:* Ibid.

108 *On April 10, 1969, at the president's instruction:* Memo from Alexander Butterfield to John Ehrlichman, Subject: Notes from the President (Action Item), April 10, 1969. See p. 240 in Appendix.

108 *Two days later in another:* Memo from Alexander Butterfield to John Ehrlichman, Subject: Note from the President (Action Item), April 12, 1969. See p. 241 in Appendix.

### CHAPTER 17

109 *On March 24, 1972, CIA director:* Memo from Richard Helms to President Nixon, March 24, 1972, with two enclosures totaling 18 pages. See pp. 242–259 in Appendix.

110 *The source of one attachment:* Ibid., Attachment A.

110 *On September 26, 1972, Bruce Kehrli:* Memo from Bruce Kehrli to Alexander Butterfield, Subject: Security Violation, September 26, 1972.

111 *The CIA bulletin showed:* Central Intelligence Bulletin, September 23, 1972. See pp. 260–261 in the Appendix.

111 *An equivalent report and satellite photograph:* Ibid.

111 *Top Secret "intercepted messages":* Ibid.

### CHAPTER 18

112 *He forwarded an email:* Email from Jason Schultz to Michael Ellzey, forwarded to Bob Woodward, June 5, 2015. I said I would supply the Nixon Library with copies of any relevant memos in my possession after publication of this book.

Thomas S. Blanton, director of the National Security Archive at George Washington University in Washington, D.C., said they have no such memo. This archive has the world's largest nongovernment library of declassified documents from the United States. After a thorough search, Blanton also said there is no evidence of a follow-on study of the effectiveness of the bombing.

Blanton did find a one-page January 10, 1972, memo that Kissinger sent to Nixon reporting on a CIA source saying that raids one day in December "were more effective than past raids." But Nixon is quoted downplaying its significance, telling Haig in a telephone conversation, "It was a routine protective reaction strike" and he didn't want the White House to get involved in commenting.

113 *John Negroponte, a foreign service officer:* Interview with John Negroponte in 2015.

113 *In the president's own handwriting:* Memo from Henry Kissinger to President Nixon, January 3, 1972. See p. 116 in the text.

113  *On January 2, 1972, five days before:* Richard Nixon: "A conversation
     with the president," Interview with Dan Rather of the Columbia
     Broadcasting System, January 2, 1972. Online by Gerhard Peters and
     John T. Wooley, *The American Presidency Project,* http://www.presidency
     .ucsb.edu/ws/?pid-3351. Audiovisual recording also available at the
     Richard Nixon Presidential Library and Museum, Yorba Linda,
     California.

113  *Up to that point, Nixon had ordered:* Electronic Records of the Air War
     Over Southeast Asia: A Database Analysis. Holly High, James R.
     Curran and Gareth Robinson, *Journal of Vietnamese Studies,* Vol. 8, No. 4
     (Fall 2013), pp. 86–124. Published by University of California Press.
     Retrieved from: http://www.jstor.org/stable/10.1525/vs.2014 .8.4.86.
     Figure 4, p. 104. CACTA/SEADAB refers to the Combat Air Activities
     File and the Southeast Asia Data Base. See p. 262 in Appendix.

*104*  HIGH, CURRAN, AND ROBINSON

| Year | Laos | Vietnam S | Vietnam N | Cambodia | Thailand | Other | Total |
|---|---|---|---|---|---|---|---|
| 1965 | 36,967 | 43,284 | 536 | | | 44 | 80,830 |
| 1966 | 63,447 | 193,254 | 128,280 | | 41 | | 385,022 |
| 1967 | 93,623 | 292,176 | 191,420 | 38 | 19 | 1,232 | 578,508 |
| 1968 | 156,619 | 338,042 | 198,670 | | 102 | 1,280 | 694,713 |
| 1969 | 489,037 | 596,147 | 651 | 6 | 62 | 964 | 1,086,866 |
| 1970 | 631,658 | 403,882 | 1,691 | 78,220 | 5 | 59,320 | 1,174,775 |
| 1971 | 414,792 | 178,506 | 6,754 | 63,253 | | 15 | 663,320 |
| 1972 | 167,370 | 706,894 | 207,284 | 57,042 | 104 | 337 | 1,139031 |
| 1973 | 82,869 | 68,595 | 14,490 | 273,728 | 521 | 572 | 440,774 |
| 1974 | | 21,717 | | | | | 21,717 |
| 1975 | | 10,205 | | 27 | 6 | 681 | 10,918 |
| Total | 2,136,380 | 2,852,701 | 749,776 | 472,313 | 863 | 64,445 | 6,276,477 |

FIGURE 4: Totals (Tonnage) by Country and by Year Based on CACTA/SEADAB
Database.

114  *I reached Kissinger:* Interview with Henry Kissinger, June 29, 2015.

119  *In an entry for Saturday, January 1, 1972:* H.R. Haldeman, *The Haldeman
     Diaries* (New York: G.P. Putnam's Sons, 1994), p. 391.

## CHAPTER 19

120 *The next month, February 1972:* Memo from Henry Kissinger to Melvin Laird, Subject: Additional Authorities for Southeast Asia, February 4, 1972, *Foreign Relations of the United States, 1969–1976*, Vol. VIII, Vietnam, January–October 1972, Document 15, http://history.state .gov/historicaldocuments/frus1969v08/d15.

121 *Nixon was very worried:* OVAL 228-1; November 20, 1972; White House Tapes, http://www.nixontapes.org.

121 *On May 9, 1972, Nixon dictated:* Memo from President Nixon to Henry Kissinger, May 9, 1972. See pp. 263–266 in Appendix.

122 *The seven paragraphs that Nixon uses:* Richard Nixon, *RN: The Memoirs of Richard Nixon* (New York: Grosset & Dunlap, 1978), pp. 606–7.

123 *When the State Department declassified:* Memo from President Nixon to Henry Kissinger, May 9, 1972, *Foreign Relations of the United States, 1969–1976*, Vol. VIII, Vietnam, January–October 1972, Document 139, footnote 1, http://history.state.gov/historicaldocuments/frus1969 -76v08/d139#fn1.

123 *In his 2015 book:* Ken Hughes, *Fatal Politics* (Charlottesville: University of Virginia Press, 2015).

123 *It stated that 66 percent:* Ibid., pp. 55–56; and David R. Derge, Vice President and Dean of Indiana University, to President Nixon, "The Public Appraises the Nixon Administration and Key Issues (with Particular Emphasis on Vietnam)," 11 August 1969, "E.O.B. Office Desk—August 10, 1974" folder, Box 185, President's Personal File, Materials Removed from President's Desk, 1969–74 [EOB office desk . . . Administration] to [Blank stationery– . . . August 9, 1974], Nixon Library.

124 *Nixon would later claim:* Richard Nixon, *No More Vietnams* (New York: Arbor House, 1985), p. 149.

124 *The Official History of the People's Army:* Merle L. Pribbenow, trans., *Victory in Vietnam: The Official History of the People's Army of Vietnam, 1954–1975* (Lawrence: University Press of Kansas, 2002), p. 301, quoted in Hughes, *Fatal Politics*, p. 63.

124 *According to a September 8, 1972, tape recording:* OVAL 773-12; September 8, 1972; White House Tapes; http://www.nixon tapes.org.

124 *Nixon wrote that his popularity in 1972:* James Mann, *The Rebellion of Ronald Reagan: A History of the End of the Cold War* (New York: Viking, 2009), p. 233.

124  *According to the tape of an October 6, 1972, meeting:* OVAL 793-6;
     October 6, 1973; White House Tapes; Presidential Recordings Digital
     Edition, Miller Center, University of Virginia, http://prde.upress
     .virginia.edu/conversations/4006749; and Hughes, *Fatal Politics,*
     pp. 88–97.

124  *"I see those poor North Vietnamese kids":* EOB 366-6; October 12, 1972;
     White House Tapes; http://www.nixontapes.org; and Hughes, *Fatal
     Politics,* pp. 103–6.

124  *"We're not going to lose. Haha.":* CDST 149-14; October 15, 1972; White
     House Tapes; http://www.nixontapes.org; and Hughes, *Fatal Politics,*
     p. 107.

124  *"May 8 was the acid test":* OVAL 799-9; October 16, 1972; White House
     Tapes; http://www.nixontapes.org; and Hughes, *Fatal Politics,* p. 109.

### CHAPTER 20

125  *For example, Kissinger:* Backchannel message from Henry Kissinger to
     Al Haig, October 22, 1972, *Foreign Relations of the United States, 1969–
     1976,* Vol. IX, Vietnam, October 1972–January 1973, Document 43,
     http://history.state.gov/historicaldocuments/frus1969-76v09/d43.

126  *"I did not feel that I could":* Richard Nixon, *RN: The Memoirs of Richard
     Nixon* (New York: Grosset & Dunlap, 1978), p. 701.

126  *On the very next page:* Ibid., p. 702.

126  *"I immediately sent a message":* Ibid.

126  *In his memoir, Kissinger also does not mention:* Henry Kissinger, *White
     House Years* (Boston: Little, Brown, 1979), p. 1388.

126  *"Here you would add orally":* Backchannel message from Henry Kissinger
     to Al Haig, October 22, 1972, *Foreign Relations of the United States,
     1969–1976,* Vol. IX, Vietnam, October 1972–January 1973, Document
     43, http://history.state.gov/historicaldocuments/frus1969-76v09/d43.

127  *It was among more than 4,000 pages:* See *Foreign Relations of the United
     States, 1969–1976,* United States Department of State Office of the
     Historian, http://history.state.gov/historicaldocuments/Nixon-ford.

127  *The next day, Monday, October 23:* Kissinger, *White House Years,* p. 1390.

127  *But a five-page TOP SECRET:* Memo from Henry Kissinger, Subject:
     Dr. Kissinger's Meeting with President Thieu, October 23, 1972. See
     pp. 267–271 in Appendix.

128  *"Outrageous as Thieu's conduct had been":* Henry Kissinger, *White House
     Years,* p. 1387.

128  *The North called this "extermination bombing":* Nixon, *RN: The Memoirs of
     Richard Nixon,* p. 741.

128  *"they did not require":* Ibid.

128  *"This glorious victory in our initial battle":* Merle L. Pribbenow, trans.,
     *Victory in Vietnam: The Official History of the People's Army of Vietnam,*
     *1954-1975* (Lawrence: University Press of Kansas, 2002), p. 320.

129  *"The enemy's massive strategic offensive":* Ibid., p. 327.

129  *In the midst of the new bombing:* Nixon, *RN: The Memoirs of Richard Nixon,*
     p. 737.

### CHAPTER 21

130  *On April 8, 1972, Nixon dictated:* Memo from President Nixon to John
     Ehrlichman, April 8, 1972.

133  *It was a cabinet dinner at Camp David:* See the President's Daily Diary
     for August 8, 1972, http://www.nixonlibrary.gov/virtuallibrary
     /documents/dailydiary.php.

133  *A tape of a discussion Nixon had with Butterfield:* OVAL 763-18; August 7,
     1972; White House Tapes; http://www.nixontapes.org.

133  *That afternoon he spent another 10 minutes:* OVAL 763-25; August 7,
     1972; White House Tapes; http://www.nixontapes.org.

134  *A 17-page transcript:* Richard Nixon, "Remarks of the President at a
     Cabinet Dinner at Camp David," August 8, 1972.

135  *On the first page of that day's summary:* News summary for October 25,
     1972. See p. 272 in the Appendix.

### CHAPTER 22

137  *That day Butterfield and all appointees:* Memo from H.R. Haldeman to
     Alexander Butterfield, Subject: Future Plans, November 7, 1972. See
     p. 273 in Appendix.

137  *In his memoir, Kissinger calls:* Henry Kissinger, *White House Years*
     (Boston: Little, Brown, 1979), p. 1407.

137  *Haldeman asked for "a basic book":* Memo from H.R. Haldeman to
     Alexander Butterfield, Subject: Future Plans, November 7, 1972. See
     p. 273 in Appendix.

138  *He compiled a 16-page memo:* Undated, untitled memo by Alexander
     Butterfield describing his duties and responsibilities at the White House.

138  *On November 10, Butterfield dictated:* Memo from Alexander Butterfield
     to H.R. Haldeman, November 10, 1972. See pp. 274–276 in Appendix.

141  *Hays would later become famous:* Marian Clark and Rudy Mara, "Closed
     Session Romance on the Hill," *Washington Post,* May 23, 1976, p. A1.

141  *A full 39 years later Butterfield wrote:* Alexander Butterfield,
     Unpublished book draft.

142  *He wrote, "As I excused myself"*: Ibid.

144  *"I want control of these"*: OVAL 836-6; January 9, 1973; White House
     Tapes; Richard Nixon Presidential Library and Museum, Yorba Linda,
     California.

## CHAPTER 23

145  *He called me to his office*: Carl Bernstein and Bob Woodward, *All the
     President's Men* (New York: Simon & Schuster, 1974), pp. 246–49.

146  *Bernstein and I had written about*: Carl Bernstein and Bob Woodward, "Bug
     Suspect Got Campaign Funds," *Washington Post*, August 1, 1972, p. A1.

146  *At the trial, Sirica asked*: James Robenalt, *January 1973: Watergate, Roe v.
     Wade, Vietnam, and the Month That Changed America Forever* (Chicago:
     Chicago Review Press, 2015), p. 109.

146  *"I have not been satisfied"*: Bernstein and Woodward, *All the President's
     Men*, p. 241.

147  *In March, James McCord*: Ibid., pp. 275–76.

147  *By the end of April*: Lee Byrd, "Mitchell Testifies to 'White House
     Horrors,' " Associated Press, July 12, 1973.

147  *After the last day of Dean's testimony*: James M. Naughten, "Dean Ends
     Testimony, Story Unshaken; 3 Senators Hint They Want Nixon Reply,"
     *New York Times*, June 29, 1973, p. A1.

148  *"The most interesting thing that happened"*: Bernstein and Woodward, *All
     the President's Men*, p. 331.

149  *"There was, however, one unchecked entry"*: Ibid., p. 330.

149  *Even before Dean's testimony*: Ibid.

150  *"The staff member said the committee"*: Ibid.

151  *When I interviewed Charlotte*: Interview with Charlotte and Alexander
     Butterfield, December 8, 2014.

## CHAPTER 24

154  *In an account of the session written in 1989*: Scott Armstrong, "Friday the
     Thirteenth," *The Journal of American History*, Vol. 75, No. 4 (March 1989),
     pp. 1234–44, and interviews with Scott Armstrong, August 19–21, 2015.

154  *In his version for the 1989 history journal*: Donald G. Sanders, "Watergate
     Reminiscences," *The Journal of American History*, Vol. 75, No. 4 (March
     1989), pp. 1228–33, http://www.jstor.org/stable/i305670.

## CHAPTER 25

157  *He later recalled for the history journal*: "Conversations Between
     Alexander P. Butterfield and David Thelen About the Discovery of

the Watergate Tapes," *The Journal of American History*, Vol. 75, No. 4 (March 1989), pp. 1245–62, http://www.jstor.org/stable/1908639.

158 *"I was, at times, impatient for the truth"*: Ibid.

159 *I noted that Graham Greene:* Graham Greene, *The Quiet American* (New York: Penguin Classics, 2004), p. 205.

159 *Immanuel Kant, the German philosopher:* Immanuel Kant, *Fundamental Principles of the Metaphysics of Morals* (Mineola: Dover Philosophical Classics, 2005), p. 24.

159 *Here the young protagonist:* J.D. Salinger, *The Catcher in the Rye* (Boston: Little, Brown, 1991), p. 213.

160 *He wrote in his 1979 spy thriller:* John le Carré, *Smiley's People* (New York: Penguin, 2011), p. 229.

160 *Much later I came upon:* Joseph Conrad, *Lord Jim* (Oxford: Oxford University Press, 2008), p. 27.

## CHAPTER 26

164 *"There is little I don't remember":* Alexander Butterfield, Unpublished book draft.

164 *It was such a change that* Time: "The Nation: The Making of the Newest Nixon," *Time*, January 18, 1971. See also Carl Bernstein and Bob Woodward, *The Final Days* (New York: Simon & Schuster, 1976), p. 428.

167 *Butterfield felt the meeting:* Alexander Butterfield, Unpublished book draft.

168 *The afternoon news had a report:* "Mystery Witness Adds Fireworks to Hearings," Associated Press, July 17, 1973.

168 *Butterfield sat erect, looking hesitant:* Video of the first minute and 48 seconds of Butterfield's July 16, 1973, testimony can be viewed on YouTube courtesy of the Newseum at http://www.youtube.com/watch?v=MeQXXopJ5U-Q.

169 *"Wonders of Watergate do not cease":* William Greider, "Wonders of Watergate," *Washington Post*, July 17, 1973, p. A1.

169 *During his testimony he was asked:* The full text of Butterfield's testimony is available at The Internet Archive, "Presidential Campaign Activities of 1972, Senate Resolution 60, Watergate and Related Activities," http://www.archive.org/stream/presidentialcamp05unit/presidentialcamp05unit_djvu.txt. Video is available (with subscription) at NBC Learn Higher Ed, http://highered.nbclearn.com/portal/site/HigherEd/browse?cuecard=66796.

## CHAPTER 27

173  *An article in* The New York Times: Christopher Lydon, "A Forthright Witness: Alexander Porter Butterfield," *New York Times,* July 17 1973.

173  *"I was shocked by this news":* Richard Nixon, *RN: The Memoirs of Richard Nixon* (New York: Grosset & Dunlap, 1978), p. 900.

173  *"Tapes—once start":* Ibid., p. 903.

173  *"This was the first I had heard":* Alexander M. Haig, Jr., with Charles McCarry, *Inner Circles* (New York: Warner Books, 1992), p. 373.

173  *"It never occurred to me":* Ibid., p. 374.

174  *Always the options man, Haig:* Ibid., p. 375.

174  *"Destroy the tapes":* Ibid., p. 378.

174  *"Mr. President":* Ibid.

174  *"Al, I've thought about this":* Ibid., p. 379.

174  *One immediate consequence, as Haig wrote:* Ibid., p. 375.

175  *A year after he disclosed:* The full text of Butterfield's July 2, 1974, testimony before the Judiciary Committee is available at http://Watergate.info/judiciary/BKITOW.pdf.

176  *After the testimony on July 2, 1974:* See "The Nation: Dialing Butterfield Hate," *Time,* February 10, 1975.

177  *Just 15 days later:* Richard Nixon: "Address to the Nation Announcing Decision to Resign the Office of President of the United States," August 8, 1974. Online by Gerhard Peters and John T. Wooley, *The American Presidency Project,* http://www.presidency.ucsb.edu/ws/?pid =4324.

177  *Perspiring, Nixon talked about:* Richard Nixon: "Remarks on Departure from the White House," August 9, 1974. Online by Gerhard Peters and John T. Wooley, *The American Presidency Project,* http://www.presidency.ucsb.edu/ws/?pid=4325.

## EPILOGUE

178  *"What extraordinary vehicles":* Henry Kissinger, *White House Years* (Boston: Little, Brown, 1979), p. 1475.

179  *On December 1, 1974:* Jim Walters, "92 Killed as Plane Crashes in Virginia," Associated Press, December 2, 1974.

179  *In July 1975, Fletcher Prouty:* "Butterfield Denies He Worked for CIA," *New York Times,* July 14, 1975; and Charles B. Seib, "The Prouty-Butterfield Flap," *Washington Post,* July 22, 1975.

180  *Charles B. Seib, the ombudsman:* Charles B. Seib, "The Prouty-Butterfield Flap," *Washington Post,* July 22, 1975.

# APPENDIX: DOCUMENTS

church services in which Haldeman writes, "The basic purpose will be to use it as a political opportunity." (See p. 219.)

9: Haldeman's November 23, 1970, memo informing Butterfield that White House church services should be used "as an opportunity to be nice to our enemies." (See p. 220.)

10: An August 10, 1971, memo from Haldeman barring the religion editor of *The New York Times* from attending worship services at the White House. (See p. 221.)

11: A memo to Butterfield from Haldeman on August 19, 1971, stressing that "the *New York Times* and *New York Post* must never be invited to these services." (See p. 222.)

12: A February 22, 1971, memo from Haldeman telling Butterfield to "hold up on Arthur Burns on any social invitations, just keep him off the list for a little while." (See p. 223.)

13: Butterfield's undated handwritten notes on his yellow legal pad regarding Nixon's concerns about Kissinger's behavior. (See p. 224.)

14: A February 9, 1971, memo establishing a new seating policy for Henry Kissinger at state dinners. (See p. 225.)

15: A handwritten note and typed letter, both dated May 8, 1969, from then–Circuit Court of Appeals Judge Warren E. Burger with advice to Nixon concerning Supreme Court Justice Abe Fortas. (See pp. 226–228.)

16: Chief Justice Warren Burger's May 10, 1971, letter to Nixon following the "gross rudeness" he felt was leveled at the president during the White House Correspondents' Association annual dinner. (See p. 229.)

17: An August 5, 1972, letter from Chief Justice Burger to Haldeman seeking military transportation for himself. (See pp. 230–231.)

18: Al Haig's June 20, 1972, memo to Haldeman, with his political analysis and advice for the 1972 presidential campaign. (See pp. 232–235.)

19: The September 7, 1972, "Dear Al" note Butterfield wrote to Haig upon Haig's promotion. (See p. 236.)

20: A memo from Butterfield, dated June 10, 1969, saying the president believed the administration should "treat the press with a little more contempt." (See p. 237.)

21: Butterfield's May 16, 1972, memo of when and how he notified Haldeman that George Wallace had been shot, marked with Haldeman's comments. (See pp. 238–239.)

22: An April 10, 1969, "Action Item" memo from Butterfield to Ehrlichman with Nixon's request that they find a way to put Ted Kennedy "squarely on the spot." (See p. 240.)

23: A second "Action Item" memo, this one dated April 12, 1969, directing Ehrlichman to "get something out on how 'very amateurish'" Kennedy had been at a briefing. (See p. 241.)

24: A Secret/Sensitive March 24, 1972, memo from CIA director Richard Helms to Nixon that includes attachments with verbatim quotes from a secret meeting between King Husayn [Hussein] of Jordan and Prime Minister of Israel Golda Meir. (See pp. 242–259.)

25: Two pages from a September 23, 1972, TOP SECRET CIA bulletin detailing surveillance of Israel. (See pp. 260–261.)

26: Table showing the tonnage of bombs dropped in Laos, Vietnam and Cambodia by year from 1965 to 1975. (See p. 262.)

27: Nixon's full May 9, 1972, memo on bombing in Vietnam to Kissinger. (See pp. 263–266.)

28: Kissinger's five-page TOP SECRET October 23, 1972 cable to Nixon and Haig detailing his conversations with Thieu. (See pp. 267–271.)

29: The October 25, 1972, news summary with Nixon's handwritten praise to Pat Buchanan at the top. (See p. 272.)

30: Haldeman's request for Butterfield's future plans and "pro forma letter of resignation," dated November 7, 1972. (See p. 273.)

31: Butterfield's November 10, 1972, response to Haldeman, detailing his fears of being "typed" and desire to leave the White House in favor of becoming secretary of the Air Force or the Navy. (See pp. 274–276.)

**THE WHITE HOUSE**

WASHINGTON

8:10 a.m.
February 19, 1969

MEMORANDUM FOR THE PRESIDENT

Subject:   Wire from the Virgin Islands Legislature

In the attached wire addressed to you the Virgin Islands
legislature, in what appears to be a purely political move,
states its inability to reasonably and responsibly proceed
with its budget hearings without a new Governor, and
petitions you to make an immediate appointment to fill
the vacancy left by former Governor Paiewonsky on
February 12th.

It is the opinion of your staff - particularly Bryce Harlow
and myself - that on the admittedly odd but still possible
chance that this subject will be brought up (even in casual
conversation) during this morning's meeting with the bi-
partisan leadership, you should not be "caught short," but
made aware of the matter as it now stands.

I first learned of the issue when Secretary Hickel called
me early yesterday evening.   I obtained a copy of the wire
and learned simultaneously that Bryce Harlow, Peter Flanigan,
and Harry Flemming were at that moment hashing it out in
Bryce's office.   As of this morning, things are on track.
We are going ahead with Peter Bove without further delay.

Meanwhile, I would recommend that:   Secretary Hickel respond
to this wire (1) stating, on your behalf, an appreciation for the
legislators' concern; (2) reminding them (gently) that the law
provides that the Government Secretary "shall have all the
powers of the Governor...in case of a vacancy in the office
of Governor...or temporary absence of the Governor"; and

·-2-

(3) assure them that a man of outstanding qualifications is
in the process of being appointed.

ALEXANDER P. BUTTERFIELD

AGREE:

DISAGREE:

COMMENTS:

June 19, 1969

MEMORANDUM FOR:      THE PRESIDENT

There are 22,354,000 U. S. blacks in America,
which is 11.1% of our 200 million (plus) population.
(This comes from three reliable sources.)

ALEXANDER P. BUTTERFIELD

TOP
Secret

P Notes enrte to KB
(Nov 27ᵗ)

(1) P talked to Laird + K — rumor it was going (MyLai)
to break before it broke. Some possibility of
a fix — event 1½ yrs ago, yet suddenly...

✓ out Claremont man. Do we have his ltr —
the one sent — supposedly sent to me?

✓ all letters — Army photog — Cleveland P/D
man sold met to Life + to C P/D. How
much?

They're vulnerable on 2 counts
— Ⓐ Photog mother + dad are Cleveland
peaceniks
— Ⓑ Meadlo too smooth for a
farmer

P thinks Pentagon too scared to investigate
adequately

Another vulnerable spot — $ passed
— Claremont fellow jewish
(lib jew)

We need some ammo in the hands of some
Senators. ✓ with Nof + Ther — very discrete.

TOP
SECRET

4 What about Dominick. What has he been
saying?

Take "a Dominick" on this. We need a
big senator - a gut fighter - a stand up
Sen. Have Lynn & Her pick a Sen
or two - or some Congressmen who could
dig into this one on a personal basis.
We can feed info to them.

Get backgrounds of all involved - all
must be exposed — Mecallo too smooth

Zero in on this. Photos too -
You handle — E can get investigator

Follow up on Caird sending over atrocity
pics (to W H)

3 pts to be made
(1) extent to which it happened
greatly exaggerated — prove
fix &/or exagg

(2) backgrounds on all

(3) any the big delay

Lets ✓ this Mike Wallace too — He's far left.

TOP
Secret

on  - phone fix
    - discredit witnesses
    -   "    Time & Life for using this
    - is def going to go after the fix angle?

    -  - For enemy, it's policy
       - For us, it's a breach of policy

No.          - get right companies with us. Salvator
(say Sal tells      should help finance — get pics in
for much to        his hands
get into this)

WHITE HOUSE

ASHINGTON

December 17, 1969

SECRET

MEMORANDUM FOR:     THE PRESIDENT

FROM:               ALEXANDER P. BUTTERFIELD

RE:                 Ronald Lee Ridenhour (And Other
                    Information re My Lai)

The attachment to this memorandum responds to your request for a
report on Ridenhour. It is the first of two which were due in my
hands last week. The other should reach me no later than December
18th ... and whatever is new will be passed on to you without
delay.

In addition to the specific matter of Ridenhour, you will be interested
in the following items relative to our earlier talk:

--  An investigator was provided by John Ehrlichman. The
    man was given a clear set of guidelines and sent into
    the field where he remains today. A summation of his
    reports will be the subject of a near-future memorandum.

--  Bryce Harlow and Lyn Nofziger put their heads together
    and came up with Senator Fannin as the "right man to
    tackle this job". Eddie Hebert was their second choice
    but, as you know, he was recently given the My Lai
    project within Congressman Rivers' investigation sub-
    committee. (I'm not familiar with their reasons for not
    selecting Peter Dominick.)

--  Senator Fannin has been provided all of the documents which,
    by instruction, I made available to the Vice President on
    December 3rd and 4th ... i.e. with the exception of Mel
    Laird's personal September 3rd memorandum to you.
    Those things are:

        -   A chronology of My Lai press coverage and
            information as to how the stories were handled.

SECRET

SECR

- Atrocity photos (12 taken in Hue and 53 taken elsewhere).

- 8 fact sheets, news releases, and other documents concerning the Hue atrocities.

-- Lyn Nofziger claims that Henry Salvatore should not be counted on as a financial backer for this project in that he (Salvatore) would "never be able to keep his mouth shut".

-- Ron Haeberle, a former Army Sergeant and combat photographer, admits that he appeared more than once before civic meetings in the Cleveland area showing color slides of alleged My Lai atrocities. Following the break of the My Lai incident in the news, he took the photos to a college friend named Joseph Eszterhas, a Cleveland Plain Dealer reporter, and on November 20th they flew together to New York City where, in room 801 of the Gotham Hotel, they invited bids from the communications media for 18 of the "more revealing color slides."

-- Seymour Hersh, the 32-year-old former McCarthy campaign press secretary, received a $1,000 grant to pursue development of the My Lai story. The grant came from the Edgar B. Stern Family Fund which is clearly left-wing and anti-Administration.

-- The Edgar B. Stern Family Fund was founded in 1936 in New Orleans by Edith Rosenwold Stern and Edgar B. Stern as a non-profit educational fund. Its present location is at 21 East 40th Street, Manhattan, and a Mr. David R. Hunter serves as Executive Director. The fund is known to have supported organizations engaged in extremist activities. In 1964 it made a grant of $4,849 to the then infant SDS ... in connection with an Appalachian conference of SDS leaders. In 1965 it gave $32,500 to the League for Industrial Democracy, a group identified with militant left-wing civil rights endeavors. In 1968 it was ascertained that the Stern foundation was promoting dissatisfaction among migrant workers in the King Ranch area of Texas. Additionally, Mrs. Edgar B. Stern, currently a Vice President of the foundation, is known to be a sister of the first wife of Alfred K. Stern who fled this country as a spy in the 1950s and accepted asylum behind the Iron Curtain.

2

SECRET

S̲.̲ ̲ ̲ ̲T̲

-- F. Lee Bailey ha___ ___n made aware of the fact that he is welcome to call ___ ___me at DoD and that officials there will not only "p__ __ll" but also give thought to additional ways of furthe_in_ _is objectives.

-- Several persons, __ their public statements, have helped to cast some doubts as to the validity of Ridenhour's story . . . . e.g. Congressman Rivers, Congressman Hebert, Congressman Ichord, Captain Medina, etc. Moreover, SVN's Senator Don reported that "no bodies of alleged massacre victims have been found in or around the My Lai area," and little credence is being given to the "massacre event" in that country.

-- The investigator is now in the Cleveland area gathering data on Haeberle.

-- Our current aim is to compile discreet investigative reports on Ridenhour, Haeberle, Hersh, Meadlo, the Edgar B. Stern Family Fund, and the Dispatch News Service (to include a run-down on its present editor, 22-year-old David Obst).

-- We believe now that the emphasis should be on:

- Putting a good lawyer in touch with Ridenhour, with instructions to make the most of Ridenhour's "bitter feeling" toward Hersh.

- The activities of Hersh and the Edgar B. Stern Family Fund.

I will keep you abreast of developments.

3

SECRET

SUBJECT:   DISCREET INTERVIEW OF RONALD LEE RIDENHOUR
           ON DECEMBER 4, 1969 AT CLAREMONT COLLEGE,
           CALIFORNIA

On December 4, 1969, Ronald Lee Ridenhour, principal in the release
of the My Lai massacre story, was discreetly interviewed by a confidential investigator posing as a news reporter. The purpose of the
interview was to ascertain:

--   The extent to which Ridenhour is aligned with left-wing
     elements.

--   The depth or degree of any relationship between Ridenhour
     and Mr. Seymour Hersh, the apparent driving force behind
     the non-government release of alleged massacre information.

Ridenhour was open and candid with respect to questions concerning
his possible left-wing affiliations. He admitted that he had been
approached by moratorium leaders on the Claremont campus following the publicity given to his letters to government officials. He
stated these campus leaders hoped to promote him as a front and
leader for a movement to take left-wing advantage of the My Lai
massacre. Ridenhour advised that he had no interest whatever in
such proposals and that he was not in sympathy with moratorium
aims. He said his letters were written solely as a matter of conscience and that his intention was to correct whatever wrongs might
have been committed.

Equally discreet interviews of several students and faculty members
at Claremont Men's College essentially supported Ridenhour's statements. It was ascertained that he actively participated as a defensive
tackle on the school's football team and that he has not, since his
enrollment on September 1st, been absent from class or otherwise
away from school. Two leftist leaders on campus were interviewed
also, and they referred to Ridenhour with derision, presumably
because of his lack of sympathy with, and non-participation in,
their activities.

SECRET

SECRET

Ridenhour made a series of startling charges against Seymour Hersh.
He stated that Hersh flew out to interview him on or about November 20.
He had not known Hersh prior to that interview. He said that Hersh
implied that he (Hersh) was a Washington "government official". He
realizes now, of course, that Hersh is not with the government, but
his distinct impression at the time of the interview was that he very
definitely was. Having been interviewed previously by military
investigators, Ridenhour did not feel that Hersh's coming to him (as
a government official) was at all unusual. Ridenhour stated that he
"innocently" supplied Hersh with the names of G.I.'s whom "he had
heard" were participants or witnesses to the alleged massacre. One
of these names provided Hersh was Paul Meadlo.

Ridenhour was very upset by Hersh's subsequent (post-interview)
activities. He bitterly charged Hersh ("He's a no-good son of a
bitch.") with manipulating the story to make it appear that he
(Ridenhour) had conducted extensive interviews of alleged participants and witnesses. Ridenhour was particularly incensed by the fact
that Hersh had realized financial gain at his expense. He said he was
hurt and embarrassed by the whole affair, and he asked the confidential
source if he could supply a lawyer "to help him bring suit against Hersh."
No promise was made to this request, but the door was left open.

Miscellaneous Information:

-- Admits he did not get along well in the service .... "I'm one
   of those guys who question orders."

-- Born in California in 1946 .... single and never married.

-- Vietnam veteran.

-- Parents reside in Phoenix, Arizona.

SECRET

MEMORANDUM

**THE WHITE HOUSE**
WASHINGTON

CONFIDENTIAL                        January 14, 1970

MEMORANDUM FOR ALEX BUTTERFIELD

The President would like you to check to find out who the
woman is in the EOB who has the two Kennedy pictures.
What's her background ... is she new, old, someone we
can trust, etc.  Please get a report back to me on this
quickly.

Thank you.

H

H. R. HALDEMAN

*This has now delayed —
nearly a month
And he asks about
it once a week —
at least.*

January 16, 1970


MEMORANDUM FOR:       MR. HALDEMAN

FROM:                 ALEXANDER P. BUTTERFIELD

RE:                   Pictures in the EOB


I have just received your January 14th memorandum concerning pictures
in the EOB ... and my delay (for nearly a month) in getting certain information back to the President.

I remember precisely what the President said when he spoke to me about
this and there was no request for a report back -- only a clear directive
that action be taken.  Whereas I am not in the habit of dragging my feet
over (especially on a matter of expressed priority interest to you or the
President) I did in this case adhere to the President's word of caution
that a sweeping order to bring down all pictures of past Presidents --
coming on the heels of his December 24th "walk-through" -- might well
be taken as "Presidentially-directed".

There are 2 parts to the project: (1)  Discreetly institute the proper
"picture policy" ... and ensure that its merits (indeed its justification)
are clearly understood by all personnel in the Executive Office of the
President, especially GS employees on the White House Support Staff;
and (2)  Assign one of our own people to every support office, or in some
other way set up a system which will ensure across-the-board loyalty of
White House Support Staff personnel .... even if it is necessary to "abolish
all offices and start over from scratch."  The first half of the project --
admittedly the easiest half -- was begun with my own "walk-through" the
EOB offices on January 1st, less than 48 hours after the President's
departure for San Clemente.  It was completed on January 14th, just 13
days later.  The second half of the project is just beginning -- and will not
be done overnight.  I am looking at personnel files now, and when I finish
I will recommend to you 1 or 2 possible courses of action .... that is,
unless you want to stay out of it entirely and give me a full rein.

Finally, let me say that it was only this past Tuesday when I first
learned from you that the President was asking for a progress report
on this subject.  On Wednesday I reported to you by memorandum that
I would have a rundown for you today (January 16th).  In that I did not
hear from you, I assumed that schedule was satisfactory; then came
your note expressing impatience, itself delayed by a day and a half.

A written report to the President is attached.


Attachment

January 16, 1970

MEMORANDUM FOR:    THE PRESIDENT

FROM:              ALEXANDER P. BUTTERFIELD

RE:                Sanitization of the EOB

Recalling your word of caution to me that a sweeping order to take down from EOB walls all pictures of past Presidents -- coming on the heels of your December 24th walk-through -- might well be taken as "Presidentially-directed", I did not move on this project until after your departure for San Clemente. However, on New Year's day I made my own inspection of EOB offices occupied by White House Support Staff personnel and less than a week later spoke to Bill Hopkins about general policy on the matter, his views, etc. I couched my pitch to Hopkins in terms of my surprise discovery ... i.e. learning that civilian government employees, unlike military personnel, do on occasion display pictures of past commanders or commanders-in-chief on (Federal) office walls. I took time to elaborate on the fact that the taking down of pictures of former chiefs, in offices or other official business environments, is only a gesture of common courtesy to new chiefs -- a gesture of "pledged loyalty" ... with no disrespect whatever intended for those who have served and moved on. Bill Hopkins knew all of this, of course, so was naturally understanding of the position I was taking. I asked him to make a detailed check (not telling him of my earlier check) ... which he did prior to your return to Washington. Here is a recapitulation of results:

-- Of 35 large and small offices occupied by White House Support Staff personnel, 6 displayed photographs of one or more former Presidents ... in addition to your own.

-- 27 offices (including the 6 mentioned above) displayed your picture.

-- 8 offices displayed no pictures of U.S. Presidents.

-- The office which you mentioned to me specifically -- the one
   in which you noticed 2 pictures of President Kennedy -- is
   supervised by Edna Rosenberg, a civil servant at the GS-9
   level, who has the distinction of having served on the White
   House Staff longer than anyone else .... 41 years this coming
   March 7th. I have checked her file very carefully and found
   that the House Committee on Un-American Activities, the
   Civil Service Commission's Bureau of Personnel Investigation, the State Department and its Passport Office, the CIA,
   the Secret Service, and the FBI have all rendered continual
   reports to the effect that she is a "completely loyal American
   whose character, reputation, and associations are above
   reproach." Born in 1902 here in Washington, D.C., she
   has remained single all of these years, and lives now with a
   sister (Miss Janette Rosenberg) in Silver Spring, Maryland.

   — One of the Kennedy pictures bore a personal
      inscription of good wishes to the personnel of
      that office, and undoubtedly for that reason had
      been retained and displayed by those who work
      there.

-- Using to best advantage the fact that your new official photographs have just been printed and made accessible to Federal
   offices and employees, I instructed Bill Hopkins to see to it
   that every office supervisor received one and in the process
   of hanging it on the wall took all others down ... "in accordance
   with normal policy".

-- On January 14th the project was completed and all 35 offices
   displayed only your photograph.

The second half of this project -- i.e. to ensure across-the-board
loyalty of all White House Support Staff personnel even if we find it
necessary to "abolish current office arrangements and start over
from scratch" -- is underway; but I cannot yet report results. I
am in the process of screening personnel records and within 2-3
days will be ready to suggest possible courses of action to Bob
Haldeman.

MEMORANDUM

### THE WHITE HOUSE
#### WASHINGTON

November 13, 1970

MEMORANDUM FOR:      MR. BUTTERFIELD

RE:      Church Services

The President has said that he would like to have church every
other Sunday during the winter period.    Obviously, the schedule
will not work out to the every other Sunday sequence.    However,
we will be having church on a rather frequent basis.

The basic purpose will be to use it as a political opportunity.    We
should invite potential candidates, finance people, new GOP-type
leaders from around the country, those people from the eastern
and southern portions of the United States who would find it easy to
come in to town for a church service and our other friends.

We will try to lock in the church dates as far in advance as possible.
This is just to alert you to the President's current thinking.

The President also feels that we should have guest lists developed so
that once a church service is decided upon, we can go forth with the
invitations with what few alterations might be necessary due to
instructions from him.

H. R. HALDEMAN

MEMORANDUM

**THE WHITE HOUSE**
WASHINGTON

November 23, 1970

MEMORANDUM FOR :               MR. BUTTERFIELD
                               MR. COLSON

Attached you will find a newspaper clipping from the New York
Daily News which takes on our partisan use of the White House
Church Services.

*Dems &
others on the
"other side" to
Worship Services*

We should, instead be using these services as an opportunity
to be nice to our enemies--and their families--as well as to
reward our friends.

Please be sure we always include Democrats and others known
to be non-supporters of the Administration--but not to outright
opponents.

*H.*

H. R. HALDEMAN

Attachment

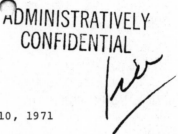

THE WHITE HOUSE

WASHINGTON

ADMINISTRATIVELY
CONFIDENTIAL

August 10, 1971

MEMORANDUM FOR:     ALEX BUTTERFIELD

FROM:               H. R. HALDEMAN

It's absolutely imperative that it clearly be
understood by all concerned that Edward B. Fiske,
the Religion Editor of the New York Times, is not
to be invited to any White House Church Services
again in the future under any circumstances
whatsoever.

### THE WHITE HOUSE

WASHINGTON

August 19, 1971

MEMORANDUM FOR:                    ALEX BUTTERFIELD

FROM:                              H. R. HALDEMAN *H.*

Please be sure that we are enforcing the regulation
that invitations to the press for White House Church
Services are on a totally controlled basis and handled
by invitation.  There should be no press pool or any
general press admission to these services.

The New York Times and New York Post must never be
invited to these services.  No one from either of the
papers - at any time.

MEMORANDUM

THE WHITE HOUSE
WASHINGTON

February 22, 1971     CONFIDENTIAL

CONFIDENTIAL

MEMORANDUM FOR:        ALEX BUTTERFIELD

FROM:                  H. R. HALDEMAN

For the time being, hold up on Arthur Burns on any social
invitations, just keep him off the list for a little while.
Check with me in three or four weeks to see if he should be
put back on for something or other.  In the meantime keep
him off of Church, etc.

CONFIDENTIAL

See Al Haig

———————

(1) Too often says that he absolutely _must_ get in to
see the President. Frequently not all
as urgent as K intimated, or stated.

Like the boy who cried "Wolf"

Presidential statement (Aug 7) re ME. ceasefire ex. of
President's current reaction — + attitude

(2) Enters President's office w/o checking. President may
have sent for Henry, but Henry must
check with Bull's office before going in.
The President could be on the phone — etc.

(3) Late to meetings in the President's office — mtgs
in which he is to participate, etc

(4) Slow to respond when called at odd time of day —
unusually slow.  Ex 1.  20 min + 3 phone calls
                       Ex 2.  22 min + 7 phone calls

(5) Imprecise re amount of time he needs.  2 minutes
develops into 20 minutes.  He should
state time needed + try harder to follow
that lead. Entire day's schedule is affected.

(6) Briefing papers: (1) timely submission ; (2) more accurate re participants ; (3) address news &/or photo plan

MEMORANDUM

**THE WHITE HOUSE**

WASHINGTON

*lucy*

**CONFIDENTIAL**/EYES ONLY

February 9, 1971

MEMORANDUM FOR:        ALEX BUTTERFIELD

FROM:        H. R. HALDEMAN  *H.*

In seating at State Dinners, the President feels that
Henry should not always be put next to the most
glamorous woman present.  He should be put by an
intelligent and interesting dinner partner and we should
shift from the practice of putting him by the best looking
one.  It's starting to cause unfavorable talk that serves
no useful purpose.

*Relayed to Lucy personally*

UNITED STATES COURT OF APPEALS
WASHINGTON, D. C. 20001

THE PRESIDENT HAS SEEN.
MAY 8 1969

CHAMBERS OF
WARREN E. BURGER

Dear Mr Erlichman
          Here is a letter
which I wish you would
hand to the President. I
am willing to risk
annoying him for
what I consider is important
to the Country - and to
him.
                    Cordially
                    WEB

WARREN E. BURGER
3111 NORTH ROCHESTER STREET
ARLINGTON, VIRGINIA

May 8, 1969


Dear Mr. President:

I had thought to write you Tuesday on what seemed
to me an unwise course followed by some in contrast
with the carefully correct course you followed in the
Fortas matter. I wish now I had expressed my views
promptly, for as a member of the Judiciary, I conclude
I have a right to do so on a matter so significantly
involving the courts. The developments since Monday -
and particularly the utterances from members of the
Congress - are, in my view, very damaging to the country,
the courts generally and potentially to you.

This week is a time for Republican leaders to "view
with dismay" and to "be saddened" and "disturbed" but
largely silent. They should not "attack." First there
is the matter of basic fairness. Second there are
political consequences which will have an impact on the
courts and the Supreme Court in particular and especially on the first nomination you send to the Senate.

As to basic fairness: if the facts condemn the
conduct of a Supreme Court Justice then let the facts
do it in their own good time. If the facts do not
warrant condemnation then oratory ought not destroy
what the facts cannot. Oratory such as most of that
emitted on the Hill tends to obscure the facts and
their significance.

As to political consequences: first the public,
which is so often more correct than its leaders, may
well resent "prejudgment"; second the 1968 Senate
supporters of Fortas for Chief Justice have really
nothing to say now but they should be left in the center
of the stage and not pushed aside by others. At the
present rate of oratory they are forgotten but they
are bound to be bitter over the harsh attacks - including

WARREN E. BURGER
3111 NORTH ROCHESTER STREET
ARLINGTON, VIRGINIA

- 2 -

the curiously and surprisingly hasty condemnation
by the Washington POST.  As a consequence when your
first nomination goes to the Senate, this suppressed
rage will likely assert itself and your nominee may
become their "whipping boy."  That in turn will
exacerbate the distressing situation in which the Court
now finds itself;  it will be very damaging to the
country and it may be bad for your objective of restoring the Court to its former high standing.

      I hope that someone will point out, gently but
firmly, that the American system gives every man the
benefit of the presumption of innocence in the face
of any charge and that everyone should suspend judgment.  Time, then, - and the facts - will carry this
crisis of the Court to its inevitable conclusion.

                          Cordially,

The President
The White House

Supreme Court of the United States
Washington, D. C. 20543

CHAMBERS OF
THE CHIEF JUSTICE                    May 10, 1971

Dear Mr. President:

    I was tempted to phone you Saturday night after
the dinner but feared I might disturb your household.
Your fortitude and forbearance in the face of gross
rudeness by your hosts will always have my unbounded
admiration.  In my many personal observations of the
press corps over the past 18 years this was one of their
worst performances.  To respond as you did with dignity
and charity is a mark of your qualities and I suspect it
was not lost on all those present.

    It is no comfort but it is perhaps instructive to
remember how the press treated your predecessors,
and particularly Washington and Lincoln.  Having been
reading closely some of the events from 1789 to 1800,
fairness to the present day press corps compels ac-
knowledgment that they are now slightly less savage,
less sadistic and less cruel than 150 to 200 years ago.
So viewed, this is progress of sorts.

    I repeat that Saturday night marked a new
measure of your capacities that will in time be recognized, and enlarged my respect and esteem.

Sincerely,

Warren E. Burger

The President

    The White House

Supreme Court of the United States
Washington, D. C. 20543

CHAMBERS OF
THE CHIEF JUSTICE                    August 5, 1972

CONFIDENTIAL

Dear Mr. Haldeman:

I write you with some reluctance to clarify the matter of security transportation when I travel by air.

Shortly after I took office in 1969 the President inquired about what security measures were provided for me. I advised him that the security of our building was very high; that we lived in an isolated place and had random, periodic checks on the house by local police arranged by Edgar Hoover who was concerned about the risks. We subsequently had my driver commissioned as a Deputy United States Marshal.

At the time of this conversation the President urged me to take nothing for granted on security measures and to especially avoid use of commercial airlines. He was aware, as I was, that since the advent of "skyjacking" Earl Warren, at the direction of Presidents Kennedy and Johnson, had been provided with Air Force facilities, including travel overseas. He said my office should work the air travel with your office.

Subsequently this was done and General Hughes, at your direction, I assume, provided transportation on three occasions since 1969. Because I was reluctant to call for this service I have traveled by train or car whenever possible and have severely limited all travel.

When I went to London last July for the American Bar Association meeting and in February 1972 to London for another important meeting, I used commercial transport with special checks on passengers under the direction of the FBI and the U.S. Marshal. I preferred not to ask overseas facilities, although on one trip I was able to "hitchhike" on a military flight.

Some months ago my staff routinely requested transportation to San Francisco for the August American Bar Association meeting. At the same time I requested transportation to Europe but only on a "space available" basis on a regular Air Force flight between August 20-25. The trip to Europe was to attend the International Bar Association Conference. Both the President and the Secretary of State urged me to attend that gathering.

- 2 -

Meanwhile a new White House transportation officer has been dealing with the matter and reported that no flights were available August 20-25 to Europe and I cancelled that engagement.

My appearance at the ABA in San Francisco, however, is a regularly scheduled annual event and I must attend. However, General Scowcroft advised that some arrangement must be made to reimburse the Defense Department. Having gone over this ground with General Hughes several years ago, we advised General Scowcroft that the Supreme Court has no budget provision of the proportions called for by Air Force rates. The suggestion was made that the cost be charged to the Justice Department, which I am unwilling to do. I cannot be placed in that position with the principal litigants in the Federal courts. Neither am I willing to be placed in the position of a supplicant asking for a "favor" since it is distinctly not my idea that I have government transportation. I therefore directed my office to advise General Scowcroft yesterday to cancel all plans for Air Force transportation to San Francisco and return and to make no further requests hereafter.

I write you at this unfortunate length so that you will have the whole picture and will understand that I am not voluntarily disregarding the President's request that I avoid commercial air flights.

I repeat that I regret to burden you with this matter but in light of the pattern established by Presidents Kennedy and Johnson and the request of President Nixon in 1969, I feel I must clarify the record. I want it to be clear that I am not ignoring the strong request of the President.

Cordially,

Honorable H. R. Haldeman
Assistant to the President
The White House
Washington, D.C. 20500

MEMORANDUM

THE WHITE HOUSE

WASHINGTON

EYES ONLY                              June 20, 1972


MEMORANDUM FOR:     H. R. HALDEMAN

FROM:               AL HAIG

Here are my views and accompanying analysis on the four points raised
in your memorandum of June 12:

    1.  What should the President's posture be between the
        Conventions?

       Unquestionably the events between now and the Democratic Conven-
tion and most importantly events at the Convention itself will influence the
ultimate strategy on the President's posture.  Nevertheless at this juncture
it is quite evident that the President is in a very strong position which is
best retained and reinforced  by maintaining a posture which is totally
consistent with the achievements that have most decisively contributed to
his popularity.  These achievements are a solid statesman-like performance
in the international area.  They have been premised on flexible and progressive
attitudes and the willingness to take risks in search of world peace and were
masterfully combined with: (a) strength and decisiveness when U. S. interests
are challenged; (b) the retention of initiative and momentum which has
consistently enabled the President to stay ahead of the pessimism normally
associated with stagnation, inactivity and lack of imagination; (c) the
solidification of the world statesman role through which the President has
captured national empathy based on his masterful performances in Peking
and Moscow which were well-covered on national television; and (d) the
development of a "Mr. & Mrs." team image which would not have been
possible had total emphasis been on the President alone.

       Based on the foregoing, the President's posture should be one of
a statesman who is above the frantic gut-fighting and politicking of the
campaign, whose strength and competence is taken fully for granted by a
Party machine whose major task should be to engage in the cool organizational arrangements which are designed to exploit a solid posture of
accomplishment.

       I sense one possible distortion creeping into current assumptions
about the Democratic candidate.  Many of our political strategists are
taking for granted that McGovern will emerge as the Democratic candidate.

EYES ONLY

This was evident in the strategy discussions held in last week's Cabinet meeting. We must be prepared for an emotional convention consensus in favor of Teddy Kennedy. It is difficult to conceive of the old Democratic Party machinery, which relies essentially on a power base of Labor, Jewish money and nouveau riche resources, merging to support a candidate of McGovern's ilk since each of these sources of power could be seriously threatened by his stated policies. For this reason our contingency planning must not overlook the possibility of a surprise popular surge in July which would settle on Kennedy as the only hope for the Democratic Party.

2. What should the President's posture be from the Republican Convention to the election? When should he start campaigning? How much travel should he do, where should he go, what type of activities should he engage in?

Following the Republican Convention in August and taking full cognizance of events between the Democratic and Republican Conventions, I think the President should pursue a strategy totally consistent with that of a self-confident, competent statesman who is above frantic political campaigning. This means that his travel and public appearances should be most carefully contrived. Above all, they should be paced to avoid over-exposure in the national media, especially television. I do not believe we should succumb to a strategy which would portray him rushing from one adulatory situation to another. Rather, these should be carefully paced and only those which can guarantee maximum effect should be undertaken. That should involve exposure situations which underline the President's attention to the affairs of state and which avoid any appearances of contrived ballyhoo. In my view the greatest danger will be over-exposure and excessive campaign energy.

3. Any general thoughts you have as to strategy for the campaign on issues, timing, points of attack, etc.

Obviously McGovern is our most vulnerable opponent. We should therefore be very careful about adopting too strong an anti-McGovern posture between now and the Democratic Convention. The one theme which I believe is best stressed between now and the Democratic Convention is McGovern's irresponsible posture on the war in Vietnam in which we emphasize the fact that he is pushing a strategy which can only encourage the enemy not to negotiate and which in many respects is less stringent on Hanoi than even Moscow and Peking contemplate. Concurrently, we should prepare, but not use, a host of themes which attack McGovern's strategy on domestic spending, inheritance, welfare programs, busing, aid to schools, national defense, etc., that can be used following the

-3-

Republican Convention in August.  The most important aspect of our anti-
McGovern strategy should be to keep the homerun  balls to the last phase
of the campaign in a way which ensures that the President peaks off in
the last three weeks of October.  Television will dominate this year more
than in any campaign in the past and it is conceivable that national attitudes
can be influenced at the last moment in an overriding way.  We should also
have themes in reserve which can be used on a contingency basis to counter-
balance bad news for us  which is bound to occur in unforeseen patterns
between now and November.  A compulsive tendency to exploit McGovern
vulnerability from the outset should be tightly controlled to ensure that we
do not end up on a wave of criticism against the Republican Party and most
importantly that we are able to quickly adjust to unforeseen setbacks which
can come from scandle, setbacks in the international environment, or
domestic shortcomings.  To ensure this is done, a most careful analysis
should be made of all McGovern vulnerabilities, a program should be
tailored to exploit each of these then the exploitation program should be
tightly time-phased to ensure continuing and growing momentum rather
than to fire all of our shots simultaneously thus enabling the Democrats to
develop compensatory neutralization programs.

    **4.**  Your thoughts as to what the opposition strategy will be
        and how we should meet it.

    In the international area the Democrats will probably exploit the
following:

    **(a)**  The war in Vietnam, bombing of North Vietnam, mining, etc.
The only sound way to attack this is to keep constantly in the forefront
Hanoi's intransigence and the solid pace of accomplishment represented by
our continuing _ disengagement.  It is obvious that we will have to get some
break between now and November which will confirm the wisdom of our
policy.  I am somewhat optimistic that this will occur and the question will
therefore become moot.

    **(b)**  The Democrats will try to exploit the inadequacy of the SALT
agreement with the Soviet Union by stressing the theme that the President
has favored an agreement which replaces a quantitative arms race by a
qualitative arms race.  This charge should be taken head on with straight
factual elaboration on the provisions of the agreement.

    **(c)**  The Democrats, if McGovern is the candidate, will obviously
try to exploit the President's image as a knee-jerk patriot who is hidebound
by outmoded conceptions of U. S. honor and power.  This attack is easily
blunted by a track record of accomplishments which should focus on the

Peking and Moscow Summits and a carefully paced follow-up program of improved relations with both the Soviets and Chinese. Barring no unforeseen setbacks, this kind of momentum is definitely in the cards and should be counted as a strong continuing asset.

(d) Perhaps the most serious danger area is that of international economics, balance of payments, lack of progress in the monetary stabilization and a growing unfavorable balance of trade. This area, I believe, affords the Democrats the most fruitful grist for criticism. We will need a careful assessment in the weeks ahead of where we are going with respect to international trade and economics and to develop some new initiatives which will flesh out the initial philosophical advantage that resulted from the international monetary agreement. We have a long way to go in the area and I doubt that statistics which can be easily drawn upon by the Democrats will confirm that we have not done more than scratch the surface. We should achieve some advantages from improved US-Soviet trade but more dramatic steps have to be taken with respect to our European and Japanese allies.

(e) Accomplishments in Latin America leave room for criticism but we should not overreact to a vulnerability which does not have a particularly strong popular base.

On the whole, the President's performance and accomplishments in the international area constitute his strong suit. For this reason his statesman and world leader role should be carefully but fully exploited.

THE WHITE HOUSE

WASHINGTON

September 7, 1972

Dear Al:

You and I know better than most people how important it is for
civilians who come to high office in our country's military establishment
to keep their hot hands out of the grade selection processes. But when
they don't, it's nice, I'm sure, to be one of those selected.

Actually, I've been on the speechless side since first hearing the
news and have wondered to myself when you're going to get off this
"outstanding officer" kick. I seem to have spent the better part of the
past three years writing you notes of congratulations on your ability to
hoodwink superiors. (Not that I don't enjoy it. I do ... I do; but I'm
running out of eloquence. )

You will recognize the attachments for what they are -- a copy of
the gen-u-ine original document and a simple fact sheet. The latter I
prepared with Brent Scowcroft's assistance to help Ron Ziegler through
the Q & A period which I felt certain would follow his announcement of
your caper. I doubt that he even read it, but you may find it of interest.
The little historical section puts you in very fine company, indeed -- and
while showing that this kind of promotion is not entirely unprecedented,
it makes clear to even the dumbest bastards that it doesn't exactly happen
every day.

In all seriousness, Al, I couldn't be more pleased for you and Pat.
The Vice Chief's slot and the four beanies that go with it are nothing more
than just rewards for your years of dedication and labor above and beyond,
and for your maintaining through it all a really perfect balance. I feel
good just knowing you.

Sincerely,

Alexander P. Butterfield
Deputy Assistant to the President

Enclosures

Major General Alexander M. Haig
Deputy Assistant to the President
    for National Security Affairs
The White House

June 10, 1969

PLEASE TREAT AS CONFIDENTIAL

MEMORANDUM FOR:      MR. EHRLICHMAN

The President read in a recent news summary that many of his
critics complain about the Administration's not being "as open
as promised." His only comment, addressed to you, appears
below:

> "John -- Tell Herb and Ron to ignore this kind
> of criticism.  The fact of the matter is that we
> are far too open.  If we treat the press with a
> little more contempt we'll probably get better
> treatment."

ALEXANDER P. BUTTERFIELD

cc:  Mr. Klein
     Mr. Ziegler

PLEASE TREAT AS CONFIDENTIAL

MEMORANDUM

THE WHITE HOUSE
WASHINGTON
May 16, 1972

MEMORANDUM FOR:     MR. H. R. HALDEMAN

FROM:               ALEXANDER P. BUTTERFIELD

SUBJECT:            Notification of Wallace Shooting

You asked for particulars concerning my delay in getting word to
you about the attempt on Governor Wallace's life yesterday afternoon.
The answer, in a word, is that I had nothing but unconfirmed bits
and pieces of information until 2-3 minutes before you called me on
the telephone (4:19 or 4:20). Toni was at that moment typing a very
short paragraph of alleged facts which you were to receive ... before
anyone else (so help me!).

The sequence of events was almost precisely as indicated below:

-- 4:00 p.m. - Taylor was in my office meeting with me on
   matters unrelated to Governor Wallace.

-- 4:06 p.m. - Ron Pontius stuck his head in my office doorway
   to tell Bob (and me) that the Secret Service radio net had just
   been informed by the Maryland State Police that "there had
   been a shooting in the Wallace detail, and that they thought
   the principal was involved". Steve had just come to my office
   on other business and heard the report.

-- 4:07 p.m. - Taylor went to my phone and called the Secret
   Service command post to direct that all further news be
   relayed to him in my office ... "as it was received".
   I told Steve to go back to his office and to keep quiet until
   something was known about Wallace's involvement --
   and physical condition, if involved.

-- 4:11 p.m. - Steve called me on the IO to suggest his alerting
   Ray Price to the news and the possibility of the need rather
   quickly of a Presidential statement. I agreed, and Steve
   called Ray.

*First mistake*

- 2 -

-- 4:12 p.m. - Taylor received his second report (Pontius'
statement being the first). It came from the Secret Service
command post and confirmed that there was a shooting and
that Wallace was hit and then en route to Leland Memorial
Hospital in Riverdale, Maryland. We learned nothing at that
time about the seriousness of the Governor's condition.

-- 4:15 p.m. - Taylor's third report came in: "Wallace has
just arrived at the Holy Cross Hospital in Silver Spring.
Three others were hit during the shooting. The
assailant has been apprehended and is being held at the
Hyattsville police station."

-- 4:16 p.m. - I dictated to Toni what was fairly certain knowledge
up to that point. Exactly 10 minutes had transpired since
Pontius' interruption of our meeting.

-- 4:19 p.m. (approx.) - You called me and I told you all that
I knew, including the fact that Price had been alerted.
I mentioned, too, that I was purposely withholding distribution
of news items being given to me pending their confirmation --
and that I had no intention of notifying the President, at least
until his meeting with Kendall and Flanigan concluded. You
sounded as though you approved.

*Right*

Again, your call preceded by only a few minutes -- as long as it
was going to take Toni to type an 8-line paragraph -- my hand
carrying a note to your office. Every action that I took was premeditated.


cc: Mr. Stephen B. Bull

*Would appreciate immediate notification
in the future — even if unconfirmed.
— and no notice to others until
we decide on a procedure.*

April 10, 1969

MEMORANDUM FOR:     MR. EHRLICHMAN

Subject:   Notes from the President (Action item)

The President would like for you to get together with the 5 o'clock group
and come up with a way to put EMK "squarely on the spot".  (For example,
he favors student demonstrations yet opposes actions intended to deal
with them.)

Additionally, the President wants the 5 o'clock group to see to it that
Teddy's support of all-out integration and bussing is widely publicized.


                                        ALEXANDER P. BUTTERFIELD


cc:  Mr. Keogh

MEMORANDUM

## THE WHITE HOUSE

WASHINGTON

### April 12, 1969

MEMORANDUM FOR:     MR. EHRLICHMAN

Subject: Note from the President  (Action Item)

An article in the latest issue of the "New Republic" discusses
the recent hearings on the Office of Federal Contract Compliance
and contrasts Senator Dirksen's "clowning performance" with
Ted Kennedy's "cool and clever handling" of both himself and
the situation.  The article's author, TRB (Dick Strout), goes
so far as to say (about Kennedy), "If we had been political scouts,
and had never heard of his brothers, we'd have made note of him."

The President suggests that you and the 5 o'clock group get
something out on how "very amateurish" Teddy was when he
(the President) briefed the leaders on the Safeguard System.

ALEXANDER P. BUTTERFIELD

cc: Mr. Keogh
    Mr. Klein

**CENTRAL INTELLIGENCE AGENCY**
WASHINGTON, D.C. 20505

*OFFICE OF THE DIRECTOR*

24 March 1972

MEMORANDUM FOR:   The President

Herewith are copies of two memoranda which I have
sent to Secretary Rogers. I would not trouble you with
this material if it were not for the fact that I have just
learned the Secretary will not be back in Washington until
late Monday. If this information is to be useful to you
in your talk with King Husayn on Tuesday morning, I thought
it should be in your hands well in advance.

You will recall that early in this Administration,
you told me to deal solely with the Secretary on this
issue of secret Israel/Jordan contacts. This I have done
on all reports originating with the Jordanian side. As
for the brief, recent accounts of the secret meetings
from the Israelis, these have been sent to you via
Dr. Kissinger at their request.

For the foregoing reasons I am sending these two
memoranda directly to you. No one on the White House
staff has seen them or is familiar with their content.

Richard Helms
Director

Enclosures - 2

23 March 1972


MEMORANDUM FOR:   The Secretary of State

SUBJECT:          Secret Israel-Jordan Negotiations


  .1.   Enclosed, as Attachment A, is an account of
a secret meeting between King Husayn and Prime Minister
Golda Meir held on 21 March 1972.  Both parties were
more specific in the presentation of their respective
positions than in previous meetings.  This served
mainly to highlight the extremely wide gap between
their positions.

  2.   In sum, Mrs. Meir rejected the Rogers' plan,
the Jarring mission, and the plan which the King presented.  She declared Jerusalem non-negotiable and
offered the Allon Plan as the maximum concession for
the West Bank.  The King declared these unacceptable.
But both agreed to continue their contacts and the
Israelis will prepare a written statement of "principles and designs" for a settlement at the next meeting.

  3.   In a personal post-mortem of this meeting
with Mrs. Meir, the King said he was now convinced
that basically Israel does not intend to give up one
inch of the West Bank and that his UAK proposal has
almost forced the Israelis to take a public stand on
the retention of the West Bank as a matter of national
policy.  He said he was further convinced that although
some of his remarks during the meeting evoked what
appeared to be a favorable reaction from some of the
other Israelis, as long as Mrs. Meir is in power no
settlement is possible.  Regarding Mrs. Meir's claim

SECRET/SENSITIVE

that peace can only be achieved through direct
negotiations, the King observed ironically that
there have now been approximately fifty meetings
between Israel and Jordan and the parties are still
at "square one".

4.  The King said he intended to discuss his
series of contacts with Mrs. Meir during his meeting
with the President and would seriously welcome any
views the President might have to offer.

N.B. ||

Richard Helms
Director

Attachments - 2

2

SECRET/SENSITIVE

PERSPECTIVE

Attachment A

Subsequent to Prime Minister Golda Meir's abrupt cancellation of the scheduled 16 March meeting between herself and King Husayn as a form of protest against the King's announced plan for a United Arab Kingdom, and the King's request that Mrs. Meir reconsider her position, Mrs. Meir sent a cordial reply requesting a rescheduled meeting on 21 March. This meeting took place, attended on the Jordan side by the King and his chief political advisor, Zayd Rafai, and on the Israeli side by Mrs. Meir, General Zamir, the Chief of Israeli External Intelligence Service, General Yariv, Director of Military Intelligence, Brigadier Eilot, Military Secretary to the Prime Minister, and Simcha Dinitz, political advisor to the Prime Minister. The following is a chronology of the highlights of their meeting:

King Husayn. Opened meeting by explaining his reasons for proposing a reconstitution of Jordan as the United Arab Kingdom (UAK). The King said that in making this proposal he had no intention of deceiving Mrs. Meir. He considered the UAK an internal plan affecting all of the people of Jordan which he viewed as a blueprint for the future. The King said he was sorry he had to announce the plan before he had discussed it with Mrs. Meir, but pointed out that he had advised her of it before he had informed the Arab chiefs of state.

Mrs. Meir. Replied she was sorry this had happened and was shocked when she heard the content of the King's announcement; her colleagues were even more shocked. She noted that Israel was not even mentioned in the proposal and that, by her interpretation, the plan would lead to the eventual liquidation of Israel. She added that it appeared to her the future border between the two states had already been decided unilaterally by Jordan.

"Is there going to be peace or not as a result
of the agreement between us?  Can Jordan sign
before, and independently of, the other Arab
states?  President Sadat is demanding pre-
conditions in any negotiations with Egypt.
Syria is impossible.  These are the principles
on which we are willing to negotiate:

   A)  Under no conditions will we return to
   the boundaries of 1967.

   B)  Secretary Rogers' proposals are totally
   unacceptable.  When Secretary Rogers visited
   Israel he told us not to call it the Rogers'
   Plan, but to call it the American Plan, since
   it was drawn up by the entire State Department.

   C)  Minor border rectifications are out of
   the question.  Changes in our borders must
   be major, something in the nature of the
   Allon Plan.

This is what we want and we will negotiate this.
Jerusalem must be a unified city, although Jordan
can control the Arab holy places.  Do you see
Jordan making peace?  Do you agree with the foregoing proposals, including the border changes?"

King Husayn.  "No!  We want peace.  The principles
of the UAK pertain to Jordanian people only.  As I
told you there are three possibilities for a
solution to our problem:

   A)  A return to the situation as it existed
   prior to 1967.

   B)  A complete separation and secession of
   the West Bank.

   C)  The establishment of the UAK, which I have
   proposed.

The latter is the only logical solution for our

2

people. We are now attempting to reorganize
ourselves and to persuade the silent majority
to say publicly what they have told me privately in support of this proposal. We are
also attempting to obtain support from Palestinian moderates living abroad. I did not mention
peace in disclosing my plan because the whole plan
is based on the premise of peace. We are now a
united people in Jordan and the UAK pertains to
our own internal situation. I did not specifically mention Israel, but you know that I recognize Israel and your problems. I am not talking
about any liberation by force. Regarding the
role of Israel, you are a partner in this plan.
The Palestinians are at the heart of the problem.
The assassination of our late Prime Minister was
a deliberate attempt to drive a wedge between the
two peoples of Jordan and we expect such actions
to continue. Does Israel intend to remain totally
isolated? I realize you are sensitive on the
question of Jerusalem. So are we. But put yourself in my position. What should I do? I want to
gather all the Palestinians together so that they
may shoulder responsibility for the development of
a peaceful and prosperous Jordan which can be the
foundation for enduring peace in the area."


Mrs. Meir. "We too feel duty bound to wage no wars.
No one wins in wars. We must change the borders in
order to provide us with the security we require
and from which we can destroy or neutralize the
plans and actions of would-be aggressors before
they can penetrate our home land. Our borders
with Lebanon are an example of the type we desire.
Such a border can be easily defended with Israel
suffering few casualties as has been the recent
case."


Zayd Rafai. "Would a demilitarized West Bank satisfy
Israel's requirements?"


3

Mrs. Meir. "No, it will not. Even the Allon
Plan is not entirely acceptable to my cabinet
but I can get it approved by popular referendum.
Why are the Palestinians now a problem?"

King Husayn. "In the past, the Palestinians were
not properly cared for or included in Jordan's
political life. This was a mistake which has to
be corrected as soon as possible. In view of your
comments, I do not see any point in presenting the
Jordanian plan which I have with me. I cannot
leave the Palestinians to stand alone, although
this might be possible later. I cannot tell my
people to give up Jerusalem. I can't tell my
people that their only link with the West Bank is
a narrow corridor. I will show you the Jordan
paper so that you may have an idea of our thinking."
[See attachment B]

Mrs. Meir. [After reading the Jordan paper] "You
really don't think we could accept this? The part
about Jerusalem sounds like a tale of horror which
I can't go into since Jerusalem is not up for discussion. As I said in the KNESSET, how you divide
Jordan is your business; but we will not go back
to the 1967 borders. I cannot give this paper to
my cabinet. In your earlier meetings with Foreign
Minister Eban and Jaacov Herzog, they presented
you with the Allon Plan and reported back to me
that this Plan was unacceptable to you. I did not
think it was categorically unacceptable to you,
but it appears I was mistaken. In view of this,
let us agree that we are not negotiating for peace
any more. The territorial aspects of your plan,
plus your position on Jerusalem, is unacceptable.
But this does not have to be the end. Everything
can remain as it is."

King Husayn. "Are you working for a Palestinian
entity?"

4

Mrs. Meir. "No. All will remain the same. You are young and can reach for the stars and you can be hopeful, but you must be realistic. Are you prepared to make arrangements for quiet cooperation? Are you prepared to:

    A) Keep Jordan out of any eastern front command?

    B) Not allow Syrian or Iraqi troops in Jordan?

    C) Keep the fedayeen out of Jordan?

    D) Continue cooperation with us on contingency planning as before?

This is the best we can do. Perhaps I was too optimistic, but I was disappointed in your UAK proposal. Will you make a small agreement with us?"

King Husayn. "Can't we work jointly to arrive at peace? Do you object to that?"

Mrs. Meir. "We can't accept your paper."

King Husayn. "I will continue to work on my plan for the UAK in order to bring the moderate Palestinians together and to isolate and possibly destroy Palestinian extremists.'

Mrs. Meir. "The West Bank is very quiet now. We will continue to keep it quiet. Nothing can be changed without peace."

King Husayn. "The question of the Palestinians has to be part of any efforts to achieve peace."

5

Mrs. Meir.  "I want to negotiate only with Jordan,
not with the Palestinians, and the question of
the Palestinians should not be brought up now.
Your plan for a UAK would only create a lot of
trouble.  The need for peace comes first and you
should not undertake any further steps before
reaching a peaceful agreement with Israel."

King Husayn.  "Do you have any strenuous objections
to my plan to isolate the extremist Palestinians
from the silent majority who have come, and are
continuing to come, to me in support of my call
for unity."

Mrs. Meir.  "I can't talk in generalities.  This
UAK plan is not acceptable.  How can you rally the
Palestinians to support your plan when you cannot
implement it?"

King Husayn.  "Are you rallying the Palestinians?"

Mrs. Meir.  "We haven't done it yet; we won't do it
tomorrow; but after five years, who knows?"

King Husayn.  "Our plan is to get the majority of
Palestinians, who are moderate, into one block in
order to isolate and destroy the extremists.  Do you
object?"

Mrs. Meir.  "Yes, you will create more extremists.
It is dangerous to call a people to a cause that
cannot be implemented."

King Husayn:  "When may we expect to receive your
plan for a peaceful settlement?"

6

Mrs. Meir. "The 1967 lines do not exist. If you accept this, then we can talk. We haven't decided yet how wide the corridor for a link-up between Jordan and the West Bank should be. Our positions are far apart."


King Husayn. "All right, we will take our paper back and await yours. This agreement does not mean that we should give up. I can't deceive my people. I either continue to work for peace or withdraw completely."


Mrs. Meir. "Fine, but if we can't agree on peace, can you accept these points in principle?"


Zayd Rafai. (Interrupting) "No peace, no guarantees."


Mrs. Meir. (Ignoring the interruption) "Can you see Jordan entering into a plan for waging war against us?"


King Husayn. "There will be no foreign troops on our soil in the immediate future. We will keep trying for peace."


Mrs. Meir. "Would Jordan join other groups to fight Israel?"


Zayd Rafai. "Jordan will only act in the best interest of Jordan."


Mrs. Meir. "Jordan never fought Israel alone. The Arabs are now preparing for war. We do not want Jordan to join them. You cannot be in two camps at once."


7

King Husayn.   "We always seem to find ourselves in the middle."

Mrs. Meir.   "We can't even seem to agree on this."

Zayd Rafai.   "Going back to your statement, Mrs. Meir, regarding Arab troops on Jordan soil, what did you mean?  No Arab troops forever?"

Mrs. Meir.   "I did not say forever.  I said for a long time to come."

King Husayn.   "There will be no Arab troops on Jordan soil for the future.  When do you intend to provide us with the Israeli plan for a settlement?"

Mrs. Meir.   "We will produce a plan outlining the principles and designs which we consider the basis for a settlement.  But one final word, Your Majesty, when you are in Washington the question of the Jarring negotiations is bound to come up.  Negotiations through Jarring will not lead to anything.  The only way we are going to reach a peaceful settlement is through direct negotiations.

The meeting broke up at this point after Rafai had retrieved all the copies of the Jordan plan.

8

( ⸺⸺⸺⸺⸺ )

Attachment B

General Remarks:

We believe that the problem of the Middle East can be solved only through political and peaceful means. We do not believe that war will solve any of the problems of any state in the area. There have already been three wars between Israel and Arab neighbors and nothing was settled by these wars. Their only achievement has been to introduce into the area chaos, anarchy, extremism, revolutions, and coup d'etats. They have opened the area wide to communist expansion. The resources and energies of the area, instead of being directed to the progress and development of its people, have been wasted on the purchase of tools of destruction. Only a just, honourable, and lasting peace can change this unfortunate state in which we find ourselves.

Security:

The kind of absolute security which Israel seeks does not exist in our age--the age of missiles and supersonic planes. At the moment Israel is the strongest militarily in the area; yet, this fact, plus her terri- torial expansion, has not provided her with the absolute security she speaks of. Security is relative. Perhaps Israel is now more secure than before June 1967, but all relative things change and the balance of power might one day in the future tip in Arab favour. Thus, security is not lines on maps, it is not rivers and canals, but rather the good will of neighbors living together in peace, accepting each other and willing to let each other live within recognized boundries, free from threats or acts of war. This is the type of security we seek for ourselves. We believe it is the type of security you also desire.

Our proposals for the establishment of a just, honourable and durable peace:

1. We believe that the basis for such a peace is the withdrawal of the Israeli forces from the occupied

West Bank of Jordan, including the Arab sector of Jerusalem. Since neither Israel nor Jordan has ever recognized the 1967 truce demarcations line as a permanent boundary and since we recognize that the line is not fit to be a permanent border--it divides villages into two and it separates villagers from their farming land, etc-- and since no border between Israel and Jordan has ever been recognized--with the exception of the 1947 partition line--we are prepared to enter into direct negotiations specifically aimed at the rectification of the June 5, 1967 line to transform it into a permanent boundary. In this, the guiding principle will be the non-acquisition of territory by force.

2. The West Bank will be demilitarized. No Jordanian or Israeli military forces will be stationed there, with the exception of the Jordanian forces essential for the maintenance of law and order.

3. No Arab troops will be stationed on the East Bank of Jordan.

4. The Palestinian people must be given the chance to exercise their right to repatriation or compensation. A certain percentage of them, to be agreed upon, should be allowed to return to their homes if they so choose. The remainder must be compensated for their losses and resettled in Jordan.

5. We are ready, willing, and able on the above basis, and with the adoption of our proposals for Jerusalem, which follow, to sign a peace treaty with Israel. This treaty will not only end the many years of war but will also normalize the relations between two states living together as peaceful neighbors.

Jerusalem:

Background: Following the six day war and as soon as the Israeli Army occupied the Jordan sector of Jerusalem, Knesset adopted on the 27th of June 1967, a law stipu- lating that the laws, jurisdiction, and administration of the state of Israel would apply to every region that would be designated by ordinance. The next day the

2

Israeli Government issued an ordinance according to which the Jordanian sector of the city, plus 100 square kilometers of the neighboring area, would constitute a region to which Israeli legislation would apply. On that same day, the Minister of Interior merged the Arab municipality of Jerusalem and the neighboring territory with the Israeli municipality. Even before the adoption of this legislation to annex the Arab city of Jerusalem, and as early as June 11, 1967, the Israeli authorities had demolished 135 homes. Israel went on to expropriate lands belonging to Arab owners and on August 30, 1970 nearly 1200 sections around the city were expropriated. Then came the accelerated construction of a ring of apartment buildings around Jerusalem which included 35,000 dwelling units for future immigrants. These facts show that the Israeli Government is pursuing a policy designed to integrate the Arab city totally and permanently with an administratively unified Jerusalem. No one can contest the fact that such measures might soon lead to an irreversible situation. This, if it happens, will irrecoverably jeopardize any hope for a peaceful settlement.

Proposals:

We believe that the future and fate of Jerusalem, the city of peace with its unique universal character, cannot and should not be decided unilaterally. This city, which has lived through so many ruins and upheavals and for which, over centuries, so much blood has been shed, must fulfill its destiny by becoming the bridge between now divided brothers. We recognize the fact that Jerusalem cannot and should not become a divided city again. It must be an open city, but it cannot and should not be an Israeli city only. We propose that the new border in the final settlement between Israel and Jordan should run around the city on both sides. Both parties will have immigration and customs offices on the outskirts of the city--each on its side. Anyone entering the city from either side will do so unimpeded. Checks will be made on the people leaving the city only. Israelis and Jordanians inside the city will have the freedom of complete movement and residence in any part of the city. The Jordanian sector of Jerusalem occupied in 1967 will be under Jordanian sovereignty and the Israeli sector under Israeli sovereignty. Details of the joint

administration of the city can be worked out.  For
example, there can be either two municipalities and
a joint municipal council to coordinate the affairs
of the city; or any similar arrangements.  Jordanian
and Israeli police will be responsible for law and
order in their respective sectors.

        These are the general outlines of our proposal
on Jerusalem.  We are, of course, prepared to discuss
details and amendments provided they do not affect the
sovereignty of Jordan over the Arab city of Jerusalem.

SECRET/SENSITIVE

24 March 1972

MEMORANDUM FOR:    The Secretary of State

SUBJECT:           Secret Israel-Jordan Negotiations

1.  I am attaching a Jordanian paper entitled
"The Real Israeli Position Regarding a Settlement
with Jordan."  It sets forth rather concisely conclusions which the King has reached regarding the
Israeli position after approximately fifty secret
meetings with Israeli leaders.  While the King and
his advisors wish to maintain their contacts with
the Israelis to insure some measure of peaceful co-
existence, they are convinced at this point that
these contacts alone will not lead to a settlement
which Jordan can accept.

2.  The King plans to present a copy of the
attached paper to the President and to seek the
President's observations and recommendations as to
"where the King and Jordan should go from here."

N.B. ||

Richard Helms
Director

Attachment - 1

SECRET/SENSITIVE

The Real Israeli Position Regarding a Settlement
with Jordan

1. Israel would like to arrive at a peace
settlement with Jordan separate from and prior to
an overall settlement of the Arab-Israel problem,
provided Jordan accepts Israel's terms for such a
settlement.

2. Security Council Resolution 242 is only a
working paper. It is not binding in any way. Besides,
Israel never really accepted that resolution and any
of its interpretations. Most of the principles contained in the resolution are unrealistic.

3. Secretary Rogers' proposals and the American
interpretation of the Security Council Resolution 242
cannot be taken seriously.

4. Israel does not object to talking with
Ambassador Jarring but that is all she is prepared to
do. Israel believes that Ambassador Jarring, or any
other third party, cannot and should not mediate a
settlement. Only direct negotiations can solve the
problem.

5. Though Israel calls for direct negotiations,
Israel has already decided what the terms of the
settlement are. Negotiations would only be to forma-
lize the Israeli dictates.

6. The proposal of minor border rectifications
is totally unacceptable. There must be substantial
changes in the June 5, 1967 line which will greatly
expand Israeli territory.

7. Jerusalem is not negotiable. It is the
united capital of Israel. The mere idea of Jordanian
sovereignty over the Arab sector of the city is unacceptable.

8.  The maximum "concessions" which Israel is
prepared to make are as follows:

A.  Israel will return most of the population of the West Bank to Jordan but not all
the territory.  Israel will annex the Jordan
valley west of the Jordan River, and will permit
Jordan to retain a corridor to join the East
Bank and the West Bank.

B.  Jordan will be given control of the
Moslem holy places in the old city of Jerusalem
and the right of access to them.

C.  Israeli citizens will have the right
to settle in certain areas of religious importance in the West Bank.

D.  The West Bank is to be demilitarized.

E.  No troops of any other Arab nation
are to be stationed on the East Bank of Jordan.

F.  Jordan must sign a peace treaty with
Israel on the above-mentioned basis.

9.  This is the final Israeli position.  Although
peace is desirable, Israel can live without it if the
above conditions are not accepted.  Things will remain
as they are now; and instead of a formal state of peace,
Israel believes there will be a gradual drift toward
peace since Israel is intent on teaching the Arabs to
coexist with her.

2

## TOP SECRET RUFF ZARF UMBRA
*HANDLE VIA TALENT - KEYHOLE - COMINT CONTROL SYSTEMS JOINTLY*

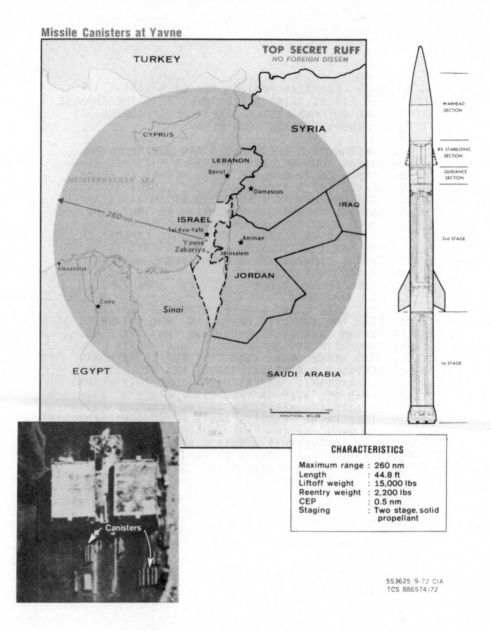

Missile Canisters at Yavne

TOP SECRET RUFF
NO FOREIGN DISSEM

**CHARACTERISTICS**

| | |
|---|---|
| Maximum range | : 260 nm |
| Length | : 44.8 ft |
| Liftoff weight | : 15,000 lbs |
| Reentry weight | : 2,200 lbs |
| CEP | : 0.5 nm |
| Staging | : Two stage, solid propellant |

553625 9-72 CIA
TCS 886574/72

## TOP SECRET RUFF ZARF UMBRA

## TOP SECRET RUFF ZARF UMBRA
*HANDLE VIA TALENT - KEYHOLE - COMINT CONTROL SYSTEMS JOINTLY*

ISRAEL:  THE JERICHO SURFACE-TO-SURFACE MISSILE
PROGRAM APPARENTLY IS NEARING THE TESTING PHASE.

SATELLITE PHOTOGRAPHY OF THE YAVNE MISSILE TEST
CENTER IN EARLY SEPTEMBER SHOWS WHAT APPEAR TO BE
AT LEAST 11 MISSILE STAGE CANISTERS.  ALL OF THE
CANISTERS ARE AROUND THREE FEET IN DIAMETER; THE
LONGER ONES ARE 18 FEET IN LENGTH AND TWO ARE SEV-
ERAL FEET SHORTER.

TO DATE, NO MISSILE ACTIVITY HAS BEEN OBSERVED
AT YAVNE DESPITE THE FACT THAT THE SUPPORT FACILI-
TIES AND TWO LAUNCH PADS WERE COMPLETED ABOUT TWO
YEARS AGO.  THE APPARENT HIATUS IN THE PROGRAM HAS
LED TO SPECULATION THAT THE ORIGINAL MISSILE DESIGNED
AND DEVELOPED FOR ISRAEL BY THE FRENCH FIRM DASSAULT
DURING THE 1960S HAS BEEN UNDERGOING MODIFICATION BY
THE ISRAELIS TO IMPROVE ITS PERFORMANCE.

FOR SEVERAL YEARS ISRAEL HAS HAD THE INDUSTRIAL
FACILITIES AND TECHNICAL EXPERTISE TO TURN OUT AT
LEAST ONE JERICHO MISSILE A MONTH.  IN ADDITION TO
PRODUCTION FACILITIES AND A TEST RANGE, THE ISRAELIS
ARE CONSTRUCTING WHAT IS BELIEVED TO BE AN OPERA-
TIONAL SITE IN THE MOUNTAINS BETWEEN JERUSALEM AND
TEL AVIV.  APPARENTLY ISRAEL INTENDS TO HAVE ALL
ELEMENTS OF THE JERICHO PROGRAM IN PLACE SO THAT AN
OPERATIONAL FORCE CAN BE QUICKLY DEPLOYED ONCE THE
MISSILE HAS SUCCESSFULLY COMPLETED A SERIES OF TEST
FLIGHTS.  {TOP SECRET RUFF NO FOREIGN DISSEM}

## TOP SECRET RUFF ZARF UMBRA

| Year | Laos | Vietnam S | Vietnam N | Cambodia | Thailand | Other | Total |
|-------|-----------|-----------|-----------|----------|----------|--------|-----------|
| 1965 | 36,967 | 43,284 | 536 | | | 44 | 80,830 |
| 1966 | 63,447 | 193,254 | 128,280 | | 41 | | 385,022 |
| 1967 | 93,623 | 292,176 | 191,420 | 38 | 19 | 1,232 | 578,508 |
| 1968 | 156,619 | 338,042 | 198,670 | | 102 | 1,280 | 694,713 |
| 1969 | 489,037 | 596,147 | 651 | 6 | 62 | 964 | 1,086,866 |
| 1970 | 631,658 | 403,882 | 1,691 | 78,220 | 5 | 59,320 | 1,174,775 |
| 1971 | 414,792 | 178,506 | 6,754 | 63,253 | | 15 | 663,320 |
| 1972 | 167,370 | 706,894 | 207,284 | 57,042 | 104 | 337 | 1,139031 |
| 1973 | 82,869 | 68,595 | 14,490 | 273,728 | 521 | 572 | 440,774 |
| 1974 | | 21,717 | | | | | 21,717 |
| 1975 | | 10,205 | | 27 | 6 | 681 | 10,918 |
| Total | 2,136,380 | 2,852,701 | 749,776 | 472,313 | 863 | 64,445 | 6,276,477 |

FIGURE 4: Totals (Tonnage) by Country and by Year Based on CACTA/SEADAB Database.

Source: "Electronic Records of the Air War Over Southeast Asia: A Database Analysis," Holly High, James R. Curran and Gareth Robinson, *Journal of Vietnamese Studies*, Vol. 8, No. 4 (Fall 2013), pp. 86–124. Published by University of California Press; accessed via JSTOR. Table is from p. 104 of the article.

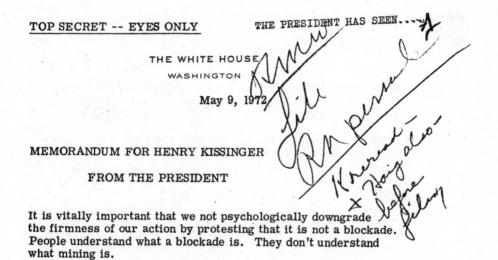

TOP SECRET -- EYES ONLY

THE WHITE HOUSE
WASHINGTON

May 9, 1972

MEMORANDUM FOR HENRY KISSINGER

FROM THE PRESIDENT

It is vitally important that we not psychologically downgrade
the firmness of our action by protesting that it is not a blockade.
People understand what a blockade is. They don't understand
what mining is.

The way everybody in the Administration should handle this
question is to say that the order of the President's action has the
purpose and effect of a blockade -- to completely stop the
delivery of all seaborne supplies to North Vietnam. We find
that we are able to accomplish this goal through mining and
through naval and other activities against shipping within the
12-mile limit claimed by Hanoi. This means that we have not
found it necessary, in order to accomplish our goal of stopping
all deliveries of supplies by sea, to stop ships in the high seas.

In other words, from a technical legal standpoint there is a
blockade only when ships are stopped in the high seas. This
we are not doing at this time -- but only because it is not
necessary to accomplish our goal of completely cutting off
seaborne delivery of supplies to North Vietnam.

What must be emphasized is that the action the President has
ordered, both on sea and on land, has as its purpose completely
denying to the enemy the supplies it needs to wage aggressive war.
We will order those actions that are necessary to accomplish this
goal. The fact that the initial order does not include stopping
ships on the high seas -- which in the parlance of international
law is a blockade -- in no way should be indicated as a sign of
weakness or firmness of resolve. We are not doing that only

- 2 -

because we find it is not necessary and that there is a more effective way to accomplish our goal -- mining and naval and air actions within the 12-mile limit claimed by North Vietnam.

I want you to make this point strongly in your briefing, and I want it circulated to all Administration spokesmen so that our action, both by the enemy and by the American people, does not run the risk of being considered so restrained as to be ineffective.

With regard to bombing strikes in the North I have decided that it is imperative that they be at the highest limit that Abrams can spare from the battle area in the next few days.

I mentioned that our primary target, except for the rail lines, should be POL. This, of course, should be our long-term goal. But over the next few days I also want some targets hit which will have maximum psychological effect on morale in North Vietnam. That is why it is so important to take out the power plants. If your operational group thinks of any other targets of this type hit them and hit them hard.

Remember that we will have more support for strong action than we will in the days ahead. As each day goes by criticism will reduce support for our action and also the failure to get results will reduce the enthusiasm of our supporters.

You have often mentioned the necessity of creating the impression in the enemy's mind that I am absolutely determined to end the war and will take whatever steps are necessary to accomplish this goal.

The time to take those steps is now.

That is why some extensive B-52 strikes in the North should if at all possible be directed against military targets in North Vietnam this week.

I am concerned by the military's plan of allocating 200 sorties for North Vietnam for the dreary "milk runs" which characterized the Johnson Administration's bombing in the 1965-68 period.

- 3 -

I cannot emphasize too strongly that I have determined that
we should go for broke. What we have got to get across to the
enemy is the impression that we are doing exactly that. Our
words will help some. But our actions in the next few days will
speak infinitely louder than our words.

I am totally unsatisfied at this time at the plans the military
have suggested as far as air activities are concerned. On an
urgent basis I want on my desk late this afternoon (Tuesday)
recommendations to carry out this directive which I am now
dictating. I intend to give the directive directly to Abrams in
the field and I will inform Laird and bring him into line if
there is any question in that direction.

Our greatest failure now would be to do too little too late.
It is far more important to do too much at a time that we will
have maximum public support for what we do.

(continued on page 4)

What all of us must have in mind is that we must punish
the enemy in ways that he will really hurt at this time.  Over a
longer period of time we can be more methodical in directing our
air strikes to two specific targets -- the rail lines, highways and
POL supply areas.  I have an uneasy feeling that your present plans
are simply too restrained and too much in the pattern of the 1965-
1968 debacle.

Now that I have made this very tough water shed decision
I intend to stop at nothing to bring the enemy to his knees.  I want
you to get this spirit inculcated in all hands and particularly I want
the military to get off its back side and give me some recommendations as to how we can accomplish that goal.

Needless to say, indiscriminate bombing of civilian areas
is not what I have in mind.  On the other hand, if the target is
important enough, I will approve a plan that goes after it even if
there is a risk of some civilian casualties.

I think we have had too much of a tendency to talk big
and act little.  This was certainly the weakness of the Johnson
Administration.  To an extent it may have been our weakness where
we have warned the enemy time and time again and then have acted
in a rather mild way when the enemy has tested us.  He has now
gone over the brink and so have we.  We have the power to destroy
his war making capacity.  The only question is whether we have
the will to use that power.  What distinguishes me from Johnson
is that I have the will in spades.  If we now fail it will be because
the bureaucrats and the bureaucracy and particularly those in the
Defense Department, who will of course be vigorously assisted by
their allies in State, will find ways to erode the strong, decisive
action that I have indicated we are going to take.  For once, I
want the military and I want the NSC staff to come up with some
ideas on their own which will recommend action which is very
strong, threatening and effective.

I want as part of the plan this week, on an urgent basis,
making strikes on all air fields in North Vietnam, particularly in
the Hanoi-Haiphong area.  I realize that they can be put back into
operation a few days after a strike, but the psychological effect
could be considerable.  On this score, I particularly want to hit
the international airfield where civilian planes land.

Also, this week I want one major strike.  Get Abrams
to collect his assets and have one 500 plane strike by Thursday or
Friday of this week so that the enemy will know that we mean business
all the way.

C

O

  P

   Y                                              October 23, 1972

SUBJECT:    Dr. Kissinger's Meeting with President Thieu,
            October 23, 1972

1.  Dr. Kissinger, accompanied by Ambassador Bunker, met with
President Thieu for two and one-quarter hours at 0800, October 23.

2.  Dr. Kissinger said that he would like to make a few observations
concerning our discussions yesterday.  The President has had a full
report of these and has asked me to repeat that he believes that the
effect of our proposal is quite the opposite of your characterization of
it and that it will indeed achieve the mutual objective for which we have
both been striving.  But we are now faced with an immediate problem.
First, I want to make it clear there never have been talks or communication with the other side which have not been communicated to you.
You have been apprised fully of every development as it has occurred
and have been consulted on every move we have made with the single
exception of the meeting on September 15 when we believed it necessary
to move before we had heard from you.  While I cannot accept what you
said yesterday, we nevertheless owe it to the sacrifices so many have
made to our common cause to make another effort.  We must let no disagreement be evident between us.  If the other side goes public, we will blame
it on the Newsweek article, although we cannot disavow  the agreement.
In the meantime, I had had to take some steps.  I have cancelled my trip
to Hanoi and have asked for a meeting in Paris to present your demands.
In the meantime, Ambassador Bunker will consult with you.

3.  President Thieu said that yesterday "I promised to avoid any confrontation and said that I would not publicly acknowledge any disagreement between
President Nixon and myself."

4.  Dr. Kissinger responded saying that yesterday you asked for my
personal opinion and I replied that I thought the course you were following
was dangerous.  I intended it as an expression of deep concern; it was not
intended to be personal in nature or any reflection on you.  You understand
how it seems to an individual who has stood against 300,000 demonstrators,

against bureaucratic and Congressional opposition, against public opinion and the press - this is why I took the liberty of speaking as I did. Both your present and former Ambassadors will tell you who stood for you and who against. As I mentioned yesterday, I believe the course you are following is suicidal.

5. President Thieu said he had expressed his views straightforwardly and had spoken frankly as a fighter, recognizing that at times we made mistakes. But after fifteen years of struggle, it does not seem too much to ask for only two changes. "If I am forced to accept, I will feel that I have been pressured by North Vietnam." He did not intend to accuse anyone. He knew that President Nixon had many other obligations which exceed the interests of Vietnam. His only question is whether the U.S. Government and people intend to support Vietnam. If they do, then they should do whatever they can concerning these two points. It is exceedingly regrettable that North Vietnam has taken advantage of his pledge to maintain secrecy in order to mislead public opinion.

6. President Thieu said he would ask Dr. Kissinger to report to the President on three specific points:

-- The observance of the DMZ as required by the Geneva Agreements of 1954.

-- The question of self-determination to be left to the South Vietnamese people. In this respect the tripartite formula does not reflect political reality.

-- The question of North Vietnam forces in the South. The Communists have lied about their invasion and want to save face. If they wish to withdraw without an announcement, this can be accepted as a de facto withdrawal.

7. President Thieu asked whether we had presented to the other side his proposals of September 13 providing for the election of a president followed by the formation of a new government, and if so how the communists had responded. He added that he would write to President Nixon and tell him what he finds it difficult to accept. The final decision, however, will be that of the Vietnamese people. "I still consider President Nixon a friend and a comrade in arms. Whether or not I am President I will strive to

create conditions so that the United States can help Vietnam. If I am
an obstacle to American aid or to peace, I will not stay on as President.
I had no intention of criticizing President Nixon. I only wish to point
out that compared to the situation which would prevail in Cambodia and
Laos I find the proposal disadvantageous to South Vietnam, but there is
no reason for hatred and enmity among friends and I propose that we
forget what has been said."

8.   Dr. Kissinger replied that we speak as friends and as admirers of
you and your country and we share your sentiment. The U.S. will never
sacrifice a trusted friend. We will not deal with anyone but the President
of Vietnam and will have no communication with anyone but the President
of Vietnam. Regarding other points which have been reached:

> -- The GVN opposition to the phrase "Administrative structure"
> used to describe the NCRC: We cannot judge the meaning of
> the phrase in Vietnamese, but to us it means something insig-
> nificant. We were determined to have nothing in the agreement
> which could be related in any way to a coalition government. In
> the U.S., the NCRC would be considered an absurdity, a tremen-
> dous defeat for Hanoi. It would, therefore, be difficult for us
> to explain the GVN's objection to it. Dr. Kissinger said that on
> the other hand, had he been able to go to Hanoi, he would have
> been prepared to request the elimination of the provision for
> the three equal segments of the NCRC.

> -- With regard to North Vietnamese forces in South Vietnam: Our
> judgment is that the provision against reinforcement, the closing
> of the Laotian and Cambodian borders and the prohibition against
> infiltration would have the practical result of diminishing the
> NVN forces. Again had he been able to go to Hanoi, he would
> have asked the DRV for the removal of three divisions from MR 1.

9.   We do not consider President Thieu's demands unreasonable. We
consider him a great patriot and soldier. But Dr. Kissinger said that
he must tell President Thieu "in anguish" that if the war goes on at its
present rate, in six months U.S. funds will be cut off.

10. Dr. Kissinger then described what it had been necessary to do in
order to maintain Congressional support. For a year, we have attempted
to isolate Hanoi. November 7 was pointed to as an unremovable deadline

TOP SECRET/SENSITIVE
EXCLUSIVELY EYES ONLY                                                            4

and, therefore, created a high degree of anxiety on the part of the North
Vietnamese. They conceded much and undoubtedly, had Dr. Kissinger
gone to Hanoi, they would have conceded more. Indeed the agreement
would have been considered a great triumph and we could have continued
with our aid and support. In both the United States and Europe it would
have been considered a defeat for Hanoi. Since July, in order to maintain
support, we have been conducting a delaying strategy. The tragedy now
is that had the agreement been presented as a surprise, it would have
enabled our continuing support which is now jeopardized. It is hardly
conceivable that Congressional support can continue. Unfortunately,
we are in the position now of having to make concessions. We thought
we had achieved victory, but obviously were mistaken.

11. "What is important is that all the sacrifices that have been made
should not have been made in vain. If we continue our confrontation you
will win victories, but we will both lose in the end. It is a fact that in
the United States all the press, the media and intellectuals have a vested
interest in our defeat. If I have seemed impatient in the last days it is
because I saw opportunity slipping away. When I say that we will maintain
our position, I do not refer to details, I refer to the integrity of our
relationship. For example, when Newsweek and Time talk about our
agreement to a caretaker government, you know there is no such thing.
I am not trying to convince you, but I want you to understand what we
have attempted to do. Had it not been for the importance we place on
our relationship, we would not have to make new plans -- this is why I
leave with such a sense of tragedy. We will do our best and Bunker will
be in touch with you."

12. President Thieu said that he agreed with Dr. Kissinger's exposition
of the American political situation presently and as it would be six
months hence. He realizes that the U.S. has many obligations, in
politics it has new obligations every day. As for himself, he does not
know in what manner he can find a way to explain to his people the diffi-
culties that have to be faced. The country must be defended, but he
understands that this is one part of a bigger problem. He would request
Dr. Kissinger to explain to the President the problems he faces. If
anything can be done to persuade the Soviets and China to use their
influence on Hanoi, it would be welcome.

13. Dr. Kissinger said that he would probably have to have a press
conference when he returned to the U.S. He will give the impression
that progress is being made, that a war which has lasted for ten years

TOP SECRET/SENSITIVE
EXCLUSIVELY EYES ONLY

cannot be settled in a week. He would give no details and would deny that there are any fundamental differences between us. A campaign against President Thieu and Vietnam must be avoided. Dr. Kissinger recommended that President Thieu and Ambassador Bunker continue discussions for "we must," he said, "dominate events." It is important that on the Vietnamese side there be no expression of the feeling that they are being let down by the U.S.

14. Dr. Kissinger said he would invite the North Vietnamese to Paris and would present the GVN demands although they will not all be achievable. He assured President Thieu that he is not an obstacle, that we have no intention of asking him to resign, but pointed out that should he become an obstacle, we cannot support him. Dr. Kissinger said that when he returned to the U.S., he will consider himself President Thieu's comrade in arms, warning, however, that we may not face the ideal way in which we can continue together.

15. President Thieu responded by assuring Dr. Kissinger that he will not be provoked into taking a position against the Americans, will not fall into the trap despite efforts to make him do so. In looking back to what happened on November 2, 1958, we can say now that had it not happened the situation today would have been better.

16. Dr. Kissinger said that he believed the proposed agreement was a good one, but assured Thieu that nothing would be done behind his back and that consultations would continue.

17. President Thieu concluded by saying that whatever may have been said in the last days we must not let the South Vietnamese people believe that Hanoi has won this long struggle. The problem in South Vietnam is that unless the agreement provides the points he mentioned, it would result in the collapse of the morale of both the military and the people.

18. Warm regards.

THE PRESIDENT HAS SEEN...

*[handwritten: Buchanan]*

*[handwritten: Tell Mort et al that I am constantly amazed at the brilliant wisdom in preparing the news summary. It is invaluable for all of us]*

NEWS SUMMARY
October 25, 1972
(nets, wires, columns)

The major stories of the day:

*[handwritten: RN]*

-- The "hard-line," "tough" Thieu speech, RN's meeting w/
HAK (film on all) about which WH said little and McG's
challenges as to why VN wasn't settled before dominated
the nets. ABC only net w/ film of RN signing vets' bill.
Thieu increasingly seen as obstacle to accord w/ Cronkite
saying it's ironic but US/NVN seemed to have reached
settlement but Thieu won't go along. However, ABC's
Koppel found "resignation to the inevitable" in his analysis
of Thieu speech. And NBC pointed out that despite Thieu's
description of coalition as suicide, both he and VC seem to
be preparing for ceasefire. ...McG on 2 nets w/ strident,
pointed questions of RN on VN, Watergate etc. -- as if he
were an "acid-tongued evangelist" challenging the devil,
said CBS. ...Brinkley said if war is ended -- after all the
deceit and "entertainment" the government has provided in
recent years -- the 1st task is to restore public trust in
Washington.

-- All nets noted speculation that bombing cutback over North
was tied to talks and on WH orders. Also the heaviest B-52
attacks ever in Saigon area were noted by all.

-- VP on NBC/CBS -- 1 as he received applause at Brigham
Young defending US role in VN; the other w/ film as he
whistled heckler to silence. ....Shriver on NBC w/ less-
than-spectacular street reception but the Mayor's boys are
apparently back in tow.

-- Tricia/Volpe on NBC/CBS dedicating a "people mover" in
Morgantown. NBC emphasized protest and the election-
timing of ceremony for a project which won't be operable
for a year while CBS focused on the technological advance.
On both nets Tricia effectively handled rabble as she pointed

### THE WHITE HOUSE
#### WASHINGTON

November 7, 1972

MEMORANDUM FOR:        ALEXANDER P. BUTTERFIELD

FROM:                  H.R. HALDEMAN

SUBJECT:               Future Plans

The President has requested that you forward to him an
indication of your personal plans or preferences regarding your possible service in the next Administration.
This should be done by memorandum and forwarded directly
to my office by no later than Friday, November 10.  This
should accompany your pro forma letter of resignation to
become effective at the pleasure of the President.

Between now and December 15, please plan on remaining
on the job, finishing first-term work, collecting and
depositing Presidential papers, and making plans for
next term.  This should not be considered a vacation
period.

Regardless of your future plans, you should put together
a basic book about your current assignment.  It should
be divided into four sections as follows:

    A.  How you define your current assignment.
    What is its objective?

    B.  What is its current status?  Where does
    it stand?

    C.  Where should it go?  What are the oppor-
    tunities for improvement in accomplishing the
    objectives of your assignment?

    D.  How should it get there?  What are the
    steps to fulfilling the objectives?

This should be as comprehensive as possible -- and should
cover the full range of your responsibilities.  This proje
should be completed by December 15.

THE WHITE HOUSE

WASHINGTON

November 10, 1972

<u>CONFIDENTIAL</u>

Dear Bob:

I know that you are confronted with a gigantic reorganization task, so despite the importance of this letter to me personally, and to my family, I will be as brief as possible ... hoping, of course, that you will read between the lines and understand many of the whys and wherefores which over the past four years have generated my present government service preferences and their particular priorities.

First, let me say in all sincerity that in no way will I ever be able to repay <u>you</u> for taking the chance you did with me and my abilities. You alone gave me the honor and opportunity of a life-time, and although it may be a bit embarrassing for you to hear it, or read it, I must tell you that I will be forever grateful. I'm sure I join all others on the staff when I thank you also for allowing such highly personal expressions to be forwarded and considered.

Secondly, I want both you <u>and</u> the President to know that my "position preferences" are most certainly not overriding -- that if asked, I will serve <u>either</u> of you in <u>any</u> capacity whatever.

Now, to the information requested in your November 7 correspondence. Frankly, and for the reasons cited below, <u>I seek a change.</u> I am anxious to find something which will give me greater challenge, greater responsibility, a somewhat higher salary, and more and better employment opportunities when the transitory appointee period comes to a close.

1)   I fear being "typed", especially in my current Valenti-like role. Perhaps unwisely I have kept myself in check around the President and refrained from commenting on any issue ... political, international, domestic or personal. I assumed you preferred it that way. But my guess is that he considers the good, fairly efficient, man-servant in the outer office akin to the village idiot -- one without mind

-2-

or opinion. Yet I have done many other things in my
lifetime, more by far than most people, and proved
to myself and others a host of capabilities quite
unassociated with the military environment. Prospective
employers, however, will have no idea of what I might
be able to offer if I remain here on the White House
Staff, so "contained." This is not to say that I want
to be in the limelight. I am not built that way. But
because I am not a lawyer who upon leaving Uncle
Sam's employ can go off to a senior post in a renowned
law firm, or a one-time businessman, advertising
executive or financier who has a multitude of corporations
waiting for him anxiously, I must now, during this next
2-4 year period, surface sufficiently to make contact
with the outside world.

2) I will be 47 years of age almost immediately after the
second term begins, and on the threshold of 51 if I am
kept aboard for the duration.

3) Alex and Susan are in college now, and in approximately
20 months Lisa will join their ranks. I have no debts but
neither do I have an outside income.

4) I have a strong desire to do things, to organize, to innovate,
to put ideas to work ... and to achieve much more than I
have done to date.

Here then, in order of preference, are the positions in government in
which I feel confident that at this stage of my total development I could
serve well and contribute genuinely:

1) Secretary of the Air Force
2) Secretary of the Navy
3) Under Secretary of the Interior
4) Under Secretary of Transportation
5) Personal Assistant to the President or Administrative Assistant
   to the President ... with considerably increased responsibility
   and freedom to operate, and a salary of preferably $42,500 per
   year but at least $40,000 per year.

CONFIDENTIAL

- 3 -

This seems a helluva presumptuous note on which to close, but then
you <u>did</u> ask.

Sincerely,

Alexander P. Butterfield

Honorable H. R. Haldeman
The White House
Washington, D.C.

<u>CONFIDENTIAL</u>

# ACKNOWLEDGMENTS

Special and enduring thanks to Alex Butterfield for putting up with the 11 months I haunted him for information, recollections and documents. He relinquished editorial control to me with grace and understanding, agreeing to let me tell his story. At the same time he was always the gentleman host, welcoming numerous visits from Evelyn Duffy and me.

This is my eighteenth book over 43 years with my Simon & Schuster editor Alice Mayhew. Her energy and wisdom guided me as she instantly recognized the importance of continuing to report the Nixon story. She is a book idea machine like no one else and devoted many days to reading, editing, rereading and reediting the manuscript.

More than thanks to Jonathan Karp, the publisher, who provided countless ideas, editing and substantive suggestions. He is a master of the craft of publishing with a depth and range found nowhere else. The CEO at Simon & Schuster is Carolyn K. Reidy who over the decades has given me the full support of her empire. I am indebted to her once again.

At Simon & Schuster I am grateful for the work, attention and professional support of Elisa Rivlin, the counsel; Jackie Seow, Executive Art Director; Joy O'Meara, Design Director; Lisa Healy, Senior Production Editor; Stuart Roberts, Assistant Editor; Julia Prosser, Deputy Director of Publicity; Stephen Bedford, Marketing Specialist; Lisa Erwin, Senior Production Manager; Richard Rhorer, Associate Publisher; Irene Kheradi, Executive Managing Editor.

My thanks to Fred Chase, the terrific copy editor and counselor. He spent a week in Washington working with Evelyn and myself. He knows the business of words like no other. I thank him for his special, near-round-the-clock efforts and guidance.

As always, many thanks to former colleagues at *The Washington Post*, especially Carl Bernstein, Don Graham, Sally Quinn, David Maraniss, Rick Atkinson, Christian Williams, Paul Richard, Patrick Tyler, Tom Wilkinson, Marcus Brauchli, Katharine Weymouth, and John Feinstein for direct and indirect assistance—and life-long insights and friendships.

Editors and colleagues at the *Post* have always given me the support and flexibility to pursue such in-depth projects. My sincere gratitude to Marty Baron, the executive editor; Kevin Merida, the managing editor; Cameron Barr, the national editor; Jeff Leen, the investigations editor; and Steve Luxenberg, Carlos Lozada, Steven Ginsberg, Fred Hiatt, and the new publisher Fred Ryan.

I hope all these book and newspaper people know how much I am thankful for the role they have played in my life. Special appreciation to Jeff Bezos, the Amazon founder and CEO who is now owner of *The Washington Post*. May he and his paper—our paper—have every success.

Archivists have helped immensely, especially Michael Ellzey, director of the Nixon Library and Museum, and experts at the Nixon Library, especially Pamla Eisenberg, Ryan Pettigrew, and Jon Fletcher.

Also many thanks to Thomas S. Blanton, director, National Security Archive at George Washington University, for his extra efforts.

Deep appreciation to David Killian, research librarian at the George Washington University, for locating the Vietnam bombing statistics cited in this book.

Many thanks to Potomac Indexing LLC for the indexing.

Now to another essence of modern publishing—selling the book. Robert B. Barnett is my lawyer, counselor and friend extraordinaire.

Invaluable, informed and energetic, he got behind this book and deployed all his talents and knowledge. Simply put, there is no one like him in Washington or publishing. And no one looks out for the interests of his client with equivalent skill and devotion.

Evelyn and I thank Rosa Criollo and Jackie Crowe for all the care and kindnesses they have provided around Q Street and elsewhere.

Tali Woodward, my elder daughter and director of the Master of Arts program at Columbia Journalism School, helped edit this book, offering many suggestions for improved clarity and context. She, her husband, Gabe Roth, and their two children, Zadie and Theo, are in our lives more and more, making everything better.

My daughter Diana Woodward is off to Yale for her freshman year. Her love of learning is palpable, and we miss her around the house. As she says, "Happy to go, sad to leave." She has been the spark and a joy.

Most relevant to a sensible life is my wife Elsa Walsh. This is the fifteenth of my books in the 34 years we have been together. I am blessed. She is author and former reporter for *The Washington Post* and *The New Yorker*. Elsa is editor, leader, chief enforcement officer, and the indispensable partner and love of my life. Human kindness is her virtue. She frequently quotes Henry James, "There are only three things important in life. The first is to be kind. The second it to be kind and the third is to be kind." She is the foremost believer and practitioner of kindness.

# INDEX

# ABOUT THE AUTHOR

Bob Woodward is an associate editor at *The Washington Post*, where he has worked for 44 years. He has shared in two Pulitzer Prizes, first for the *Post*'s coverage of the Watergate scandal with Carl Bernstein, and later for coverage of the 9/11 terrorist attacks. He has authored or coauthored 17 national nonfiction bestsellers, 12 of which have been #1 national bestsellers.

Woodward has two daughters, Tali and Diana, and lives in Washington, D.C., wtih his wife, writer Elsa Walsh.

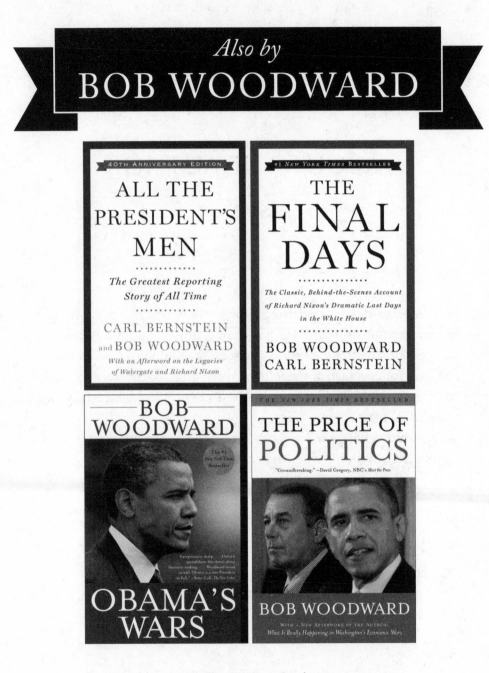

53648